History of the World

HISTORY OF THE WORLD

From the Late Nineteenth to the Early
Twenty-First Century

Arjun Dev

Indira Arjun Dev

Orient BlackSwan

HISTORY OF THE WORLD

ORIENT BLACKSWAN PRIVATE LIMITED

Registered Office
3-6-752 Himayatnagar, Hyderabad 500 029 (A.P.), INDIA
e-mail: centraloffice@orientblackswan.com

Other Offices
Bangalore, Bhopal, Bhubaneshwar, Chennai,
Ernakulam, Guwahati, Hyderabad, Jaipur, Kolkata,
Lucknow, Mumbai, New Delhi, Patna

© Orient Blackswan Private Limited
First published by Orient Longman Pvt. Ltd. 2009
Reprinted 2010, 2012 2013 ,2014

ISBN: 978 81 250 3687 6

Typeset by
Bukprint, Delhi

Printed in India at
Yash Printographics, Noida

Cover Photograph
Mladen Lukic. Reprinted by kind permission of the photographer

Published by
Orient Blackswan Private Limited
1/24 Asaf Ali Road, New Delhi 110 002
e-mail: delhi@orientblackswan.com

> The external boundaries and coastlines as depicted in the maps
> are not to scale. They are neither correct nor authentic.

Contents

Contents

List of Maps

Introduction

PERIODISATION IN HISTORY

The history of any country or region or of the world as a whole is generally divided into periods and sub-periods. This is done on the basis of some specific criteria. One criterion which is common in traditional historical writings is to divide the history of a country in terms of the dynasties that ruled over it. In this sense, we refer to, for example, the Mauryan, the Gupta and the Mughal periods in Indian history, the Han and the Manchu periods in Chinese history; and the Tudor and the Stuart periods in the history of England. This kind of division is still common as the period of rule of a dynasty provides a convenient chronology for the study history. The division of history into periods is also based on other criteria. For example, we have divisions like the Renaissance and the Industrial Revolution, which denote broad chronological periods in the history of some countries. The criteria of division in these cases are developments in certain aspects of cultural and economic life. Such divisions (unlike the divisions based on dynasties) indicate broad periods and not any specific date or year, as developments in culture and economy cannot be traced back to any particular date. To give an example from Indian history, the period of the rise of Indian nationalism cannot be ascribed to any particular event taking place on a particular date. Sometimes, division into periods is done on the basis of centuries. We have, for example, the history of England, let us say, in the fifteenth century, the sixteenth century, the seventeenth century, and so on.

Another, more important, kind of division of history into periods, or simply periodisation, is done on the basis of demarcation of stages in the development of society. In this kind of periodisation, each period denotes not only a broad chronology but a distinct form of society, economy, political system and culture, which has a well-defined character of its own, distinguishable from other periods. The broadest and commonly accepted periodisation of the history of most countries and of the world as a whole is the division into ancient, medieval and modem periods. In terms of chronology, these periods vary from country to country as society in different countries and regions moved from one stage to another at different times. For example, in the history of Western Europe, the ancient period came to a close by the early centuries of the Christian era and the medieval period began when a new form of social system characterised by feudalism began to take shape. Similarly, the medieval period in the history of Western Europe may be said to have ended by the fifteenth–seventeenth centuries and the modern period began with the decline of feudalism and the emergence of a new kind of social system, called capitalism. Comparable developments denoting the passing of one type of social system and the emergence of a new one in other countries or regions, say in Asia and Africa, took place at different times. Therefore, the specific chronology of the ancient period, the medieval period and the modem period differs from country to country and region to region.

It should also be remembered that the ancient period or the medieval period in the history of all countries do not have the same characteristic features. There are variations in many essential features of social and economic life, political system and culture. Thus, medieval China or medieval India do not necessarily denote the same kind of society, economy, political system, etc., as medieval Europe. However, while periodising the history of the world as a whole, the variations in different regions of the world are ignored for the sake of convenience and new forms of society and economy, even though they might have emerged only in one region of the world, are taken to mark the beginning of a new period. For example, the period between the fifteenth and seventeenth centuries, which marks the beginning of the modern period in Western Europe, is also taken to mark the beginning of the modem period in the history of the world as a whole. This is done because some of the new trends that first emerged in Western Europe during these centuries also became the major features of the history of many other countries and regions of the world or exercised a powerful influence on the history of other countries in the subsequent period.

CONTEMPORARY HISTORY

As mentioned above, the period of world history beginning from the fifteenth–seventeenth centuries is generally regarded as the modern period. The term 'modern' implies that it would cover the developments from its beginning right up to the present time in which we live. Until three or four decades ago, however, historians generally were reluctant to write about the period in which they or even their contemporaries (some of whom would be much older than them) lived. Many histories of the world written and taught in the 1950s, 1960s and even in the 1970s would stop with the year 1945 (the year when the Second World War ended) or 1939 (the year when the Second World War began). Some would stop even earlier in 1918 or 1914 (the years, respectively, when the First World War ended and began). Some of the reasons given for not indulging in such an endeavour are not without base. Many important sources which the historian requires to write the history of the period in which he is living would not be available to him. For example, many important official papers regarding the activities of governments are open to historians for study only after a lapse of 50 years (in the case of some countries, 30 years). Many people who are involved in the formulation of policies and in the activities of the government, such as prime ministers, various ministers and high officials, maintain diaries of their activities and notes of meetings or write their memoirs. These diaries and memoirs (called 'private papers') are generally not published in the lifetime of their authors and even when they are published or made public, care is taken to see that such portions as may show them or the government in a bad light are removed or not made available to the historian. The official records and the private papers often deal with matters of a sensitive nature or with persons still living. Thus, making such documents public may cause embarrassment to the government/s or the individual/s about whom they deal with. Some records of discussions between the leaders of different countries, if made public, may embitter relations between them or between them and other countries. Sometimes, governments release documents in support of their policies and actions. Such documents tends to project governmental policies as representing the best interests of their countries or even of the world, and malign others that may lead to a different conclusion. Because of the non-availability of all relevant sources of information, many historians would rather not venture to write the history of recent years.

There are other, stronger, reasons why some historians are unwilling to write about the period in which they are living. The art of writing history is a valid and useful intellectual activity only if it is practised without bias. A historian who writes about the present is, in a sense, a participant and is emotionally involved in the events and developments that he is writing about. Therefore, it is said, a historian's writings cannot be unbiased and objective.

The first reason, mentioned above, regarding the historian's reluctance to write about the present or contemporary history (we shall define what we mean by 'contemporary history' later) carries less weight than is sometimes made out. There is such a wide variety of materials available about contemporary history, and in such abundance, that the absence of some official records and private papers may not really make much difference. This, of course, precludes such historical questions as can be resolved only if all relevant official documents, private papers and the like are available. One can think of many such questions from recent history, for example, the events that took place in August 1991 in Moscow. However, reliable materials on the aspects of history which are of great importance to the historian, such as social and economic life, political institutions, science and technology, various components of culture, are more readily available for contemporary history than for any other period of the past. And these materials are available for almost every part of the world. For earlier periods, even the facts with regard to the population of most parts of the world are not available with any degree of certainty.

The question of bias is more relevant, even though a reader of Indian newspapers of recent years may say that the writings on ancient Indian history, at least the popular writings, including those by some professional historians, reflect more bias on ancient Indian history than on the history of a more recent past. The danger of bias, however, is real and it need not be seen only or even mainly as narrow-mindedness or prejudice. The historian's view may be coloured by his philosophical outlook or his general approach to the problems of the world. While narrow-mindedness of any kind has no place in the historian's profession, no historian can be free from some philosophical outlook or other, as every historian views contemporary problems and issues from a certain standpoint. The historian's general viewpoint or philosophical outlook is, in fact, an important aid to her or his study. It is crucial in formulating a hypothesis which forms the basis for further study and for forming a coherent picture of the event or the phenomenon being studied. There is no getting away from it. The historian, however, has to guard against the danger of her or his general viewpoint degenerating into narrow-mindedness and becoming a stumbling block rather than an aid to understanding. It is also important that the reader of a work of history studies it critically, and is aware of the general viewpoint of the historian as well as of the influence it has exerted on the historian's work.

A more serious problem which arises while studying contemporary history is one of historical perspective or, as one historian has put it, of "knowing what happened in the end". A historian dealing with the events of an earlier period, say, the civil war in England or the battle of Plassey, knows how those events ended and is also able to see and relate the long-term consequences of those events. One cannot write with the same certainty about, say, the end of the Cold War or about the changes which are taking place in the republics which constituted the USSR.

Since there was the possibility that one's views might colour one's historical study and since not enough time had elapsed to provide sufficient historical perspective, some historians thought it was not safe to write even the history of the nineteenth century. Many more, of course, would hesitate to write about recent history with much greater justification. An example from recent history will illustrate how 'unsafe' it can be to write about contemporary history. In 1928, a scholar wrote an article on capitalism for the new edition of *The Encyclopaedia Britannica*. In this article, he wrote, "Capitalism is still accused of responsibility for avoidable unemployment, arising from periodic alternations of climaxes and depressions in trade activity, of 'booms' and 'slumps'. It is certain, however, that though there must always be some tidal movement of rise and fall, the former violence of these rhythms is now much abated...." This article was published in the *Encyclopaedia* in 1929, the year which saw the beginning of the worst economic depression in history affecting almost all parts of the world. The 1920s had been the years of economic growth and prosperity for many capitalist countries in the West. The scholar who wrote the article was convinced that the capitalist system had finally attained stability, but his opinion was proved wrong just at the time it was published. Similar examples can be quoted to show how some recent events have proved false the views of some socialist scholars regarding the growing strength of the world socialist system. The historian's perceptions of the post-1917 developments in Russia or of the socialist movement during the past seven decades would be different today from what they were ten years ago.

It may be useful in this context to quote Eric Hobsbawm, author of a published volume on the twentieth century. In the preface to this book, he writes,

> Nobody can write the history of the twentieth century like that of any other era, if only because nobody can write about his or her lifetime as one can (and must) write about a period known only from outside.... My own lifetime coincides with most of the period with which this book deals, and for most of it, from early teenage to the present, I have been conscious of public affairs, that is to say I have accumulated views and prejudices about it as a contemporary rather than as a scholar. This is one reason why under my professional hat as a historian I avoided working on the era since 1914 for most of my career, though not refraining from writing about it in other capacities.

It is now possible, according to him, to see the history of the twentieth century "from 1914 to the end of the Soviet era in some historical perspective."

From the above, it is clear that much of contemporary history is 'provisional' or 'open-ended'. The events of the past fifteen years have, for example, rendered obsolete much of contemporary historical writings published before 1990. The Soviet Union, which was described along with USA as a pre-eminent military power, ceased to exist. The kind of socialism which was built in the Soviet Union and other socialist countries lost its appeal as the alternative to the capitalist system. Yugoslavia, which had emerged as an independent state at the end of the First World War and had played a leading role in the Non-Aligned Movement, disintegrated. The division of Germany into two independent states, each following a different path of development, came to an end. The system of apartheid in Africa has collapsed and a non-racist, democratically elected government has come to power in South Africa. Some of these developments, and the pace at which these have taken place, have been completely unanticipated. Thus, much of contemporary history lacks the definitiveness or the finality, which the history of earlier periods has.

It should also, however, be remembered that *all* contemporary history, is not 'provisional' or 'open-ended'. For example, the statement that the system of imperialism built by the European powers since the nineteenth century or before collapsed within about two decades after the Second World War is not going to be proved false in the same way as no new scientific researches are going to prove false the statement that the earth is not flat. The statement about the collapse of European imperialism describes a very important historical development in the contemporary world. There are many other significant developments in contemporary history about which our knowledge is much more than 'provisional' though there would also be quite a few about which our knowledge would remain 'provisional'. However, our knowledge of contemporary history is crucial to our understanding of the world in which we live and its problems even if such knowledge is 'provisional'.

What is 'contemporary history'? There are many different answers to this question. Literally, it might mean "only the history of what is already happening at the moment of writing" or "a record of events through which the historian has lived". But most historians consider it to be a specific period of history with its own specific characteristics, in the same way as ancient history, medieval history or even modern history denote. Some historians consider recent modern history to be contemporary history. According to one historian, writing in the early 1960s,

> ... our era has such a well-defined character that it is possible to speak of contemporary history in a specific sense.... (It) is the crucial years from 1945 to the present day which can be regarded as especially the sphere of contemporary history.

A Soviet historian, in his book on contemporary history published in 1986, described the period from 1917 to 1945 as the first stage of contemporary history. He further wrote:

> Contemporary history begins with the Great October Socialist Revolution of 1917 in Russia. This revolution provided the impetus for a radical change in the fate of mankind, its transition from the domination of the exploiter classes to the elimination of exploitation, to the establishment of social justice....

Many Western historians considered the years between 1914 and 1945 as the domain of contemporary history. This was perhaps a reflection of the view that European developments were central to the history of the world. In 1965, a French historian published a book entitled *Major Controversies of Contemporary History*. He studied 65 controversies covering the period 1914 to 1945, by analysing 11,000 published works and numerous personal interviews. Most of the controversies dealt with certain events of European history, a few concerned the US policy vis-à-vis Europe and two related to Japan's relations with Russia and the United States. No other part of the world figured in the book.

There is an increasing trend among historians the world over to treat the history of the twentieth century as the specific sphere of contemporary history. The history of the twentieth century is viewed as contemporary history not only because it is a convenient period in terms of chronology or as recent modem history but because it is regarded as having a 'well-defined character' which makes it a distinct period of history, distinct even from modern history.

Contemporary history, or the history of the twentieth century, is also increasingly viewed as contemporary world history. This is because of the awakening of mankind "to a sense of world community in which all were inescapably involved". For the Europeans, according to the editor of a work on the twentieth century, it was possible to take a short-sighted view of the history of the period preceding the twentieth century and to think that Europe played a leading role in world history. Such a view, according to him, "is no longer even plausible, and any history of the 20th century has to take a view of the whole world in a way that was not true of earlier periods". Geoffery

Barraclough, in his book *An Introduction to Contemporary History*, has written, "One of the distinctive facts about contemporary history is that it is world history and that the forces shaping it cannot be understood unless we are prepared to adopt worldwide perspectives". He considers the period designated by him as 'contemporary' to be different in "quality and content" from what is known as modern history. According to him, contemporary history has characteristics which mark it off from the preceding period in much the same way as what we call 'medieval history' is marked off from 'modern history'. While no fixed dates can be given, contemporary history, according to Barraclough, "begins when the problems which are actual in the world today first take visible shape". He puts this in the last decade of the nineteenth century.

Eric Hobsbawm's book *Age of Extremes*, carries the sub-title *The Short Twentieth Century 1914–1991*. According to him, "the years from the outbreak of the First World War to the collapse of the USSR which, as we can now see in retrospect, form a coherent historical period that has now ended" and that "there can be no serious doubt that in the late 1980s and early 1990s an era in world history ended and a new one began".

Contemporary History: Some Characteristic Features

The main characteristic feature of contemporary history, is that the world has become "integrated in a way it had never been before". There are still many things that divide the world. There are countries that have highly developed economies and there are also countries with extreme economic backwardness. There are ideological and political divisions such as capitalist, socialist and others, though some of them appear to be less important now than they were even ten years ago. Much of contemporary history has been a history of confrontation and conflict. In spite of these divisions and conflicts, "the common problems of mankind" have "become the common concern of all".

Contemporary history is characterised by tremendous changes in every aspects of social, economic and political life and in every other areas of human activity. Winston Churchill, British prime minister during the Second World War and again from 1951 to 1955, mentions in one of his books the advice that an elder statesman gave him when he was entering politics. "My dear Winston", the elder statesman told him, "the experiences of a long life have convinced me that nothing ever happens". Churchill, commenting on this advice, wrote, "Since that moment, nothing has ever ceased happening." He also described this century as "this terrible Twentieth Century". In many ways, the contemporary period, which is mainly the twentieth century, has been truly "terrible". No other century has experiences such colossal destruction of human lives and property as this century has seen and experienced. This period has seen the collapse of imperialism and colonialism on a world-wide scale, the ending of the hegemony which Europe exercised over the world since the beginning of the modern age, and the rise of what is commonly known as the Third World—the peoples of Asia, Africa and Latin America— as a major force in world affairs. The period also saw the emergence of the United States of America and, for many decades, of the Union of Soviet Socialist Republics as world powers, or 'super powers' as they were commonly called. Thus, world politics has been completely transformed during the past one hundred years.

There have been changes in the nature and functions of the state the world over and new forms of state have emerged. In spite of many differences between different forms of state, the powers of the state everywhere have increased and the state now performs many more functions than it did in the past. There is much more active participation by the people in the political affairs of their countries and in the making of history than ever before. It may be recalled that in the year 1890 universal adult franchise was unknown in almost every part of the world. Now it is a common feature of political life in most countries.

There have been tremendous changes in economy and society. The Industrial Revolution, which began in England during the last decades of the eighteenth century, had spread to a few countries of Europe and North America by the end of the nineteenth century. In the twentieth century, industrialism has become a world-wide phenomenon. The advances in science and technology have been so far reaching and fundamental that we often speak of them as revolutionary. Their direct application in industry has further accelerated the rate of change in economic life. In the process, however, the countries that do not have the advantage of modern science and technology, have been left behind and the gap between the economically developed, the developing and the underdeveloped countries has increased tremendously.

All societies have undergone major transformations. There has been an unprecedented increase in what is called "human expectations—a much higher percentage of human race demanding much more and believing that it is possible to provide it". Ideological challenges such as those represented by the rise of socialism in the mid-nineteenth century became powerful forces in the twentieth century influencing hundreds of millions of people in all parts of the world. Even though many regimes which professed socialism have collapsed, the socialist ideal has enriched the concepts of human rights and democracy. The principles of social justice have received universal acceptance.

There has been what may be called a growing secularisation of political and social life, of art and literature, and of ideas, although some parts of the world continue to be plagued with sectarian conflicts and violence. There has generally been a loosening of the hold of religion and what has been called "the growing impatient demand for greater satisfaction in man's present life". The art and literature of the contemporary world are distinguishable from the art and literature of any previous period. Many artists and writers rebelled against the traditions of art and literature; they experimented with new forms and techniques and gave expression to new experiences. In the countries where there was conscious revival of traditions as a part of national awakening, the art and literature that grew were distinctly new and not merely a continuation of the traditional forms, much less their imitation. The art and literature in almost every part of the world have been influenced by the developments in other parts of the world much more than in any other period of human history.

The most significant characteristic of contemporary history, which is increasingly becoming the dominant characteristic, is the awakening "to a sense of world community in which all were inescapably involved". There has been a growing common concern over the common problems of mankind. The most important of these problems has been the common danger that the development of thermonuclear and other weapons of destruction posed to the very survival of human life. There are other problems, such as those of poverty and backwardness, of over-population and, more recently, but one that is increasingly recognised, of environment. Human beings the world over have developed a shared destiny, as never before experienced in the past.

CONTEMPORARY HISTORY AND MODERN HISTORY

If contemporary history is distinct from modern history (and not merely the most recent part of it), it is useful to have an overview of modern history. It should be remembered that no historical period is totally new, every historical period carries within itself much of the preceding period. There are always many elements of continuity. It is also necessary to know the preceding period in order to adequately grasp the *new* in the following period.

The modern period of history may be said to have begun in the fifteenth–seventeenth centuries, if we take an overall view of the world. This statement, of course, is not true for all regions and countries of the world. These centuries marked the transition from the medieval period in some countries of Western Europe. The major historical developments in these centuries of transition were the Renaissance, the Reformation, the beginning of modern science, the discovery of new lands and new routes (particularly new sea-routes) by Europeans leading to the colonisation of the Americas and parts of Asia and Africa, and the emergence of nation-states. All these developments were related to a fundamental change in the way the social and economic life of the people was organised. This change was marked by the disintegration of the feudal system and its replacement by a new system, called capitalism. A large part of the world was brought together as a result of these developments, often by brute force and, in the case of many parts of Africa, by enslavement. Another development which began to take place in the second half of the eighteenth century, and which brought about even more fundamental changes, was the Industrial Revolution. It began in

England with the use of machines for producing goods. By the last quarter of the nineteenth century, the Industrial Revolution had spread to many countries of Europe, though in varying degrees, and to North America, particularly to the US. The countries to which the Industrial Revolution had spread had their social and economic life completely transformed. The centre of economic activity shifted from rural to urban centres, and from agriculture to industrial production and related activities. An ever-growing share of a country's wealth started coming from industry rather than from agriculture. Two new social classes emerged in society—the capitalist or the *bourgeoisie*, who were the owners of industries and controlled trade and commerce, and the industrial working class or the *proletariat*, who worked for a wage. This was a period of terrible misery for the working classes of the industrialised countries of Europe. The workers began to organise themselves into trade unions even though in many countries these were illegal. They also began to organise themselves as a distinct political force under the influence of the ideas of socialism. Thus arose the socialist movement which strove not only to promote the economic demands of the workers but also to mobilise them to overthrow the system of capitalism itself. Karl Marx and Frederick Engels played a leading role in giving a scientific shape to the ideas of socialism and in organising the socialist movements in many countries of Europe. The ideas of socialism also reached the United States. In 1864, the International Working Men's Association, popularly known as the First International, was formed. By the time it was formally abolished in 1876, socialist parties came into being in many countries of Europe. Some of them had a large following. In 1871, the first revolution inspired by the ideas of socialism had taken place in Paris. This is known in history as the Paris Commune which, though it lasted for barely three months, was an event of great historical importance. In 1889, the Second International was formed and socialist parties of various countries were affiliated to it. In the meantime, laws were passed in many countries to safeguard workers against some of the worst effects of the Industrial Revolution and capitalist exploitation.

Simultaneously with these developments, there were significant changes in the political sphere. The formation of nation-states was one of the major developments that marked the period of transition from the medieval period to the modern period. The formation of nation-states in Europe continued during the nineteenth century and, in the case of some countries, during the first two decades of the twentieth century. Nationalism arose as a major factor in the history of Europe.

Nations that were divided into a number of states, such as Germany, or were under the rule of another country, such as Italy, strove to unite themselves into independent states. There was another major development regarding the political system in many countries of Europe. The political system in almost all countries of Europe was monarchical and autocratic. Only England, after a civil war in the seventeenth century, had succeeded in establishing the supremacy of the parliament. During the eighteenth and nineteenth centuries, ideas of democracy and popular sovereignty gained ground. In 1789, the French Revolution took place which proclaimed the ideals of liberty, equality and fraternity, and the Rights of Man and Citizen. Earlier, the English colonists in America had issued the Declaration of Independence which declared, that "all men are created equal" and had certain "inalienable rights", and that the people had a right to overthrow an oppressive government. The colonists had succeeded in their war of independence and had set up a new independent republic, the United States of America.

Along with nationalism, democracy was a major force in the history of nineteenth century Europe. A number of revolutions and movements took place in most countries of Europe to establish democratic political systems. Although almost all the countries of Europe continued to have a monarchical form of government, in many cases the monarchies were constitutional, that is, they were governed by a constitution and real power was exercised by the parliament. In most countries, however, the franchise was not universal, and many men and all women were excluded from the right to vote.

All these developments were confined to Europe and North America, but even in Europe there were some countries that remained unaffected. The rest of the world had neither an Industrial Revolution, except Japan during the last decades of the nineteenth century, nor the kind of social and political changes that have been mentioned above. The eighteenth and nineteenth centuries also witnessed the colonisation of the Americas and parts of Asia and Africa, which took place as a result of the discovery of new lands and sea-routes. A new wave of imperialism arose during the last three decades of the nineteenth century and before the end of the century almost every part of the world had come under direct or indirect subjugation of a few European powers and of the United States. In the case of some countries, the actual occupation took much longer in the face of resistance put up by the people of the colonies. The imperialist conquest of some other countries, such as India, had been completed even earlier. The countries of the world which today constitute the Third World, were subjected to economic exploitation by the imperialist countries even when they were not under direct imperialist rule. The people of the colonies resisted the imperialist rule from the very beginning. Even before the nineteenth century ended, powerful forces had begun to emerge in some countries under colonial domination, which sought to end the colonial rule, not for restoring the pre-colonial systems in their countries but for transforming them into independent modern nations, industrialising them and building their societies on the principle of equality.

Though the world of the nineteenth century was very different from the world which came into being in the twentieth century, particularly during the times in which we live, it should, however, be remembered that some of the forces that were to build the world of the twentieth century, had already begun to emerge in the nineteenth century.

ONE

The World from the 1890s to the First World War

Europe dominated the world from the last decade of the nineteenth century to 1914 when the First World War broke out. However, there were already signs that the beginning of the end of European hegemony had started. Outside Europe, two countries—USA and Japan—had already emerged as major powers. Within the colonies, nationalist movements had begun to take shape. The rivalries among the European imperialist powers over colonial possessions and the conflicts among various European states over European affairs led to the First World War. Within many European countries, powerful movements had emerged which aimed at radical changes in the existing social, economic and political systems. Even before the war was over, the biggest country of Europe, Russia, had a successful revolution. The world which emerged after the First World War was very different from what it had been in the preceding three decades.

EUROPE

Europe's Hegemony and Inter-Imperialist Rivalries

From the 1870s, when the new phase of imperialist expansion began, to 1914, almost the entire continents of Asia and Africa and some areas in other parts of the world had come under the control of one European imperialist country or the other. In Asia, India, Malaya (now Malaysia), Ceylon (now Sri Lanka) and Burma (now Myanmar) were under British rule; the countries comprising Indo-China were under French control and Indonesia was under Dutch hegemony. China was not directly ruled by any single imperialist country but was divided into 'spheres of influence' among the imperialist powers. She thus, was reduced to the status of an international colony. Her dismemberment was prevented by the Boxer Rebellion (1899–1900).

COLONIAL POSSESSIONS IN ASIA IN 1914

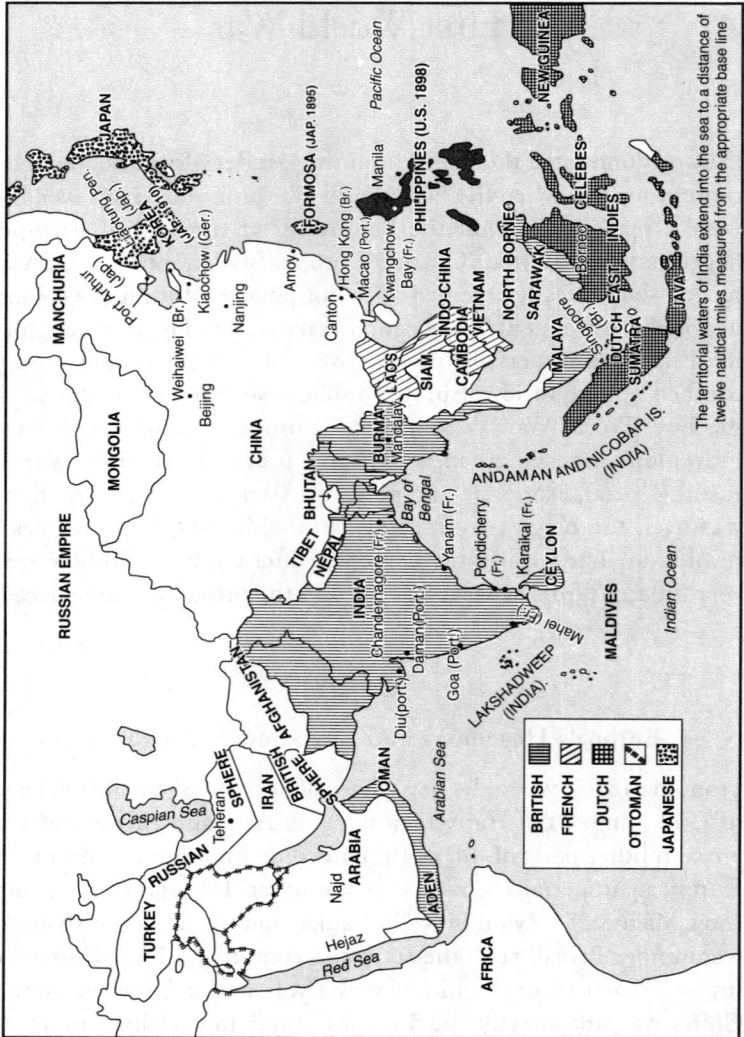

RUSSIAN EMPIRE

MANCHURIA

MONGOLIA

JAPAN

KOREA (JAP. 1910)

Shantung Pen. (dep.)

Port Arthur (dep.)

Weihaiwei (Br.)

Kiaochow (Ger.)

Beijing

Nanjing

CHINA

Amoy.

Canton

Hong Kong (Br.)

Macao (Port.)

Kwangchow Bay (Fr.)

FORMOSA (JAP. 1895)

Manila

PHILIPPINES (U.S. 1898)

Pacific Ocean

NEW GUINEA

CELEBES

NORTH BORNEO

SARAWAK

Borneo

DUTCH EAST INDIES

Singapore

MALAYA

SUMATRA

JAVA

INDO-CHINA

VIETNAM

CAMBODIA

SIAM

LAOS

BURMA

Mandalay

TIBET

BHUTAN

NEPAL

Bay of Bengal

ANDAMAN AND NICOBAR IS. (INDIA)

INDIA

Chandernagore (Fr.)

Daman (Port.)

Diu (port.)

Goa (Port.)

LAKSHADWEEP (INDIA)

Yanam (Fr.)

Pondicherry (Fr.)

Karaikal (Fr.)

Mahel

CEYLON

MALDIVES

Indian Ocean

Arabian Sea

AFGHANISTAN

BRITISH SPHERE

RUSSIAN SPHERE

IRAN

Teheran

Caspian Sea

TURKEY

OMAN

ARABIA

Najd

ADEN

Hejaz

Red Sea

AFRICA

The territorial waters of India extend into the sea to a distance of twelve nautical miles measured from the appropriate base line

BRITISH

FRENCH

DUTCH

OTTOMAN

JAPANESE

Though the rebellion was suppressed by a joint Anglo-German-Russian-French-Japanese-American force, which occupied Beijing, but it prevented the partition of China. In 1907, Iran was divided into three spheres of influence. Russia dominated the northwest, while Britain controlled the southern portion of Iran. The central part was kept as a buffer between Russia and Britian. Britain also exercised some degree of control over Afghanistan. Central Asia had come under the rule of the Russian empire. The only major country in Asia which was independent was Japan. She had defeated China in 1895 and occupied Formosa and in subsequent years had extended her influence over China. She also defeated Russia in a war over Manchuria. In 1910, she occupied Korea.

Africa, with the exception of Ethiopia and Liberia, was divided among the European powers. In 1876, Leopold II, King of Belgium, had taken possession of Congo, more or less as his private property. In 1908 it was handed over to the Belgian government. Britain's empire in Africa included Egypt and Sudan, Rhodesia (Zimbabwe), Uganda, British East Africa, Sierra Leone, Gold Coast (Ghana), Nigeria and South Africa. The French had taken possession of Algeria, Tunisia, Morocco, the Sahara, French Congo, French Guinea, Senegal, Dahomey (Benin) and Madagascar. Germany had acquired German East Africa, South-West Africa, Cameroon and Togoland. The Italian conquests included Libya and Somaliland. Portugal held Angola, Mozambique and Portuguese Guinea. Spain had acquired Rio de Oro and Spanish Guinea. Italy's ambition to conquer Ethiopia had been thwarted when her troops were defeated by the Ethiopian army at the famous Battle of Adowa in 1896.

The British empire was the biggest in the world, both in terms of the number of people over whom it ruled and the area under her control. Britain, at this time, had a population of about 45 million, but the population of her colonial possessions extending over an area of 23 million square kilometres was about 400 million. France with a population of about 39 million ruled over an empire of over 10 million square kilometres inhabited by over 50 million people.

Europe dominated the world not only politically but also economically. Three countries of Europe—Britain, Germany and France—controlled about 45 per cent of the world trade and about 60 per cent of the world market for manufactured goods.

COLONIAL POSSESIONS IN AFRICA IN 1914

The process of the imperialist conquest of Asia and Africa was accompanied by intense rivalries and conflicts among the European imperialist powers. The competing claims over colonies often created conditions of war. However, most of these conflicts were resolved in the conference rooms of Europe and wars were generally avoided. The European powers generally settled their disputed claims over territory on the basis of quid pro quo or 'something for something', by giving away something in exchange for something else. For example, in 1904, after a long period of conflicting claims, which had brought them almost to the point of war, Britain and France entered into a secret agreement whereby Britain was given a 'free hand' in Egypt, while France was given uninterrupted right of domination over Morocco. When Germany came to know about it, she demanded that France relinquish her claim to Morocco. A series of international crises followed, bringing Europe to the brink of war. The Moroccan issue was finally settled in 1911 when France agreed to give a portion of French Congo to Germany and Germany relinquished her claim over Morocco. Both in creating these crises and in resolving them, the people of French Congo or Morocco, whose territories were being bargained, had no say.

In spite of the "Gentlemen's Agreements", which resolved most disputes over colonies, there was growing militarisation of the European states. Every country feared and suspected the others and tried to increase its military and naval strength. Most European countries introduced conscription, that is, making military training compulsory for everyone. Europe was being gradually converted into armed camps. Each country, of course, claimed that the increase in her armed strength was for purely defence purpose, while disputed that of others as an instigation for war. Britain opposed Germany for building a strong navy, saying that it was a luxury for her as she had a strong army. On the other hand, Kaiser William II, the German Emperor, declared, "The German Fleet is not built against any one and not against England, but according to our need.... I want to make myself safe, against France and Russia and England too. And I am all for the white man against the black." Britain was determined to maintain her naval superiority, which she had enjoyed for about three centuries. The feverish manner in which the armed strength of various European states was increasing and the preparations for war were made, led to the steady growth of a feeling that war was inevitable. Further, war came to be considered a part of the natural order of things and was even extolled as a virtue. Preparations for war were accompanied by an extensive propaganda for war. Some philosophers and politicians even started viewing war as one of the "divine elements of the universe" and "a condition for progress".

When we speak of the economic and military might of Europe, it should be remembered that this was not true of all countries of Europe. When war broke out in 1914, there were about twenty-five states in Europe, big and small. The most industrialised of these were Britain,

Germany and France while most of the rest—Spain and Portugal in the Iberian Peninsula, the Balkan states such as Albania, Serbia and Bulgaria, Greece and countries of Eastern Europe—were still primarily pre-industrial economies, even though some of them had acquired colonial possessions. Russia, the most populous country in Europe and with a big empire was primarily an agricultural country, where industrialisation had just begun, and that too, mainly through investments by other countries. Nor were there any notion of the principle of nationality. The Baltic states of Estonia, Latvia and Lithuania, and Finland were part of the Russian empire. Poland as a state did not exist—one part of it was under Russian occupation, another part was ruled by the Austro-Hungarian empire and the third part lay in Germany. Czechoslovakia was a part of the Austro-Hungarian empire as were many areas of the Slav people (comprising parts of what was till recently Yugoslavia). Ireland had been a British colony for centuries. The political system in these countries also varied. Some were republics, though not all republics were democratic; some were constitutional monarchies, the powers of the monarch varying from country to country; and the rest were autocracies.

Conflicts within Europe

The conflicts among European countries were not confined to the question of colonies. There were tensions and antagonisms between them over European affairs. Of the twenty-five European states, five may be said to have been powerful. These were Britain, Germany, France, Austria-Hungary and Russia. Of these, Britain was the richest and the most powerful. Britain had a parliamentary form of government, though monarchy had been retained. Even after the various Reform Acts passed during the nineteenth century, the House of Commons of the British parliament, which comprised elected members (the other being the House of Lords which comprised hereditary members), was not truly democratic. All men still did not have the right to vote and women had no voting rights at all. One of the major problems that Britain faced was the demand for Home Rule by the Irish. A powerful movement for independence had been growing in Ireland, though many people in northern Ireland, mostly settlers from England and Scotland, were opposed to it.

Germany was emerging as the strongest power, both in terms of her economic capabilities and armed might, and was Britain's main rival. She too had a parliamentary form of government though the position of the German emperor was much stronger than that of the British monarch. The territory of Germany included a part of Poland and Alsace-Lorraine which she had taken from France after a war in 1870–71. France, the third most industrialised state of Europe, had been a republic since 1871. She looked forward to the day when she would avenge her humiliating defeat at the hands of Germany and recover Alsace-Lorraine by a war of *revanche* (revenge). The dominant power in Central Europe was the Habsburg Empire, or the dual monarchy of Austria-Hungary. Emperor Francis Joseph was simultaneously the emperor of Austria and king of Hungary. Politically, Austria-Hungary was the most troubled state in Europe, extending over a large area of Europe. Her territories, besides Austria and Hungary, included areas inhabited by many nationalities, like the Czechs of Bohemia and Moravia, Slovaks, Poles, Romanians, Serbs and Croats, and Italians. In all these territories, there was a resurgence of nationalism, creating deep discontent and divisions. The nationalism of the Slav people in Austria-Hungary was also fanned by Russia and Serbia and created strong antagonism between these two countries and Austria-Hungary.

Russia was the biggest country in Europe and she had established a vast empire which included the Baltic states, Finland and parts of Poland in Europe, and Northern and Central Asia. Economically Russia was a backward agricultural country with an outdated political system—there were some industries concentrated in a few big cities. She was under the autocratic rule of the Czars, as the Russian emperors were called, and until 1905 she did not have even the semblance of a parliament. After the revolution of 1905, a parliament, called the Duma, was created with very limited power. Discontent was rife in the Russian empire among the non-Russian nationalities, because of the oppressive social, economic and political system. Another country of Europe which pretended to be powerful was Italy. She had vast colonial ambitions, but, except for her northern parts, she was industrially backward.

Some of the tensions in Europe were connected with the dismemberment of the Ottoman empire. Till the early nineteenth century the entire Balkan Peninsula was a part of the Ottoman empire. Throughout the nineteenth century Russia and the Ottoman empire fought each other. Russia's attempts to extend her control over the Ottoman territories in Europe were thwarted by other European countries, notably Britain, Germany and Austria-Hungary. By the early twentieth century, the Ottoman rule over the Balkans had all but ended. Serbia, Bulgaria and Albania had emerged as independent states. However, the dismemberment of the Ottoman empire did not solve the problem of nationalities in Europe. Serbia had emerged as a champion of the Slav people, many of whom inhabited the Austro-Hungarian empire. She depended on Russia's support in her ambition to create Greater Serbia which would include the Ottoman provinces of Bosnia-Herzegovina, that were under Austria-Hungary, and the southern areas of Austria-Hungary which were inhabited by the Slav people—the Croats, Slovenes and Serbs. She encouraged discontent in these areas and organised conspiracies against Austria-Hungary. This region became the source of increasing tensions in Europe and finally provided the incident which brought about the First World War.

In 1908, Austria-Hungary formally annexed Bosnia-Herzegovina which, though formally a part of the Ottoman empire, had been under her control. Serbia wanted Russia to go to war with Austria-Hungary on this issue but Germany's threat of supporting Austria-Hungary in the event of a war restrained Russia. There was further intensification of bitterness in Serbia against Austria-Hungary as a result of the Balkan Wars (1912–13). Some of the Balkan states, including Serbia, had united, with Russian support, to conquer Macedonia from the Ottomans. However, after the Ottomans had been defeated, Austria-Hungary, with the support of Britain and Germany, succeeded in making Albania an independent state rather than a part of Serbia, which Serbia had earlier hoped.

Formation of Alliances

During the period, treaties and secret agreements were signed, and threats of war issued and withdrawn, indicating alignments and realignments. There were no permanent friends or enemies amongst them and thus no country could rely on the support of another country.

This mistrust persisted till the very outbreak of the First World War and was an additional source of tension. Coupled with this there was the confusion of who was a friend or an enemy. For example, Russia had threatened to go to war on the question of Bosnia-Herzegovina. In fact, she had earlier reached a secret understanding with Austria-Hungary promising her not to interfere in her plans to annex Bosnia-Herzegovina in exchange for her support in Russia's ambition to have the straits leading to the Mediterranean opened to her. However, in spite of these uncertainties, two rival alliances had emerged by the first decade of the twentieth century. Already in 1882, the Triple Alliance comprising Germany, Austria-Hungary and Italy had been formed. Although Germany and Austria-Hungary remained friends, by 1890 it was clear that Italy's loyalty to the alliance would be uncertain. Russia and France had signed secret agreements in 1894 which had brought them together against the Triple Alliance, particularly against Germany and Austria-Hungary. In 1904, Britain and France—who had long been enemies and had often reached the brink of war for their competing claims over colonies—entered into what is known as the *Entente Cordiale*, which was a sort of friendly agreement rather than a formal alliance. The secret clauses of this 'friendly agreement' included France giving up her claims on Egypt in return for freedom to do what she liked in Morocco. The next stage in the process was an agreement in 1907 between Britain and Russia—the two had a long history of hostility and war. The purpose of this agreement was to divide Iran. With this was formed the *Triple Entente* comprising Britain, France and Russia. It was an Entente (understanding) and not a formal alliance. The formation of alliances (or understanding), in spite of doubts about the loyalty of allies or friends, in case the war broke out, further built the atmosphere of war and added to the mistrust and fear of each against the other. The alliances also made it, in a way, inevitable that, when the war breaks out, it would not be a local war confined to one or two countries and that it would almost certainly assume wider proportions.

Social Tensions

Besides the conflicts between states, there were serious tensions and problems within states. The problem of nationalities, which has been mentioned, was not the only source of internal tension. The socio-economic changes that had come about as a consequence of the Industrial Revolution and the rise of capitalism made Europe's hegemony over the world possible. However, the social system in almost all countries of Europe was marked by gross inequalities. In the countries where industrialisation had not taken place on any significant scale, the peasantry, which constituted the bulk of the population, continued to live in conditions of misery and oppression. For countries that were marked by industrialisation and had become mighty economic powers, the social setup was based on undisguised exploitation of the workers. In spite of the growth of industries which produced an increasing quantity of goods, vast masses of people lived in unhealthy conditions and led lives of semi-starvation, with the ever-present danger of being thrown out of employment. Their abject provety became apparent on many occasions. In Britain, for example, during her war against the Boers (Dutch settlers) in South Africa between 1899–1902, the need for recruiting additional men to the army was urgently felt. A large number of people who flocked to the army recruiting centres were, however, rejected, for they were either diseased or considered too weak, to serve as soldiers. Efforts were made to mitigate some of the worst effects of capitalism, but the situation of the downtrodden had not significantly improved even up till the end of the nineteenth century. A British historian of twentieth century Europe has thus remarked:

> The poor who thronged the overcrowded slums of the big towns and industrial districts were a lower order of humanity and treated as such, valued only as the necessary pool of labour, always in surplus, on which the social as well as the economic system depended.

Socialist Movement

The period witnessed the rise of the trade union movement and the spread of the ideas and movements of socialism. Since the last quarter of the nineteenth century the socialist view that capitalism was a system based on exploitation was gaining increasing popularity among the workers of Europe. There was a spate of strikes in pre-First World War Europe. In almost every country of Europe, socialist parties had been formed and were steadily growing both in strength and popularity. By 1914, the number of people who voted for the various socialist parties in Europe also steadily increased. In 1914, the socialist parties of Germany, France and Italy were the single largest parties in the parliaments of their respective countries.

In 1889 the Second International was formed. One of the decisions taken at the Congress at which the Second International was formed was "to organize, for 1st May, a great international demonstration organised in such a way" that on the same day "the workers in all the lands and cities will simultaneously demand from the powers-that-be a limitation of the working day to eight hours". Since then, May Day is observed throughout the world as the working-class day and a day of solidarity of the workers throughout the world.

There were many differences within the socialist movement and among the parties of each country on the meaning of socialism and the methods of achieving it. Some socialists held the view that capitalism could be ended only by overthrowing the ruling class through a revolutionary struggle while others held that capitalism could be transformed gradually through the growing influence of the working class without a revolution. However, almost all the socialist parties were agreed on the eventual overthrow of the capitalist system. These differences were also reflected in the policies of the Second International and continued to divide the socialist movement in later years.

Colonialism, Militarisation and War

Two major issues which all socialist parties and the Second International were concerned about were that of the colonies and of militarisation and war. There were differences on both these issues although on certain aspects of these issues almost all socialists were agreed. Some advocated the view that the right of every nation to freedom and independence was a fundamental concept of socialism and that colonialism should be totally rejected. Others, while condemning capitalist colonial policies, held that under a socialist government colonialism could play a positive civilising role. The latter view was often used by some sections in the socialist movement to directly or indirectly support the colonial policies of their respective governments. These differences persisted for many decades and it was only after the collapse of the colonial system that the 'civilising role' of colonialism, under a capitalist or a socialist government, lost all its 'socialist' adherents.

In spite of these differences, however, the socialist parties of Europe, including those of the imperialist countries, kept themselves aloof from the colonial policies of their respective governments. The Second International, at its Congress held at Stuttgart in Germany in 1907, unanimously passed a resolution which committed the socialist members of the parliaments of different countries to oppose the robbery and subjugation of the colonial peoples and to fight for reforms which would better their lot, protect their rights and "do everything possible to educate them for [their eventual] independence". The leaders of the freedom movements often established close relationship with the socialist parties and leaders of the colonial countries. Dadabhai Naoroji, the Grand Old Man of India's freedom movement, attended a Congress of the Second International, and was greeted with "tumultuous cheers and applause, lasting for several minutes". The president of the session asked the delegates "to treat with the greatest reverence the statement of the Indian delegate, an old man of eighty, who had sacrificed fifty-five years of his life to the struggle for the freedom and happiness of his people". Madame Cama, an Indian revolutionary, unfurled India's flag of freedom, which she had designed, at a Congress of the Second International.

From its very beginning, the socialist movement had viewed war as an extreme expression of the evils inherent in the existing capitalist system and a barbaric instrument with which the ruling classes of various countries tried to promote their economic and political power. The establishment of peace and human brotherhood had been one of the inspiring ideals of the socialist movement. With the growing militarisation and the danger of war, the socialist parties and the Second International increasingly concerned themselves with these issues. One of their major preoccupations throughout this period was the "question of how the workers of the world could unite to prevent wars". All socialist parties were agreed that every effort should be made to prevent wars. They were committed to opposing the arms race and voting against war credits in the parliaments of their respective countries. Many socialist leaders suggested that workers should go on a general strike to prevent war and, in case it broke out, to bring about its speedy termination. Keir Hardie, the British socialist leader, advocated the idea of a strike in the arms industry, transport and mining for preventing wars. The Stuttgart Congress of the Second International unanimously adopted a resolution on "Militarism and the International Conflicts". The resolution stated that wars "are part of the very nature of capitalism" and declared that the struggle against militarism was inseparable from the struggle for socialism. It pledged the socialist parties and their representatives in parliaments "to combat the naval and military armaments with all their might ... and to refuse the means for these armaments. It is their duty to work for the education of the working-class youth in the spirit of the brotherhood of nations and of Socialism...." The resolution ended by saying:

> If a war threatens to break out, it is the duty of the working classes and their parliamentary representatives in the countries involved ... to exert every effort in order to prevent the outbreak of war by the means they consider most effective....
>
> In case war should break out any way, it is their duty to intervene in favour of its speedy termination and with all their powers to utilize the economic and political crisis created by the war to rouse the masses and thereby to hasten the downfall of capitalist rule.

The concluding parts of the resolution quoted above were drafted by three socialist leaders—Lenin and Martov from Russia and Rosa Luxemburg from Germany. They remained steadfast in their adherence to the resolution. A great leader who fought all his life against the forces of militarism and war was Jean Jaures of France. He had earned the wrath of the French *revanchists* (the revenge-seekers) for his propaganda against militarism and war. During the Balkan War in 1912 when a European war seemed imminent, he had declared,

> Let governments remember that in conjuring up the danger of war they invite the peoples to make a simple calculation—how much smaller a sacrifice a revolution would involve, when compared with the war they are preparing.

On 28 July 1914 Austria-Hungary declared war on Serbia. Soon after, a meeting of the Second International was held in Brussels. A call was given at this meeting to the workers of all countries threatened by war to organise peace meetings and to work for the settlement of the dispute between Austria-Hungary and Serbia. The meeting also decided that "the German and French workers will bring even greater pressure on their own governments to make Germany exercise restraint on Austria while France persuades Russia to keep out of the conflict". There was a workers' demonstration in Brussels with the slogan "War on War". Jaures was among the leaders who addressed the demonstrators. After his return to Paris on 31 July, he went in a deputation to persuade the French government to pressurise Russia, France's Entente ally, against her mobilisation for war. A few hours later, on the eve of the outbreak of the First World War, he was shot dead in a cafe.

When the war, finally, broke out, the socialist parties found themselves powerless to oppose it or to call for an uprising for its termination. Some socialist parties even decided to support their respective governments and made common cause with their respective ruling classes. The war, which was the result of the inter-imperialist rivalries and served only the narrow imperialist aims of the ruling classes, was being viewed by some of the socialists as a fight for the survival of their respective nations. With this, an important phase in the history of the socialist movement came to a close. The spirit of internationalism which had characterised the socialist movement from the very beginning, suffered a mortal blow. There were splits in the socialist movements in almost all countries and these became even deeper after the Russian Revolution.

The period of the quarter century before the First World War was one of tremendous growth in the strength of the socialist movement in Europe. The socialist movement challenged the existing order in Europe—the capitalist system on which it was based, the policy of imperialist conquest and exploitation of colonies, and militarism and war. There was a fear of revolution in Europe though none actually took place except in Russia in 1905 where it was suppressed. "Certainly no European government hesitated to go to war for fear that its subjects would refuse the call to arms or turn their weapons against their own rulers—and they were right". This statement by a

historian correctly sums up the situation as it developed in Europe—
except in the case of Russia where the rulers were proved wrong.

USA

For about a hundred years after the thirteen English colonies on the
east coast of North America had won their independence from
England and emerged as the United States of America, that country
territorially expanded at the cost of the neighbouring areas to attained
its present territorial proportion. The westward expansion of the
United States took place at the cost of the American Indian tribes
which inhabited those areas. The American Indians resisted these
encroachments, but by 1890 their resistance finally ended in a
massacre at a place called Wounded Knee in South Dakota. USA
also purchased vast territories of Louisiana and Alaska from France
and Russia, respectively, and seized Texas and California from Mexico
after a war. Between 1861 and 1865, there was a civil war when the
southern states of USA, which were primarily agricultural with
plantations worked by slave labour, seceded from the union. As a
result of the defeat of the southern states in the civil war the union
was preserved and slavery was abolished.

Within three decades after the end of the civil war, USA had become
the foremost industrial power in the world. By the end of the
nineteenth century, she was producing about one-third of the total
production of iron and steel in the world. In almost every branch of
industry, she outstripped every other country in the world. There
were over 300,000 km of railroads in the country, which exceeded the
combined railroads in the whole of Europe. She produced and
consumed more oil and natural gas than the rest of the world put
together. For a long time, the amazing growth of the US economy
went unnoticed. One reason for this was that the US herself provided
a huge market for her products. The US population had risen from
about four million in 1790 to about 92 million in 1910. About twenty-
five million Europeans had migrated to the US during the nineteenth
century and the first decade of the twentieth century. In USA there
had also been a general lack of interest in European and world affairs.

COLONIAL POSSESSIONS IN THE PACIFIC (UP TO 1914)

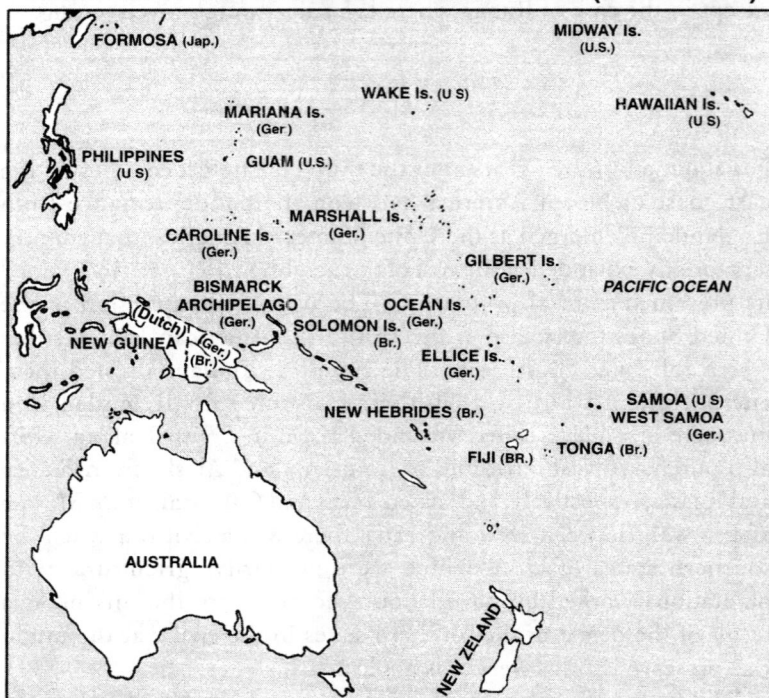

FORMOSA (Jap.)

MIDWAY Is. (U.S.)

WAKE Is. (U S)

MARIANA Is. (Ger.)

HAWAIIAN Is. (U S)

PHILIPPINES (U S)

GUAM (U.S.)

MARSHALL Is. (Ger.)

CAROLINE Is. (Ger.)

GILBERT Is. (Ger.)

PACIFIC OCEAN

BISMARCK ARCHIPELAGO (Ger.)

OCEAN Is. (Ger.)

NEW GUINEA (Dutch) (Ger.) (Br.)

SOLOMON Is. (Br.)

ELLICE Is. (Ger.)

SAMOA (U S)

WEST SAMOA (Ger.)

NEW HEBRIDES (Br.)

FIJI (BR.)

TONGA (Br.)

AUSTRALIA

NEW ZELAND

USA as an Imperialist Power

By the 1890s, USA had emerged as a new imperialist power. In 1889, a US senator said, "Today, we are raising more than we can consume. Today, we are making more than we can use. Therefore, we must find new markets for our produce, new occupation for our capital, new work for our labour". Another senator had warned that the US must not fall out of the line of march. Like many Europeans at that time, the Americans also had begun talking about the duty of the civilised nations to uplift the less fortunate ones and the domination by strong nations of the weak ones being in accordance with the laws of nature. The US expansion in the Pacific had started even earlier. By 1881, the Hawaiian Islands were referred to as being a part of the American System, though they were formerly annexed only in 1898. In the 1880s, a war-like situation had developed as a result of the US, German

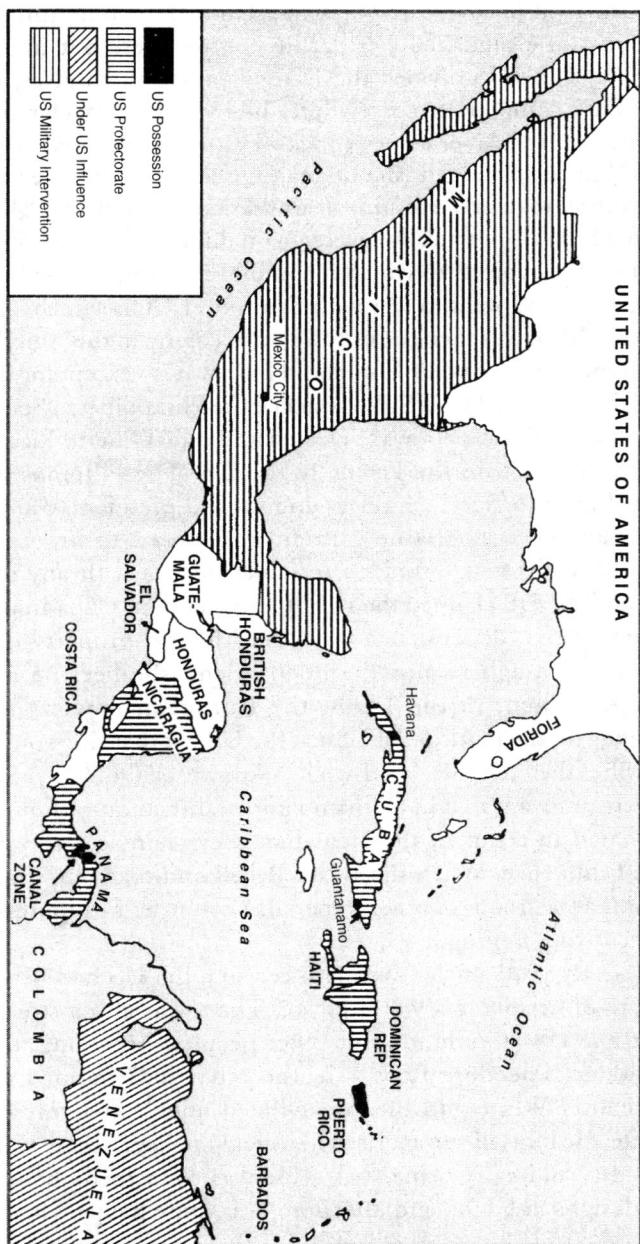

EXPANSION OF US POWER IN CENTRAL AMERICA AND THE CARIBBEAN (UP TO 1917)

Legend:
- US Possession
- US Protectorate
- Under US Influence
- US Military Intervention

and British rivalries over the Samoan Islands. For some time, the three countries established a tripartite control there but in 1899, Germany and the US divided the Islands among themselves, with Britain being compensated elsewhere. In 1893, USA declared her hegemony over the American continent. During a territorial dispute between Venezuela and British Guiana (present Guyana), she forced Britain to agree to refer the dispute to arbitration and declared, "Today the United States is practically sovereign on this continent and its fiat is law upon the subjects to which it confines its interposition".

In 1898, the US went to war with Spain over Cuba which, along with Puerto Rico, was then the only Spanish colony in the Americas. It was claimed to have been "a splendid little war"—except for those who had fought in it. The US also attacked the Philippines, a Spanish colony in the Pacific. Spain was defeated and ceded Puerto Rico and the island of Guam in the Pacific to the US. The Filipinos were considered unfit to rule themselves and the US president, claiming that he had received divine guidance, decided to annex the Philippines. Cuba was forbidden to make treaties with any other country and the US claimed the right to intervene in Cuba in order to preserve her independence, and the life and property of its inhabitants. Though nominally independent, she became a US appendage. When, in the 1890s, the European powers made preparations for the partition of China, the US felt that she would be left out. She, therefore, declared what is known as the 'Open Door policy', which meant that in China no imperialist country should be discriminated in terms of the areas that they claimed to be their spheres of influence. When the Boxer Rebellion broke out, the US troops joined the troops of other imperialist countries in suppressing it and occupying Beijing.

By the early years of the twentieth century, the US had become fully aware of her being a world power. There was also a streak of racism in the US attitude towards other peoples. According to the US president, Theodore Roosevelt, the "civilized" nations were predominantly White and the "uncivilized ones" predominantly non-White. He himself summarised his foreign policy in these words: "Speak softly and carry a big stick". He was concerned about the Russian designs in China and, therefore, was quite happy when the

Japanese attacked the Russian fleet in 1904. Later, he mediated to end the Russo-Japanese War and persuaded Russia to recognise Japan's territorial gains which included the control of Korea and southern Manchuria, and a part of the Sakhalin Island which had earlier belonged to Russia. He also entered into a secret agreement with Japan which gave the US the right to trade freely in that region. The US appeasement of Japan's colonial ambitions was to prove costly to the US later as Japan became the main rival to the US in the Pacific.

Latin America had begun to be seen as USA's special sphere of interest, which was open to intervention only by the US. In 1904, Roosevelt declared that the United States had the right not only to oppose European intervention in the American continent but to intervene in the internal affairs of her neighbours to maintain order. This is known as a new 'corollary' to the Monroe Doctrine. For over thirty years, the US kept to herself the control of the custom revenues of the Dominican Republic. In 1906, US troops landed in Cuba to preserve order and remained there for three years.

The completion of the Panama Canal is considered the "most celebrated accomplishment" of Roosevelt. A French company had completed about 40 per cent construction of the Panama Canal in Colombia. The US bought from the French company its holdings but the Colombian government refused to agree to the terms which the US had offered to her for securing the rights to construct the canal in the Colombian territory. Roosevelt called the Colombians "bandits" and "blackmailers". Soon after, a "revolution" was organised in Panama with money being supplied by an American industrialist. The US troops landed in Panama to preserve order (actually to prevent Colombia from suppressing the 'revolution') and, after three days, Panama was recognised as an independent nation. The new government of Panama signed an agreement with the US on the Panama Canal on terms that were much more favourable to the US than those which the US had earlier offered to the Colombian government and which the latter had rejected. The canal was opened in 1914. In the meantime, in 1906, Roosevelt had been given the Nobel Peace Prize for his role in ending the Russo-Japanese War.

The US policy of intervention in the internal affairs of the Latin American countries continued during the presidencies of William Howard Taft and Woodrow Wilson. Taft's policy of promoting American investments in the Latin American countries and elsewhere and establishing a de facto control through these investments did not preclude the use of gunboats and armed intervention. The US policy towards Mexico during the presidency of Wilson earned the US the lasting hostility of Mexico. In 1910, a corrupt dictator of Mexico had been deposed by a popular leader called Francisco Madero. In 1913, he was deposed, with US approval, by another dictator, and murdered. This dictator was deposed after some time but the US unsuccessfully continued to intervene in the affairs of Mexico.

Protest Movements

The industrial expansion, which had made USA a leading industrial power and was soon to make her a world power, was accompanied by corruption, intense exploitation and complete disregard for the interests of the people. The owner of one of the largest railroad companies is credited with the most ruthless but frank remark: "The public be damned". By adopting ruthless methods, a few individuals controlling a few corporations had concentrated enormous economic power in their hands. Often this concentration took place through bribery and in crass violation of the existing laws. The holder of a huge industrial empire, when told that what he was doing was against the law, declared: "What do I care about the law? Hain't I got the power." The need to control the increasing concentration of economic power in a few hands became a major issue in the politics of USA from the 1890s. It led to a movement called 'Progressivism'.

What has been said earlier about the conditions of the common people, particularly the industrial workers, in Europe was also true for USA. The working and living condition of the workers was miserable and unemployment was a common feature of their life in spite of the enormous economic growth. Workers were never very far from the prospect of poverty, losing their jobs or facing a cut in their wages. Child labour was rampant and children working at night in the textile mills were kept awake by throwing cold water on their faces. Female children in some industries worked sixteen hours a day. About 20 per cent of the workers employed in the manufacturing industries were women, who were paid much lower wages than men. Little attention was paid to prevent industrial accidents, which were a common occurrence.

The workers of USA began to organise themselves and there was a wave of strikes from the 1880s. Most of these were ruthlessly suppressed by the state police who use to terrorise the workers. The industrialists also used guards hired for the purpose of breaking strikes and terrorising workers. One agency which provided the services of its guards for this purpose was the Pinkerton Detective Agency and it continued to provide these services for many decades. Killing of trade union leaders was not uncommon. A national workers' organisation which emerged in this period was the American Federation of Labour (AFL). On its call, strikes and demonstrations were held on 1 May 1886 all over the country to press the demand for an eight-hour working day. In Haymarket Square in Chicago, on that day, the police fired at demonstrators who were protesting against police atrocities on the striking workers of the city. Four workers were killed. Someone had earlier thrown a bomb at the police, which had killed seven policemen. Eight persons were arrested on the charge of inciting the person who had thrown the bomb and in what is considered to be one of the most "injudicious trials" in American history. Seven of the accused were sentenced to death. The Second International's decision to give a call to workers to observe May Day was connected with the incidents that had earlier taken place at Haymarket Square in Chicago on 1 May 1886.

Many Americans raised their voice against the gross inequalities in society, the exploitation of child labour and of women workers, the growing concentration of wealth in a few hands, and corrupt industrialists, bankers, politicians and officials. A powerful literature of protest was produced by writers and journalists. There also developed a strong opposition to the imperialist policies being followed by the US government. Some of the earliest socialist groups outside Europe were formed in the US. In 1901, the Socialist Party of America was formed. Its most prominent leader was Eugene V. Debs, who polled about one million votes in the 1912 election for the presidency. Another important labour organisation was the Industrial Workers of the World (IWW). When the First World War broke out, the US, in the words of President Wilson, decided to remain "impartial in thought as well as deed". In April 1917, USA decided to enter the "war to end wars" and to "make the world safe for democracy". As has been mentioned earlier, the coming of the First World War brought about a permanent schism in the world socialist movement with some of the socialist parties of different Europe countries supporting the imperialist policies of their respective governments. The American Socialist Party and the IWW, however, stuck to their opposition to the war. The US government had made laws according to which any public expression of opposition to the war was sedition and sabotage. Many Americans were prosecuted for their opposition to the war. Eugene Debs was sentenced to ten years' imprisonment.

Black People's Struggle for Equality

There were other tensions and conflicts within the US some of which have persisted till our own times. Vast sections of the American population suffered from various other disadvantages besides the ones created by the concentration of wealth in a few hands. Industrial progress did not mean increased prosperity of the people. In the course of a little over a hundred years, the American Indian tribes, which inhabited North America, were deprived of their lands and their way of life was totally disrupted. By 1890, the process of their total subordination was nearly complete and they had to accept what the Whites left to them.

One of the major issues in the history of USA since the nineteenth century has been the struggle of the Black or Afro-American people for freedom and equality. For about eighty years after USA emerged as an independent nation with a republican form of government, slavery continued in that country. In 1860, in a total population of about 31 million, there were four million slaves owned by about 225,000 people. This was mainly prevalent in the southern states of USA. In 1865, after the civil war, slavery was abolished. For about ten years after the civil war, efforts were made to enforce the rights of the Black people—the former slaves in the former slave-owning southern states. In 1868, 'citizenship' rights were given to all persons "born or naturalized" in the United States and these rights could not be abridged. In 1870, the Fifteenth Amendment to the Constitution was passed, which made it a law that the right of the citizens to vote "shall not be denied or abridged on account of race, colour, or previous condition of servitude". Earlier, even in the northern states, which did not have slavery, most Black people were denied their basic citizenship rights on one ground or the other. After the Fifteenth Amendment the Black people not only got their right to vote but such a right was enforce even in the southern states. This period which lasted till the 1870s is known as the Reconstruction Period. In many respects, this was the first time that the US had a truly democratic system. It came to an end when power was handed back to the former slave-owners in the southern states. Troops of the Federal government were withdrawn from the southern states, and a period of denial of political and legal rights to the Black people and the practice of racial discrimination and oppression against them started.

By the early years of the twentieth century, the Black people were stripped of their legal and political rights, and segregation between Whites and Blacks was rigidly enforced. Blacks and Whites could not travel in the same train compartments, they could not go to the same parks and beaches, they could not eat in the same restaurants, and they could not go to the same schools, theatres and even hospitals. Segregation was combined with violence, and it is estimated that about 200 Blacks were lynched by White mobs every year during the last decade of the nineteenth century. Racism also became an instrument for perpetuating socio-economic inequalities. The Black people were the most economically depressed section of the American society. But most of the Whites were also poor and were ruthlessly exploited. By arousing racial feelings, common people, Black and White alike, were prevented from forming a united front against economic exploitation. The Black people suffered from discriminatory practices throughout the country; in the southern states, of course, the discrimination was much worse and much more brutal than in the northern states. By the early years of the twentieth century, a powerful movement of protest against racial discrimination began to emerge. The most significant figure in this movement was W.E.B. Du Bois. He remained a key figure for about halk a century. In 1909, the National Association for the Advancement of Colored

People (NAACP) was formed. Many Whites who were opposed to racism also supported the struggle of the Black people. However, it took over half a century before significant progress began to be made in ending racial discrimination and the inhuman system of racial segregation.

It has been mentioned earlier that even in those European countries that had a democratic system of government, women were denied the right to vote. The same situation existed in the US. The movement for woman suffrage had started in the mid-nineteenth century and it became an important issue in the early twentieth century. However, it was only in 1920 that American women were granted the right to vote by the US Constitution.

Japan

Rise of Modern Japan

It has been mentioned earlier that Japan was the only Asian country to have escaped imperialist control. For centuries, military generals, called *shogun*s, exercised real power in Japan while the Japanese emperor was a mere figurehead. For over two hundred years, Japan had been almost totally secluded from the rest of the world. In many respects, the Japanese social system was comparable to the social system of feudal Europe. Around the middle of the nineteenth century, Japan was rudely awakened to the modern world when her independence was threatened. Within a few decades she not only succeeded in warding off the danger of foreign domination but also underwent a process of modernising certain aspects of her society that enabled her to emerge as a world power.

In 1853, Commodore Perry went with a US fleet and delivered an ultimatum to Japan. It was stated that "positive necessity requires that we should protect our commercial interests in this remote part of the world, and in doing so, to resort to measures, however strong, to counteract the schemes of powers less scrupulous than ourselves". Eight months later, when he returned with a bigger fleet, the Japanese government signed a treaty with the US under which two ports were opened to US ships and some amount of trade was permitted. Similar treaties were then signed by several European countries. In 1863 and

JAPAN'S COLONIAL EXPANSION (1895–1918)

1864, the US and European fleets displayed their military superiority by firing on two Japanese cities.

In 1868, the rule of the shogun was ended and a new set of rulers and advisers came to the fore. They ruled in the name of the emperor, whose authority, in theory, was restored. This event is known as the Meiji Restoration, after the title 'Meiji' which the new emperor took.

Within less than four decades of the Meiji Restoration, Japan's economy and political institutions underwent speedy transformation. The Japanese government made heavy investments in industries, the money for which was raised through heavy taxation and by exploiting the peasantry. Subsequently, the industries were sold to capitalists. Afterwards, government support for starting industries was no longer required as the Japanese capitalists were able to start industries on their own. The process of industrialisation was accompanied by impoverishment of the peasants, who often rebelled. An increasing number of them migrated to the cities where they provided cheap labour for the industries. By the early years of the twentieth century, Japanese goods, particularly textiles, could successfully compete in the international market with European goods. The demand for Japanese manufactures within Japan was limited due to the extreme poverty of the common people.

In 1889, Japan was given a new constitution. The emperor enjoyed a special position as head of the executive and ministers were appointed by him and were responsible to him. He was believed to be "heaven-descended, divine and sacred; he is pre-eminent above his subjects. He must be reverenced and is inviolable". The constitution provided for a parliament called the Diet. Less than three per cent of the population had the right to vote. The Diet enjoyed little power: the ministers were not responsible to it, and even in financial matters, its powers were limited. The military enjoyed vast powers in the new political system and, in course of time, came to dominate it completely. The army and the navy appointed army and naval officers, ministers of the army and the navy, and the Diet had absolutely no control over them. The educational system which was built up made the mass of the population literate within a very short time. It enabled the Japanese to master the technical skills necessary for industrialisation. The educational system was used to promote emperor worship and an attitude of extreme nationalism and chauvinism. Civil liberties and open political struggles were lacking in Japan. The state was controlled by an oligarchy and the repressive apparatus of the state, notably the police, enjoyed wide powers to control the press and even prevent the holding of public meetings and demonstrations. Political dissent was not tolerated. In spite of severe restriction, however, the first socialist group in Asia was formed in Japan.

Japan as an Imperialist Power

By the 1890s, Japan had started pursuing her colonial ambitions. These ambitions were primarily directed at China and aimed at establishing Japanese supremacy in East Asia. Later, the object of the Japanese ambition encompassed the entire Asian continent and the Pacific region. Having built up her armed strength, she went to war with China and defeated her in 1895. She annexed Formosa (Taiwan), which was a part of China, and forced China to recognise Korea, over which she claimed suzerainty, as an independent state. The Japanese objective in all this was not to secure the independence of Korea but to end the Chinese influence there and to gain a free hand for the subjugation of Korea. In 1905, Korea was made a protectorate of Japan and in 1910 was annexed by her. In 1899, Japan's status as a great power was recognised by the US and European countries when they gave up the rights and concessions that they had obtained as a result of the treaties which Japan had been forced to sign with them after 1854. In 1902, the Anglo-Japanese Treaty or Alliance was signed, and Japan became the first Asian country to enjoy the status of full equality with other colonial powers. The British objective in signing the treaty was to deter Russian designs in China. The Russo-Japanese War (1904–5) that followed, ended in the defeat of Russia. Southern Manchuria was recognised as a Japanese "sphere of influence". Japan also obtained half of the Sakhalin Island and acquired control of the Liaotung Peninsula. During the First World War, Japan sought to establish her protectorate over China. Though she did not succeed in achieving this aim, she was able to extend her influence there.

The rise of Japan as a great power, even though she was following imperialist policies in Asia, provided an impetus to the growth of nationalism in many Asian countries. Her war with Russia proved that an Asian non-White country could defeat a major European power. It should, however, be remembered that the main victims of Japanese imperialism were not Europeans but people of other Asian countries.

The emergence of USA and Japan as great powers was an indication that the supremacy of Europe would not last long. The First World War hastened the end of European hegemony.

Asia, Africa and Latin America

We have referred to certain developments in Asia, Africa and Latin America in the context of European, American and Japanese imperialism. From the time when the imperialist countries established their direct or indirect control, they were faced with stiff resistance by the native people. In course of time, the early forms of resistance gave way to the rise of nationalist movements, which aimed at the overthrow of direct or indirect foreign control, asserted their right to equality with other nations and expressed their determination to build up the economies of their countries on modern lines and their political and social systems on the principles of democracy and social justice. These nationalist movements often had to fight against the outdated political systems in their own countries as well as those elements that stood in the way of their progress.

Rise of Nationalist Movements in Asia

Indian nationalism with its specific features was the first nationalist movements to emerge in the colonies. By the early years of the twentieth century movements for national liberation had begun to emerge in other parts of Asia, notably in Indo-China, Indonesia, Korea, the Philippines and Iran.

In Iran, after a series of revolts, the Shah of Iran had been forced to agree to transform Iran into a constitutional monarchy with a parliament, called Majlis. With the support of foreign powers, particularly Russia, the Shah re-established his despotic rule and the Majlis was abolished.

In China, a number of revolutionary organisations emerged which later consolidated to form the Chinese Revolutionary League. The president of this League was Dr Sun Yat-sen, who played the leading role in the national awakening of the Chinese people and uniting the various revolutionary groups together. The League was guided by three principles enunciated by Dr Sun Yat-sen. These principles were: nationalism, democracy, and livelihood (the last one is sometimes referred to as socialism). In specific terms, these principles meant the ending of the rule of the Manchu dynasty which had been ruling China since the middle of the seventeenth century, and the establishment of a democratic republic with equitable distribution of land among the populace. In 1911, revolution swept southern China and on 1 January 1912, China was proclaimed a republic with its headquarters at Nanjing (Nanking). Dr Sun Yat-sen was made the president of the republic. In the meantime, in northern China, some steps had been taken to introduce constitutional monarchy in China, with General Yuan Shih-kai as prime minister. To avoid a conflict between the governments in control of northern and southern China, from Beijing (Peking) and Nanjing respectively, a compromise was reached. The Manchu ruler abdicated and thus the imperial rule in China came to an end. Yuan Shih-kai was recognised as the president and he was entrusted with the task of calling the parliament. Yuan Shih-kai was supported by foreign powers. In 1913, he called the parliament but soon dismissed it. He had dreams of declaring himself emperor. In the meantime, Dr Sun Yat-sen had formed the Guomindang (Kuomintang) or the National Party and had given a call for a "second revolution". Yuan was able to suppress the Guomindang, which was banned, and Dr Sun sent to exile. In 1916, Yuan died and China came under the rule of warlords, who controlled different parts of the country and received financial support from foreign powers. When the First World War ended, the national and revolutionary movement in China entered a new phase.

By the early years of the twentieth century the Ottoman Empire had lost most of its territories in Europe. Most of her possessions in North Africa had also been taken over by European colonial powers. In the countries of West Asia—Syria, Iraq, Lebanon, Palestine and Arabia— nationalist feelings had been on the rise. Within Turkey, there were powerful stirrings against the tyranny of the Sultan and for making Turkey a modern democratic and secular state. The movement was led by a group of intellectuals, reformers and army officers, called the Young Turks. Threatened by a rebellion, the Sultan, in 1908, agreed to restore the constitution, which had been first introduced in 1876. Some Young Turks were in favour of giving equal rights to the Arabs of the Ottoman Empire while others were bent on maintaining Turkish supremacy and even extending it. Ultimately, Turkey, due to the failure of the liberal Young Turks, was drawn into the First World War on the side of Germany and Austria-Hungary, and the British succeeded in pursuing their imperialist ambitions in the Arab world by making use of the anti-Ottoman Arab nationalist feelings.

Anti-Colonial Resistance in Africa

The European partition of Africa had been more or less completed by the end of the nineteenth century, except for some parts of North Africa, which were acquired by the end of the first quarter of the twentieth century. The actual occupation of the African territories, however, took the European colonial powers much longer because of the resistance and revolts that they had to face. Some of these revolts took the colonial powers a long time to suppress. There was, for example, the Maji-Maji revolt in German East Africa in 1905–7. Unlike in many other countries of Asia, modern nationalist movements in Africa emerged only after the First World War. When they arose, they had a long tradition of resistance and revolt behind them.

Developments in Latin America

In Latin America, twenty independent states had emerged with the collapse of the Spanish and Portuguese empires. Till the end of the nineteenth century, most of them had backward economies, based mainly on agriculture. Most of them were also ruled by corrupt oligarchies, and strong governments did not emerge, which could resist the economic domination by other countries. The rich resources of these countries, instead of being used for development and welfare of the people, were bartered away to European companies and, later, increasingly, to US corporations. With foreign investments in mines, plantations, railways, shipping, electricity, and almost all important sectors of the economy, Latin America had become what has been called an 'informal empire'. Almost all the states of Latin America was dominated by the US.

Most Latin American countries had social systems which were marked by gross inequalities. In some countries, slavery had been abolished as a result of the French Revolution. In some others, however, it persisted even after it had been abolished in USA. In Brazil, for example, slavery was abolished only in 1888. However, in spite of the long persistence of slavery in some of the Latin American countries, the kind of racism, racial discrimination and segregation which marked life in USA even in the twentieth century, was absent in Latin America.

Except for later Asian immigrants, the population of Latin American countries comprised American Indians, people of European descent, and Blacks, who were descendants of slaves brought from Africa, and their admixtures. More than half of the population of Latin America was of mixed blood. However, in most countries which had a large American Indian population—such as Peru, Ecuador, Bolivia, Colombia, Venezuela—all powers were concentrated in the hands of White ruling cliques. Large estates were owned by mainly absentee landlords while the American Indians were forced to live in conditions of extreme poverty. Only in Mexico—a country with a large American Indian population—did united popular movements grow with American Indian participation on a massive scale to put an end to social inequalities, to bring about equitable distribution of land, and to build a state system based on the support of the common people. Mexico, however, underwent a long period of political turmoil, including intervention by USA before the aims of the Mexican Revolution could, to some extent, be realised. Argentina made some progress in building up her economy and democratic institutions. The city of Buenos Aires was regarded as the Paris of Latin America.

By the time the First World War broke out, there were democratic stirrings in many parts of Latin America. Even though Latin American countries had been independent for about a century, they "lingered on the margin of international life", with no independent role to play. With little industrialisation, they were reduced to the position of suppliers of raw materials. Some of them were transformed into single crop economies for the benefit of their powerful neighbour. This made them further dependent. The contrast between North America and Latin America was too glaring to be missed by the people of Latin America. There was a rise in the aspirations of the Latin American people and a growing sense of hostility to USA.

THE FIRST WORLD WAR

The inter-imperialist rivalries, the growing chauvinism, antagonism and conflicts within Europe, the formation of opposing alliance systems, and the growing militarisation and feverish preparations for war, were some of the marked features that characterised the history of Europe since the last decade of the nineteenth century. There had been a number of crises which had been at least temporarily resolved. The tensions in Europe, however, had created a situation in which war had begun to be considered inevitable. Every state was ready with its war plans and strategies. It had also become increasingly clear that once the war broke out, it would not be possible to localise it and that it would become a general war and every country would get drawn into it.

The Immediate Occasion

The assassination of Archduke Francis Ferdinand, heir to the Austrian throne, and his wife in Sarajevo on 28 June 1914 provided the immediate occasion for the outbreak of the war. Sarajevo, where the assassination took place, was the capital of Bosnia which had been annexed by Austria-Hungary a few years earlier. The organiser of the assassination was a secret society, called the "Black Hand" or "Union of Death". They were a group of extremist Serbian nationalists whose aim was to unite all Serbians into a single Serbian state. Historians are generally agreed that the Serbian government, or at least the Serbian prime minister, was aware of the conspiracy to assassinate the Archduke but did nothing to stop it. Convinced of Serbia's complicity in the assassination, Austria (short for Austria-Hungary) served an ultimatum on 23 July making eleven demands on Serbia. Austria did not expect these demands to be accepted and hence fixed a time-limit of forty-eight hours for unconditional compliance. Serbia accepted most of the demands, but not all. Total acceptance of all the demands would have meant total loss of sovereignty by Serbia. Serbia's reply of 25 July did not conciliate Austria, and Serbia, knowing that it would not, had already ordered mobilisation of her troops. Austria rejected Serbia's reply and immediately ordered the mobilisation of her army for an attack on Serbia. She was determined to put an end to this "permanent danger to my House and my territories", as the Austrian emperor called it in a letter to the German emperor. On 28 July Austria declared war on Serbia. On 29 July, the Austrian army bombarded Belgrade, Serbia's capital.

The outbreak of war between Serbia and Austria was soon followed by wars between countries that were militarily linked together. These wars led to the general war or the First World War. In order to pressurise Austria to abandon the war against Serbia, Russia ordered mobilisation against Austria. She could not permit Austrian expansion in the Balkans. Russia had her own ambitions in Serbia which would have suffered if Serbia gets defeated at the hands of Austria. As Germany would come to the aid of Austria, if Russia entered the war against Austria, Russia also prepared for war with Germany. Germany was convinced that in the event of a war between her and Russia, France would join Russia against Germany. This would mean that Germany would have to fight on two fronts, with France in the west and with Russia in the east. To be successful in the war, Germany had made plans to first defeat France in a quick war by mobilising most of her troops for this purpose and then turn to Russia against whom a quick victory was not possible. Thus, the second war was between Austria and Germany on the one side and Russia and France on the other. The British position was still unclear as the British government was divided on the issue of going to war. She responded to the French request for help by promising to defend France's northern coast against the German navy. However, German invasion of neutral Belgium finally ended Britain's indecisiveness, and Germany and Britain were at war. Thus, the rival alliances, formed in the preceding years, had come into play. Only Italy, a member of the Triple Alliance, remained neutral on the ground that Germany was not fighting a defensive war.

The Scope of the War

On 1 August 1914, Germany declared war on Russia and on 3 August on France. In the morning of 4 August, German troops entered Belgium and at midnight of the same day Britain declared war on Germany. In the meantime the Serbo-Austrian war which had led to the conflagration involving Germany, Russia, France and Britain, appeared to have become secondary. Till 6 August Austria was not at war with Russia and till 12 August she was not at war with Britain and France. Soon others joined in as a result of efforts by both sides to win allies by promising them territorial gains. In August, Japan

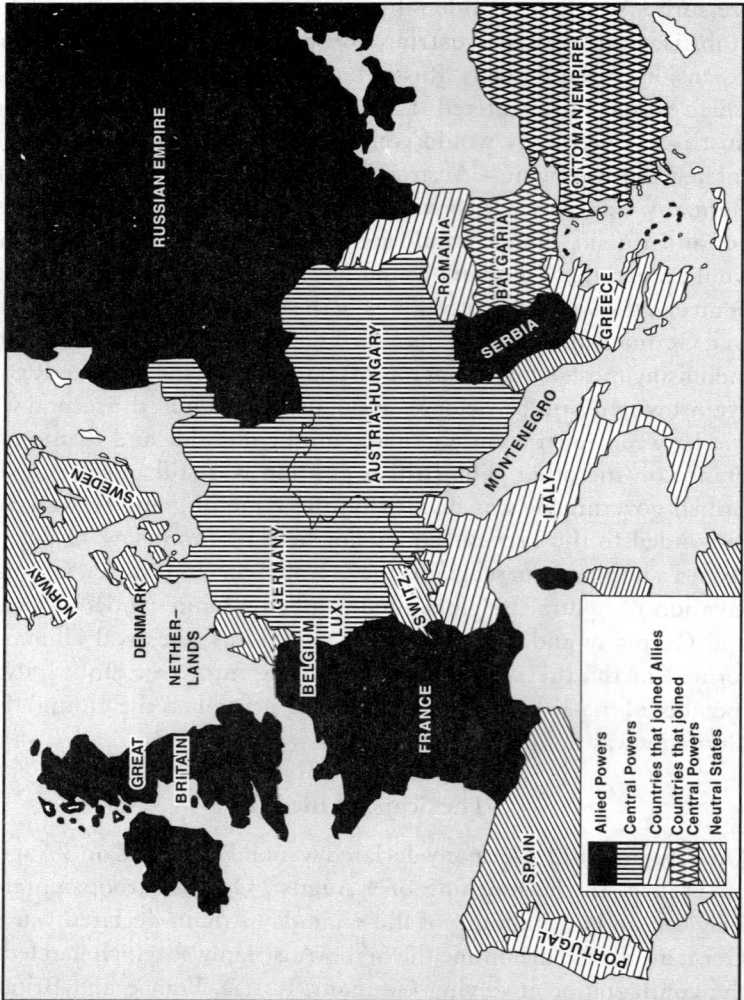

EUROPE DURING THE FIRST WORLD WAR

RUSSIAN EMPIRE

OTTOMAN EMPIRE

ROMANIA

BALGARIA

SERBIA

GREECE

AUSTRIA–HUNGARY

MONTENEGRO

SWEDEN

ITALY

NORWAY

DENMARK

GERMANY

NETHER–LANDS

BELGIUM

LUX–

SWITZ–

GREAT BRITAIN

FRANCE

SPAIN

PORTUGAL

Allied Powers

Central Powers

Countries that joined Allies

Countries that joined Central Powers

Neutral States

THE TRENCH LINE

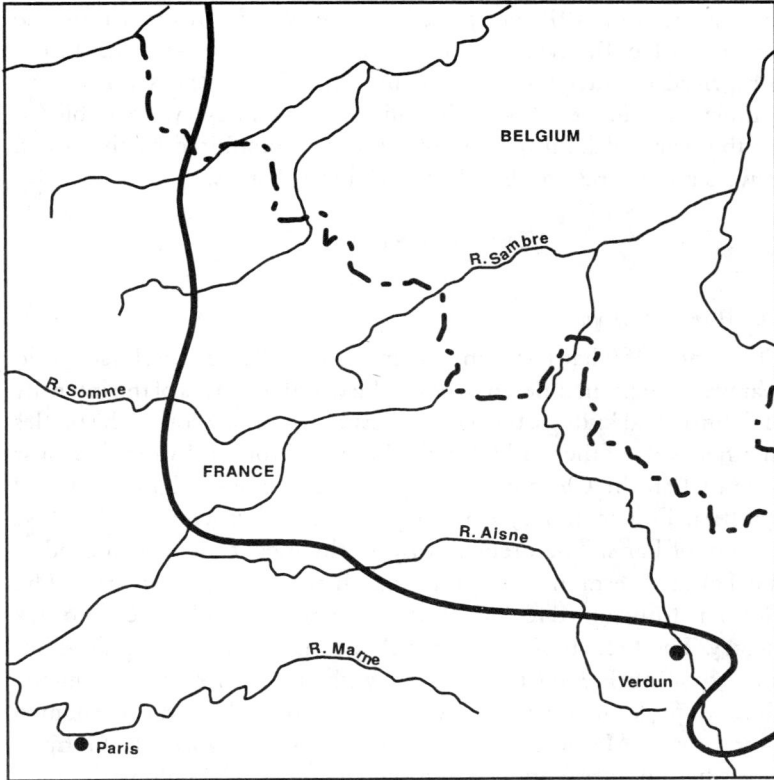

declared war on Germany. She had entered into an alliance with Britain but her main aim was to seize German territories in China and in the Pacific. Portugal, often referred to by Britain as her oldest ally, also entered the war. In May 1915, Italy declared war on Austria. Britain and France had promised her Austrian and Turkish territories. Later, Romania and Greece also joined Britain, France and Russia, and these countries along with their allies came to be known as the Allied Powers. Germany and Austria were joined by Bulgaria in October 1915, having been promised territories in Serbia and Greece. Bulgaria was also given some Turkish territories. Turkey declared war on Russia in November and joined the war on the side of Germany and Austria. These countries—Germany and Austria and their allies—came to be known as the Central Powers. Various other countries in other parts of the world also joined the war. USA entered the war in April 1917 on the side of the Allied Powers. In all, the number of belligerent countries rose to twenty-seven. These comprised countries from all continents. Thus, the scope of the conflict was widened. About 65 million men (soldiers) were mobilised for the war. Of them over 42 million were mobilised by the Allied Powers and over 22 million by the Central Powers.

The Course of the War

The War in Europe

The battles of what has rightly come to be called as the First World War were fought in different parts of the world. In terms of the intensity of fighting and killings, the battles in Europe overshadowed the battles in other parts of the world. On the Western Front in Europe, the war began when the German armies, sweeping across Belgium, entered southern France and by early September had reached in the close vicinity of Paris. The French army, in the meantime, had moved to the France-German frontier to march into Alsace-Lorraine. The German army hoped to encircle the French army and achieve a quick victory. The French offensive into Alsace-Lorraine was repulsed but the retreating French forces along with the British forces met the German forces in a battle known as the Battle of the Marne (named after the river Marne near which the battle was fought). The German forces had to retreat and they entrenched themselves along the river Aisne. There were desperate fights, but by the end of November the war entered a period of a long stalemate on the western front when neither side could dislodge the other for about four years.

Behind a long unbroken chain of opposing trenches and barbed wire extending over hundreds of kilometres from France's southern border with Switzerland to the northern seacoast of France, the opposing armies dug themselves in. Protected from the machine gun and rifle fire behind the trenches, neither side could break through the other's line of trenches. Each side conducted raids on the other in the pre-dawn hours with little success, only steadily adding to the number of the dead on both sides. Germany, in 1915, started the use of poison gas to achieve a breakthrough, and Britain, in 1916, introduced the use of tanks, devised recently, for the same purpose. Neither made much difference. The losses suffered by each side were made up for by bringing in more troops.

On the Eastern Front, Russia achieved some initial successes against Germany and Austria but these were short-lived. In 1915, the Russian armies suffered heavy defeats and the forces of the Central Powers entered many territories of the Russian empire. In 1916, Russia launched another offensive but it was repulsed. After the October Revolution, Russia withdrew from the war. On 2 March 1918, she signed the Treaty of Brest-Litovsk with Germany and ceded many of her territories as the price of peace. Out of a total of 12 million men mobilised by Russia, 1.7 million had been killed, about 5 million wounded and about 2.5 million were either missing or had been taken prisoner. In the meantime, Serbia and Romania had capitulated.

Spread of the War Outside Europe

Outside Europe, some major battles were fought in North Africa and West Asia. Germany and Turkey united to threaten the Allied possessions and influence in North Africa and West Asia. Britain and France fought these attempts and tried to seize the Arab territories of the Ottoman Empire. They also established contacts with Arab nationalists and others and fomented anti-Turkish Arab risings. While pretending to espouse the cause of Arab countries freedom from Turkish rule, Britain and France entered into a secret agreement, known as the Sykes-Picot agreement, in 1916. This agreement provided for the division of Arab countries between Britain and France. In 1917, the British government also pledged itself "to the establishment in Palestine of a national home for the Jewish people". This 'pledge' by Britain about another country, which was not considered fit to be consulted, was to have serious consequences for peace and stability in West Asia.

During the course of the war, German colonial possessions in Asia and Africa were seized by the Allied Powers. Japan made colonial gains in China by acquiring control over the German sphere of influence and forcing China to make further concessions to her. German South-West Africa was occupied by South African troops, Togoland by British and French troops and Cameroons by British, French and Belgian troops. The fighting between British and German troops in German East Africa continued till the end of the war.

The Stalemate in Europe

In the meantime, what has come to be known as the "war of attrition",
continued in Europe. It meant each side trying to wear out the other
side by mobilising more and more men and using enormous amounts
of artillery and other weapons. Two catastrophic battles were fought
as a part of this "war of attrition". In February 1916, Germany
launched a massive attack on the French fortress of Verdun. The
French in turn poured hundreds of thousands of their soldiers into
the battle. This battle, which did nothing to end the stalemate, resulted
in about 700,000 soldiers killed or wounded, more or less equally
divided between the two sides. The other was the battle of Somme
(named after the river Somme along which the battle was fought).
Here the Allied troops involved were mainly British who launched
the attack. On the very first day of the battle, the British dead or
wounded totalled about 60,000.

The Policy of Blockade

The war had become a total war. It was no longer confined to battles
between armies. It required total mobilisation of all the resources of
the main belligerent countries. An increasing amount of munitions
and other war materials were required to be produced. This meant
changing the production pattern. Every economic activity had to be
subordinated to the needs of the war. It also required that no goods—
food, raw materials, war materials, anything and everything—should
be allowed to enter the enemy's country from anywhere. This implies
a regime of economic blockade, where each side thought that the
other would be starved into submission. Britain imposed a naval
blockade on Germany and though the naval fleets of the two countries
fought only one major battle, and that too indecisive, the British
succeeded in their blockade of Germany. To prevent food and other
supplies from reaching Britain, Germany started using submarines
(U-boat, in German *Unterseeboot*) which it had developed to sink
any ship, including those of the neutral countries, heading for Britain.
This, among other things, led to the United States entering the war
on the side of the Allied Powers.

The use of aircrafts in warfare also started and though cities were
bombed from the air and German and Allied aircraft had dog fights,
air warfare played little role in deciding the outcome of the war.

End of the War

Russia had withdrawn from the war after the October Revolution and had been forced to accept a humiliating treaty by Germany. However, the war between the Central and the Allied powers was to be decided elsewhere and not on the Eastern Front. The loss of Russia by the Allies was more than made up for by the entry of USA into the war. USA had been supplying goods, including munitions and food, to the Allies from the time of the outbreak of the war and, as a result, the US economy had prospered. Now the armies and the vast economic resources of USA were to be directly used to defeat the Central Powers.

In the meantime, discontent had been rising in the civilian population and among the soldiers of all the major belligerent countries. There were demonstrations and mutinies. The autocratic Russian empire had already fallen. The discontent was much more widespread in the countries of the Central Powers. There was a wave of strikes in Germany and Austria-Hungary and a succession of mutinies in their armies and navies. In Austria-Hungary, there were desertions on a large scale among the soldiers of the "subject nationalities" and many of them were fighting on the side of the Allies. By about the middle of July 1918, the tide of the war was beginning to turn against Germany. Germany had launched a series of offensives on the western front, inflicting heavy casualties on the Allies. But by July, the German offensive was contained and the Allies launched counter-offensives. In the meantime, the Allied forces had started their military intervention in Russia. In the east, thousands of Japanese troops poured into Siberia. While the Allied intervention in Russia was to outlast the end of the First World War, the collapse of the Central Powers had begun.

By the end of August 1918 only Germany remained a major central power to be completely defeated and final Allied offensives against Germany were launched in September. On 29 September 1918, Bulgaria surrendered. By the end of October the Ottoman Empire had ceased to exist. On 12 November, the Habsburg emperor abdicated. Most people of the Austro-Hungarian empire—the Czechs, the Poles, the Yugoslavs and the Hungarians—had already declared their independence. On 3 November, revolution broke out in Germany; on 9 November, the German emperor abdicated and fled to Holland, and on 10 November Germany was proclaimed a republic. On 11 November 1918, the new government of Germany signed the armistice and at 11 o'clock in the morning of 11 November, the First World War came to an end.

The destruction caused by the war in terms of human lives was terrible. Out of about 65 million soldiers mobilised by both the powers, about nine million were killed and about 22 million wounded. To understand the true nature of this catastrophe and its impact on European societies, it should be remembered that most of the dead and the survivors, "scarred physically and mentally", were the "flower of Europe", young people between the ages of 18 and 35. Erich Maria Remarque, who had been forced to join the German army, published a novel which in the English translation is entitled *All Quiet on the Western Front*. The dedication page of the novel carries the following statement:

> This book is to be neither an accusation nor a confession, and least of all an adventure, for death is not an adventure to those who stand face to face with it. It will try simply to tell of a generation of men who, even though they may have escaped its shells, were destroyed by the war.

THE RUSSIAN REVOLUTION

Revolutionary Movement in Russia

During the war years, the Russian Revolution, an event of great historical significance took place. Certain aspects and events of Russian history—Russian colonial empire, the autocratic nature of her political system, the backwardness of her economy, her defeat at the hands of Japan, the role played by her in the European conflicts, particularly in the Balkans, and her entry into the war have already been mentioned. In the nineteenth century, there were various reform and revolutionary movements expressing discontent among the Russian peasantry who continued to live in misery even after serfdom was abolished in 1861. Vast estates were owned by the Russian nobility and the Church, and there were millions of peasants without any landholdings of their own. The industrial workers, a new class that had emerged with the beginning of industrialisation, also lived in conditions of misery. While the common people were obviously opposed to the existing system in Russia, the middle classes and the intellectuals were also united in their opposition to the autocratic political system and were thus drawn to the revolutionary movement along with the peasants and workers.

Since the last quarter of the nineteenth century, socialist ideas had begun to spread in Russia and a number of socialist groups had been formed. In 1898, the various socialist groups joined together to form the Russian Social Democratic Labour Party. Vladimir Ilyich Ulyanov, popularly known as Lenin, was the leader of the left-wing section of the party. In 1903, this section secured a majority in the party and came to be known as Bolsheviks, while the minority section were known as the Mensheviks. The Bolsheviks, while defining their final goal as the establishment of socialism, proposed their immediate tasks as the overthrow of the autocratic rule of the Czar and the establishment of a republic, ending the oppression of the non-Russian nationalities of the Russian empire and granting them the right of self-determination, introduction of an eight-hour working day and abolition of inequalities in land and the end of all feudal oppressions of the peasantry. There was a revolution in Russia in 1905, which forced Nicholas II, the reigning Czar, to agree for the establishment of a parliament, called the Duma, along with other democratic rights of the people. During this period, a new form of workers' organisation had come into being, called the Soviet. It was a body of workers' representatives set up for the purpose of conducting strikes. Later, Soviets of peasants were also formed—followed by Soviets of soldiers—and these sprang up all over the country. The Soviets were later to play a crucial role in the history of the Russian Revolution.

The February Revolution

The Revolution of 1905 had not ended the autocracy in Russia. Though the Duma existed, the power in Russia was wielded by the Czar, the nobility and the corrupt bureaucracy. Russia's imperial ambitions led her to the war but the inefficient and corrupt Russian government was incapable of carrying on a modern war. The war exposed the bankruptcy of the existing system in Russia, aggravated the crisis of the autocratic system and, ultimately, brought about its downfall. The Russian soldiers, 12 million of whom had been mobilised, were ill-equipped and ill-fed. The Russian army suffered heavy losses during the war. The war had further worsened the already poor state of the Russian economy, further adding to the growing unrest. The country, including the capital city of Petrograd (formerly St Petersburg, later Leningrad, and now again St Petersburg) with its population of two million, was facing prospects of starvation. There were long queues for bread which was in short supply. From the beginning of the year 1917, there was a spate of strikes, which took the form of a general strike. The demand for ending the war and the rule of the Czar grew and on 12 March many regiments of the army joined the striking workers, freed political prisoners and arrested Czarist generals and ministers. By the evening Petrograd had passed into the control of insurgent workers and soldiers. These events of 12 March 1917 marked what has been called the February Revolution (because, according to the old Russian calendar, the date was 27 February). The Czar, who had been away from the capital, had ordered the suppression of the insurgents and the dissolution of the Duma. However, the Duma decided to take over power in its own hands and on 15 March announced the formation of a Provisional Government. That very day, the Czar was forced to abdicate and his autocratic rule came to an end. A few months later, in September 1917, Russia was proclaimed a republic.

The end of the Czarist autocracy was welcomed the world over. But the Provisional Government failed to solve any of the problems that had led to the collapse of the Czarist government. The policy of pursuing the war was continued and nothing was done to solve the land problem. The Bolsheviks were the only party which had a clear-cut programme. As we have seen earlier that two Russian socialists— Lenin and Martov—had drafted a part of the Second International's resolution which called upon workers to utilise the crisis, created by the immanent danger of the war, if it broke out, and overthrow the system which had led to the war. The Bolsheviks were consistent in their opposition to the war. There were five Bolshevik members of the Duma. They opposed the war when it broke out. They were arrested and exiled. When the February Revolution took place, Lenin was in Zurich, Switzerland. He called it only the initial, but by no means the complete victory, and declared:

> Only a workers' government that relies, first, on the overwhelming majority of the peasant population, the farm labourers and poor

peasants and, second, on an alliance with the revolutionary workers of all countries in the war, can give the people peace, bread and full freedom.

The October Revolution

At the time of the February Revolution, the Petrograd Soviet of Workers' and Soldiers' Deputies had been formed and it became the most important force in the fast-changing situation. On his arrival in Petrograd in April 1917, Lenin addressed the people with the following appeal:

> The people need peace: the people need bread; the people need land. And they give you—war, hunger, no bread; they leave the landlords on the land.

He gave the call: "No support for the Provisional Government, All Power to the Soviets." At this time there was another threat to the Provisional Government. General Kornilov had risen in revolt in an effort to establish his dictatorship. However, the attempt was thwarted by the workers and soldiers who rose up to defend the Revolution. At this time, the Provisional Government was headed by Aleksander Kerensky, who held liberal and democratic views. He, however, failed to make any departure from the policies which had been pursued by the Russian government since the outbreak of the war, and proved himself to be totally ineffective. He was totally lacking in support.

In October, the Bolsheviks made careful preparations for an uprising. The All-Russian Congress of Soviets of Workers' and Soldiers' Deputies had been convened on 25 October. The uprising to overthrow the Provisional Government had been timed to coincide with the Congress. The uprising began in the early hours of 25 October in Petrograd and within a few hours, almost every strategic point in the city was occupied by the revolutionary soldiers and workers under the guidance of the Bolsheviks. At 10 a.m. Lenin's address, "To the Citizens of Russia", was broadcast. He said,

> The Provisional Government has been deposed.... The cause for which the people have fought, namely, the immediate offer of a democratic

peace, the abolition of landed proprietorship, workers' control over production, and the establishment of Soviet power—this cause has been secured.

The date of this event was 25 October according to the old Russian calendar, hence it is called the October Revolution. It actually happened on 7 November. At 10.40 p.m. the meeting, of the All-Russian Congress of Soviets of Workers' and Soldiers' Deputies began. At about the same time, the assault on the Winter Palace, the headquarters of the Provisional Government, started. At 1.50 a.m. on the next day (26 October according to the old calendar), the Winter Palace had been occupied and the members of the Provisional Government put under arrest. The head of the Government, Kerensky, had, however, escaped. At 9 p.m. the second session of the Congress of Soviets started. According to the eye-witness account of John Reed, an American journalist, Lenin was received with a "long-rolling ovation" as he stood up. As the ovation finished he said simply, "We shall now proceed to construct the socialist order!"

The first act of the new government was the adoption of the Decree on Peace (adopted at 11 p.m.). It expressed the resolve of the government to immediately enter into negotiations to conclude a peace without annexations or reparations. The workers of Germany, France and Britain, the Decree said,

> will understand the duty imposed upon them to liberate humanity from the horrors and consequences of war, and that these workers, by decisive, energetic and continued action, will help us to bring to a successful conclusion the cause of peace—and at the same time, the cause of the liberation of the exploited working masses from all slavery and all exploitation.

As a consequence of such a policy, Russia withdrew from the war even at the cost of losing many of her territories which Germany had made a condition for agreeing to peace.

The second step taken by the revolutionary government, headed by Lenin, was the Decree on Land, which was adopted at 2 a.m. on 27 October (9 November). This Decree abolished private property in land and declared land to be the property of the entire nation. Soon it renounced unilaterally all the unequal treaties which the Czarist government had imposed on countries such as China, Iran and Afghanistan. The right of all peoples to equality and self-determination was proclaimed.

Civil War and Foreign Intervention

The uprising in Petrograd, which led to the establishment of the Bolshevik government, was followed by similar uprisings in other parts of the former Russian empire, and by February 1918, the new government had established its authority throughout the country. Soon, however, Russia was involved in a civil war. The forces loyal to the old regime, known as the White Russians, had organised themselves to overthrow the revolution. The Allied powers—Britain, France, USA, Japan and others—also started their military interventions in Russia, to bring Russia back to the war, to exploit her resources for the war and to aid the counter-revolutionary forces. The civil war and foreign military interventions, however, ended by 1920.

The dynasty of the Czar was the first to fall during the First World War. Two other imperial dynasties—the German and the Austro-Hungarian—fell before the war was over. Another—that of the Ottoman Sultans—fell soon after the war.

The significance of the October Revolution extended beyond the boundaries of Russia. Soviet Russia, later the Union of Soviet Socialist Republics, became a major influence in the subsequent history of the world.

Two

The World between the Two World Wars

GENERAL FEATURES OF THE PERIOD

The end of the First World War, "the war to end all wars", it was believed, would be followed by a period of peace, freedom, democracy, and a better life for everyone. When USA entered the war, Woodrow Wilson declared,

> ... we shall fight for the things which we have always carried nearest our hearts—for democracy, for the right of those who submit to authority to have a voice in their own Governments, for the rights and liberties of small nations, for a universal dominion of right by such a concert of free peoples as shall bring peace and safety to all nations and make the world itself at last free....

Seven months later, the Russian Revolution took place and the Soviet government issued the Decree on Peace, which called on all the belligerent nations and peoples to enter into negotiations for a peace without annexations and indemnities. The Russian revolutionaries also hoped that their example would be followed by the working classes of some other countries of Europe. The Soviet appeal was rejected by the Allied Powers, and Germany extorted a heavy price for letting Russia withdraw from the war.

On 8 January 1918, Wilson had presented his peace proposals, called the Fourteen Points. These included the abolition of secret diplomacy, freedom of the seas, reduction of armaments, and redrawing of the boundaries of European countries on the principle of nationality. In the case of colonies, what was proposed was an "impartial adjustment of all colonial claims", and not the application of the principle of national self-determination. The last point was about the formation of "[a] general association of nations ... for the purpose of affording mutual guarantees of political independence and territorial integrity to great and small states alike". The Fourteen Points were expected to form the basis of peace.

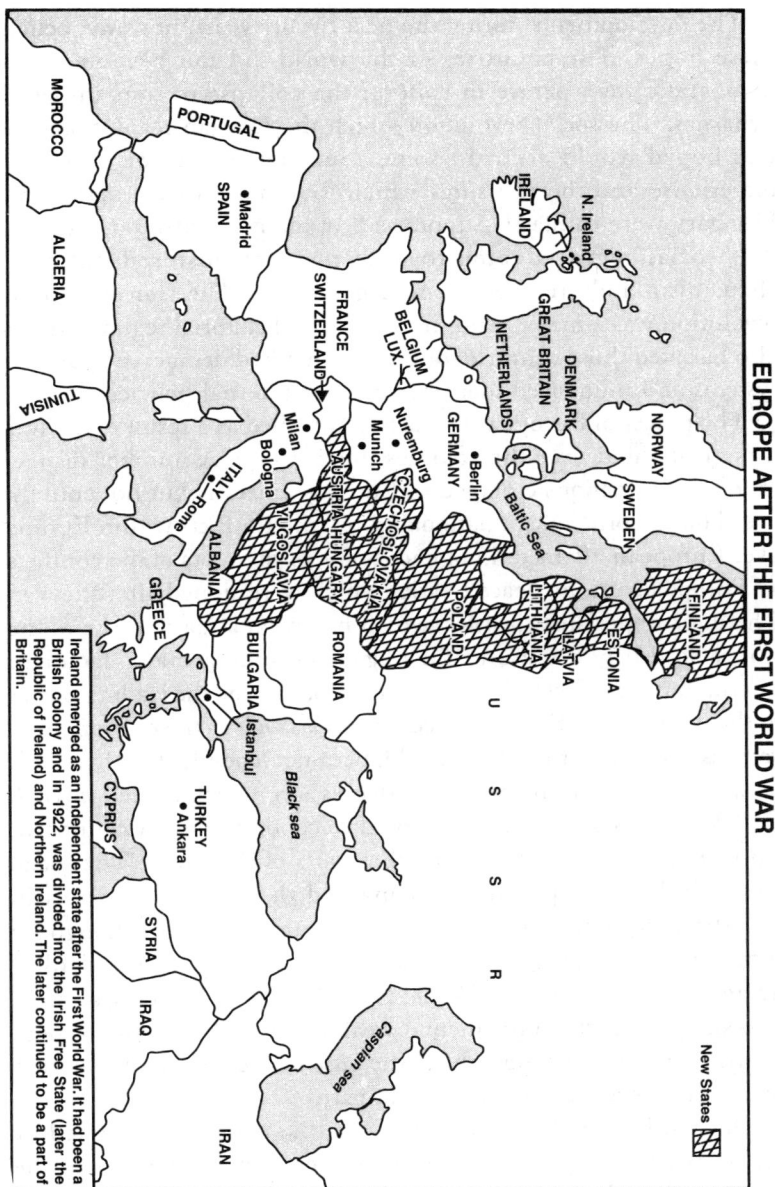

EUROPE AFTER THE FIRST WORLD WAR

New States

Ireland emerged as an independent state after the First World War. It had been a British colony and in 1922, was divided into the Irish Free State (later the Republic of Ireland) and Northern Ireland. The later continued to be a part of Britain.

The developments during the next twenty years, however, belied these hopes. The countries of the world did not become more democratic than before in spite of the collapse of four imperial dynasties. The social revolution which the Russian revolutionaries had hoped would occur in some countries of Europe, failed to materialise and the uprisings which took place in Germany and Hungary were ruthlessly suppressed. In many countries of Europe, dictatorial regimes came to power, which fostered national chauvinism and prepared themselves for war. The fear of a social revolution was a major factor in the rise of dictatorial regimes and it also haunted those countries of Europe that had democratic political systems and influenced their internal and external policies.

The power of Europe was much diminished as a result of the war though its hold over the colonies did not end. A number of new independent nations emerged in Europe, generally but not entirely, based on the principle of nationality, but the conflicts within Europe over European affairs did not end. Some of the roots of the conflicts in Europe lay in the peace treaties which were signed after the war. The inter-imperialist rivalries, which had been a major cause of the war, also did not end and they again became a major factor in international conflicts. USA in this period, became the leading power in the world. Most European economies, as well as the economies of various countries around the world, became dependent on her. This became clear when the economic depression, which started in USA in 1929, had its disastrous effects on the economy of every country in Europe (except Russia), and in other parts of the world. The social and economic inequalities that marked the pre-war societies in industrialised countries, continued during this period too though for some time some progress was made in improving the standard of living of the people. The economic crisis of 1929–33, however, brought into sharp focus the fundamental weaknesses of the existing system of which misery and poverty of the vast masses of the population seemed to have become an essential part.

Outside Europe and North America, the period was marked by the growing strength of the national liberation movements in the colonies, though their success was to come only after another world war had been fought. The League of Nations, envisaged in Wilson's Fourteen Points, came into being as a result of the peace treaties, but it proved totally ineffective in preventing the world from relapsing into another war. Since the mid-1930s a second world war seemed to have become inevitable, and when it broke out in 1939, barely twenty years after the end of the first one, it was much more widespread and many times more destructive than the first one.

THE PEACE TREATIES

Dictated Peace

The main enemy of the Allied Powers in the First World War had been Germany. The Peace Conference of the Allied nations started in Paris on 18 January 1919 to draft a peace treaty with Germany. The Conference was dominated by the US President, Woodrow Wilson, the British Prime Minister, Lloyd George and the French Prime Minister, Georges Clemenceau. The surrender of Germany had been obtained on the understanding that the Fourteen Points and other statements made by Wilson would be the basis of the peace treaty. Wilson had, besides the Fourteen Points, announced that "[t]here shall be no annexations, no contributions, no punitive damages" and that free acceptance by the people concerned would be the basis of any settlement. This principle was completely violated when the treaty was drafted. Neither Germany nor any other Central Powers were represented at the conference. When the victors had finalised the treaty, they gave Germany five days' time to sign it or face an invasion. Germany had no choice but to sign what she termed as "dictated peace". Even at the time of signing the treaty, the German representatives were humiliated. They were not asked to sit in the hall along with the representatives of the Allied Powers where the signing ceremony took place and were "escorted in and out of the hall in the manner of criminals conducted to and from the dock".

Germany was also forced to accept her "war guilt". The treaty had a chapter on reparations, which started by stating that

> Germany accept the responsibility of Germany and her allies for causing all the loss and damage to which the Allied and Associated Governments and their nationals have been subjected as a consequence of the war imposed upon them by the aggression of Germany and her allies....

When this was shown to the German foreign minister, he said,

> It is demanded of us that we shall confess ourselves to be the only ones
> guilty of the war.... We are far from declining any responsibility ... but we
> energetically deny that Germany and its people ... were alone guilty.... In
> the last fifty years the imperialism of all the European States has
> chronically poisoned the international situation....

The treaty also had articles providing for the trial of Germans
whom the Allies accused of committing war crimes. The list of the
accused included the German emperor, who had taken refuge in
Holland.

The framers of the treaty were guided by various secret treaties
and agreements that the major Allied Powers had signed during the
course of the war. The main purpose of these secret treaties was to
divide the spoils of the war. Russia was one of the signatories to these
secret treaties. After the revolution in Russia, she not only denounced
these agreements but made them public. This exposed the claims of
the Allies that they had been fighting the war for freedom and
democracy. Though these treaties were published in the American
and the British presses, it did not deter the victors from implementing
these secret treaties while deciding the fate of Germany (and later of
Turkey and others Central Powers). President Wilson, for all his
insistence on open diplomacy, was persuaded to give his consent.

Creation of the League of Nations

One of the first acts of the Peace Conference was the creation of the
League of Nations (enumerated in Wilson's Fourteenth Point). The
Covenant (or the formal, solemn and binding agreement) of the
League of Nations was approved by the Peace Conference in April
1919. The primary objective of the League as enunciated in the
covenant was the promotion of "international cooperation, peace and
security". Three articles of the covenant were particularly important
for the primary objective of the League. Article VIII mentioned that
"the maintenance of peace requires the reduction of national
armaments". Article X stated that the "[m]embers of the League
undertake to respect and preserve as against external aggression the
territorial integrity and existing political independence of all

Members.... In case of any such aggression or in cases of any threat or danger of such aggression the Council [of the League] shall advice upon the means by which this obligation shall be fulfilled". Article XVI related to sanctions. It stated: "Should any Member of the League resort to war..., it shall *ipso facto* be deemed to have committed an act of war against all other Members of the League...." This Article specifically stated that other member states sould sever all trade or financial relations with the aggressor country and, on the recommendation of the council, make collective use of armed force against her.

As will be seen, the League proved to be totally ineffective in maintaining peace and taking any effective steps against the aggressor countries. Nor was any progress made towards the reduction of armaments. Two agencies created by the League, however, did useful work. These were the Permanent Court of International Justice (popularly known as the World Court) and the International Labour Organization. Major developments relating to the League will be mentioned later.

The Treaty of Versailles

The peace treaty with Germany was signed at Versailles on 28 June 1919 and is known as the Treaty of Versailles. According to the provisions of the treaty, Alsace-Lorraine, which Germany had seized from France in 1871, was returned to France; the newly created state of Poland was provided with access to the sea by giving her about 65 km of 'corridor' which separated East Prussia from the rest of Germany. Danzig was made a free city under the political control of the League of Nations and economic control of Poland. Belgium, Denmark and Lithuania also acquired German territories. The Saar coal-mining area was brought under the control of the League of Nations for fifteen years while the mines in the area were given to France as compensation. Germany was debarred from uniting with Austria. The Rhineland was to be permanently demilitarised and occupied by the Allied troops for fifteen years. The strength of the German army was fixed at 100,000 and she was prohibited form possessing any air force or submarines. Germany was allowed to have only a limited number of naval ships. Having been forced to admit her 'war guilt', she was required to pay reparations to the Allies. These reparations were assessed later and amounted to £ 6,600 million.

Germany was also deprived of all her colonial possessions German colonial territories were divided among the victorious powers as had been earlier agreed among them in the secret treaties. Most of German East Africa—Tanganyika—went to Britain, with some portions going to Portugal and Belgian Congo. Cameroons and Togoland were divided between Britain and France. Ruanda-Urundi was handed over to Belgium and South-West Africa to South Africa. The Pacific islands under German control were divided among Australia, New Zealand and Japan. Japan also acquired Shantung, which had been a German sphere of influence. These acquisitions were given the legal sanction of a peace treaty, which Germany had signed, as well as of the League of Nations.

In theory, the German colonies were not annexed by the victorious colonial powers. The covenant of the League provided for a system of what was called the Mandates. This system was applied to the colonies of the defeated colonial powers. The covenant stated that these colonies and territories were "inhabited by peoples not yet able to stand by themselves under the strenuous conditions of the modern world" and that "the well-being and development of such peoples form a sacred trust of civilization". To give practical effect to this trust, the covenant further stated, that, the peoples inhabiting these colonies and territories should be placed under the 'tutelage' of the 'advanced nations'. However, which 'advanced nation' would bring which particular territory under her tutelage had already been determined by the 'advanced nations' themselves and, therefore, the League had no practical say in it.

Treaties with Austria, Hungary and Turkey

The Treaty of Versailles was the main treaty as it concerned the main defeated country. However, separate treaties were signed with other Central Powers. The Treaty of St Germain was signed with Austria on 10 September 1919. According to this treaty, Austria recognised the independence of Hungary, Poland, Czechoslovakia and Yugoslavia, and ceded territories to these countries and to Italy. Austria was reduced to the position of a small state and was debarred from forming a union with Germany. A separate treaty was signed with Hungary, which was now an independent state. She was required to cede territories to Yugoslavia, Czechoslovakia and Romania. The treaty with Bulgaria required her to cede territories to Romania, Yugoslavia and Greece.

The final treaty was signed with Turkey. According to a secret agreement, Britain and France had already divided the Arab territories between themselves. Syria and Lebanon had come under French control, and Iraq, Palestine and Transjordan under the British as mandates. Some Arab territories such as Kuwait, Bahrain and Qatar had come under British influence even earlier, while some others which had enjoyed autonomy under local rulers continued as before. Hejaz became a separate state but was soon conquered by Ibn Saud, the ruler of Nejd, to form Saudi Arabia.

The loss of their Arab empire by the Ottomans had been inevitable. The Allies had given support to Arab nationalist uprisings against the Ottomans, only to acquire their territories after the war. However, the dismemberment of Turkey herself led to a Turkish nationalist uprising. Greece and Italy had occupied large parts of Turkey. The Sultan of Turkey signed a treaty in September 1920 agreeing to Turkey's near-total dismemberment. In the meantime, the national uprising led by Mustafa Kemal, who had established a government in Ankara, swept the country. Kemal's armies drove the Italians and Greeks out of the country and in July 1923, the Allies were forced to sign a new treaty with Turkey. Turkey was declared a republic which laid the foundation of a modern secular Turkey. The office of the Caliph (Khalifa) was abolished.

These treaties formally brought the First World War to an end. Many provisions of these treaties, however, later became the source of new tensions in Europe. From the beginning Russia had been excluded from all negotiations, and was kept out of the League of Nations (as was Germany). In fact, while the treaties were being drafted and the terms of the League of Nations was being formulated, the troops of many Allied nations were fighting the revolutionary government of Russia. The colonial question was settled to the satisfaction of the victorious colonial powers and not of the peoples of the colonies. China had been one of the Allies in the First World

War and she was represented at the Peace Conference. However, her territories, formerly under German control, were given away to Japan.

USA, USSR and Japan between the Two World Wars

The major powers that emerged during the inter-war period were USA, USSR and Japan. All the three had been Allies for some time during the First World War until the Russian Revolution. After the war, while Russia was ostracised, USA played the most important role in the framing of the peace treaties and, therefore, in the making of the post-First World War world. She became the world's dominant economic power. Russia, later a part of USSR when it was formed, emerged from the war, the Revolution, the Civil War, and the foreign interventions, as the most ravaged country in Europe. However, by the late 1930s, she managed to become a strong industrial and military power. Her political, economic and social systems distinguished her from the rest of the world and she played a distinctive role in world affairs. Japan emerged from the war as the strongest power in Asia and the Pacific with ambitions of establishing her hegemony in that region.

USA

The Treaty of Versailles, in the formulation of which the US president, Woodrow Wilson, had played a leading role, was rejected by the US Senate. USA refused to join the League of Nations, which had largely been the creation of Wilson. In the elections held in 1920 for the offices of the president and the vice-president, the candidates of the Democratic Party, to which Wilson belonged, were defeated by the Republican Party. The candidates of the latter party also won two more successive elections held in 1924 and 1928.

Economic Misery despite Economic Growth

The immediate post-war years in USA were years of a serious economic crisis. During the war, while the European economies suffered serious damages, the US economy expanded. No battle was fought on US soil and thus her cities, industries and farms did not face any damages. With the end of the war, the economic expansion which was the result of the war, suddenly ceased, creating a serious economic crisis. About 100,000 businesses were reduced to bankruptcy and about five million people lost their jobs. The resulting labour unrest led to industrial strikes. In 1919 there were over 3,500 strikes, some of them involving hundreds of thousands of workers and lasting for many months. The strikes were put down with a heavy hand, and attempts were made to create a scare of a revolutionary outbreak like the one that had occurred in Russia.

Within a short time the US economy recovered with unprecedented growth. During this period, when the rest of the capitalist world was recovering from the ravages of the war, USA began her industrial expansion based on major advances in science and technology. She had emerged as the main creditor nation of the world, and most European countries were her debtors. An indication of the tremendous industrial expansion may be seen in the fact that in 1929, more than five million cars were sold in USA. This industrial expansion was accompanied by a further concentration of economic power. Thousands of small companies were swallowed up by the few big ones. Competition between different manufacturers, which had been a characteristic feature of capitalist economies, almost ended. In some cases, such as steel, almost the entire industry in the country was in the hands of one company. These companies exerted enormous influence on the government and enjoyed special privileges. It used to be said that what was good for General Motors, the chief manufacturer of cars, was good for America. The concentration of economic power in few hands led to increased corruption and there were many scandals involving politicians and top levels bureaucracy.

The unprecedented economic growth, however, brought little benefits to the workers, most of whom continued to lead lives of poverty and misery. Besides low wages, there was the ever-present danger of being thrown out of employment. A strong trade union movement also could not emerge due to the connivance between the companies, government officials and law courts. The capitalists often resorted to violence against the workers with the help of the police and hired gangs.

The Crash of 1929

The unprecedented expansion of the US economy came to an end with an unprecedented catastrophe. Early in 1929, President Herbert Hoover declared, "[o]urs is a land rich in resources, stimulating in its glorious beauty, filled with millions of happy homes, blessed with comfort and opportunity". The future of the country, he added, was "bright with hope". Within a few months after this comment, on 24 October 1929, the crash happened, which in history has come to be known as the Great Depression. The basic cause of the economic crisis lay in the nature of the US economy which went on expanding, while keeping the bulk of the populace impoverished. The tremendous increase in production facilitated by advances in technology and increasing profits created sharp divisions between the haves and the have-nots. This created a situation in which there were not many people who had the means to buy what was being produced. Between five and seven per cent of the non-agricultural population had been unemployed throughout the 1920s. In spite of almost a decade of unprecedented economic growth, "more than half the families in America lived on the edge of or below the minimum subsistence level". It has been estimated that, in 1929, about a third of all personal income went to just five per cent of the population. This "fundamental maldistribution of purchasing power" has been regarded as a major factor leading to the crash, even by those who were by no means critics of the capitalist system of economy.

The crash began when the prices of shares began to fall, creating a panic, and people rushed to sell their shares, which led to a further fall in the prices of shares. This led to the collapse of the stock market. This was followed by the failure of banks—between 1929 and 1932, over 5,700 banks failed and another 3,500 ceased their operations. The failure of banks wiped off the life's savings of millions of Americans. This meant that the buying capacity of the people further went down, as even those fewer people who earlier had the money to buy goods were now penniless. The industries could not get loans from the banks, and the goods they produced could not be sold, and so they began to close down. This meant that more people lost their jobs and the demand for goods further went down leading to the closure of more factories. The number of the unemployed rose from 1.5 million in 1929 to five million in 1930, to nine million in 1931 and to 13 million in 1932—the figure of 1932 being over 25 per cent of the total US workforce. The condition of farmers was no better than that of urban workers. The prices of agricultural produce fell, and millions of farmers lost their lands and were reduced to the position of destitutes.

Racial Discrimination

The 1930s were a terrible period for the American people. The worst affected were the Black people. Over 200,000 had served as soldiers in Europe during the war and on their return home they found that racial discrimination against them had further worsened. Even the war veterans were victims of humiliation, indignities and lynching. They were the first to be thrown out of employment and often their jobs were taken over by Whites. The right to vote continued to be denied to them. Racial segregation and discrimination had spread throughout the country and was no longer limited to the southern states. White terrorist gangs such as the Ku Klux Klan were active in many parts of the country. The victims of their violence now included, besides the Black people, Jews, foreigners, and other groups regarded as "racially impure". During the Great Depression, the condition of the Black people further worsened. White racists demanded that no jobs should be given to 'niggers' until every White man was employed. Hundreds of thousands of them migrated from the southern states to the north but there, too, conditions were no better. It has been estimated that, in 1932, about one-third of the Black population was unemployed besides another one-third was underemployed.

The 1930s witnessed the growth of radicalism in US society. A strong trade union movement began to emerge. There were radical political movements advocating socialism. The Communist Party of USA which had been formed earlier, grew in strength and played an important role in organising the workers, Blacks and Whites alike, and fighting against racism. The Black people also organised themselves to fight back racism. The National Association for the Advancement of Colored People (NAACP) played an important role in the fight against racism and in uniting the Black and the White workers.

Two cases of blatant injustice rocked USA during this period and aroused protests by people in many other countries. The first case concerned two Italian immigrants, Sacco and Vanzetti, who were arrested on the charge of committing a murder. The evidence against them was considered "at best questionable". They were sentenced to death. It was generally believed in USA and elsewhere that they were innocent and had been framed in a false case to add to the scare that USA was in danger of a revolution by subversive elements. There was a worldwide demand for a retrial of the case but it was refused and Sacco and Vanzetti were executed. The second, known as the Scottsboro Case, was a case of racism. In 1931 nine young Black boys were tried in Alabama on the charge of raping two White prostitutes. Eight of them were sentenced to death by a jury consisting entirely of Whites. The case was generally considered to be completely fabricated and a nation-wide campaign, supported by world opinion, was launched for the defence of the boys who had been convicted. In this case, the executions were not carried out though most of the boys languished in prison for many years.

The New Deal

The Great Depression, which had its origin in USA, has been described as "the largest earthquake ever to be measured on the economic historian's Richter Scale". It affected almost all countries of Europe and, to some extent, almost every country in the world. Its effects on Europe were extremely grave, and would be mentioned subsequently. In USA, some of the worst effects of the economic crisis began to be remedied after 1933. This happened during the presidency of Franklin D. Roosevelt, who was first elected in 1932 and won three subsequent elections. The programme of reform which he started is known as the New Deal. A large programme of welfare was initiated, which alleviated the misery of many sections of the population, though the effects of the Great Depression continued right up to the US entry into the Second World War. Though Roosevelt was generally believed to be sympathetic to Blacks, little was actually done to improve their lot.

USA and the World

The US refusal to join the League of Nations was a big blow to that organisation. The main preoccupation of USA during the period was the expansion of her economic control over the rest of the world. The growing US domination of the world economy had serious consequences for Europe and the rest of the world. USA supplied vast amounts of credits to Germany and some other countries in the 1920s, which helped in the economic recovery of Europe but the increased dependence on USA had disastrous consequences for these countries as was to happen during the Great Depression. She was initially concerned at the growing Japanese ambitions in China as it could harm the US economic interests. In 1922, a treaty was signed between USA, Japan, Britain, France and Italy, which aimed at ensuring an Open Door policy in China so that no one country established her exclusive control over China. The treaty also imposed some restrictions on Japan's naval strength but left her as the greatest naval power in the Pacific. Like other Western countries, USA refused to be involved in any efforts to curb the acts of aggression started by Japan in 1931 and later by Italy and Germany. For sixteen years, she refused to recognise the government of USSR (similarly it took her over twenty years to recognise the government of China). In Latin America, the US economic domination was further strengthened, and direct military intervention continued until the time when Franklin Roosevelt became president. The US domination of Latin America—or "Yankee Imperialism", as the Latin Americans called it—caused widespread resentment there.

USSR

Most historians consider the Russian Revolution as one of the most significant events of the twentieth century. Many people the world over, for a long time, viewed it as the beginning of a new era in human history. They saw it as "an alternative and superior system to capitalism and one destined by history to triumph over it". By all accounts, it was a major factor in the shaping of the twentieth century world. No other revolution in human history had professed to bring about such fundamental transformation of society as the Russian Revolution of 1917. Since the beginning of civilisation over 5000 years ago, if we take the world as a whole, the common feature of all 'civilised' societies had been social and economic inequalities and exploitation of one class by another. The state, whatever be its form, was used to maintain the system of inequality and exploitation. The Russian revolutionaries proclaimed as their objective the overthrow of the system of inequality and exploitation, and the creation of a society in which no one would live off the labour of another.

The immediate steps taken by the revolutionary government of Russia was the proclamation of two decrees—Decrees on Peace and Decree on Land. Soon after, all industries and banks were nationalised. A Declaration of the Rights of the Peoples of Russia was issued. It announced the end of the oppression of the non-Russian nationalities of the Russian empire and proclaimed the right of all nationalities to self-determination, equality and sovereignty. All the secret treaties signed by the Czarist government were annulled and peoples of the East were called upon to overthrow colonial rule.

In January 1918, Russia was proclaimed as the Russian Soviet Federative Socialist Republic (RSFSR). By the time the First World War ended, the Bolsheviks had established their control over the territories of the former Russian empire, except Estonia, Latvia, Lithuania and Finland, which had emerged as independent states. Poland also emerged as an independent nation and included all the Polish territories which had earlier been part of the Russian empire. In the meantime, civil war had broken out and foreign military intervention started. The Soviet policy on land and non-Russian nationalities helped in the consolidation of the Soviet power. By 1920, both the civil war and foreign intervention came to an end.

War Communism and the New Economic Policy (NEP)

The First World War, the civil war and the foreign intervention which followed the revolution had totally ravaged the economy of Russia. These, along with the famine that followed, resulted in the death of millions of people. In 1921, industrial production was 13 per cent of what it had been before 1914. The Soviet government had resorted to various stringent measures to prevent a total collapse. Landed estates had been confiscated and distributed to peasants but all that the peasants produced beyond their minimum essential requirements was appropriated by the government to feed the rest of the population. Almost nothing could be bought or sold. Whatever was produced by industries was distributed to workers and other people to meet their minimum essential requirements in lieu of wages. The system which came into being as a result of these measures is known as War Communism. It created widespread discontent and in some places there were revolts.

In 1921, a new policy, called the New Economic Policy (NEP), was adopted and the system. War Communism was withdrawn. Peasant control over their produce was restored, salaries were paid in cash, trade in goods was reopened, and efforts were made to rehabilitate the economy. In some industries, private management was introduced and many small industries were allowed to remain in private hands. A large number of cooperatives were set up. In 1921, there was a large-scale failure of crops in almost the entire country, creating conditions of mass starvation. A massive nation-wide effort was launched to provide relief. People from many other countries also organised relief aid to the Soviet people. USA, though refusing to recognise the Soviet government, also sent food supplies.

Industrial Development and Collectivisation

The NEP helped the economy to recover to the pre-war level and laid the foundation for further development. This policy remained in force till 1928 when a massive effort was launched to achieve a high level of economic development through successive Five Year Plans. The first Five Year Plan was launched in 1929 and the second in 1934. By the time the Second World War started, USSR (for short Soviet Union), which had been set up in 1924 and of which Soviet Russia was a part had become a strong industrialised and military power. No other country had industrialised herself as fast as the USSR. Also, the conditions under which her economy developed were totally different from those of other countries. This was achieved by mobilising her own internal resources, entirely under the auspices of the state. Whatever private enterprises existed during the period of the NEP were taken over by the state, and private ownership of and control over industry and trade became non-existent. It is notable that the only country to escape the effects of the Great Depression was the Soviet Union.

Vast changes took place in the agricultural sector. The changes introduced were supposed to facilitate the modernisation of agriculture with the help of machines and tractors. They had disastrous consequences in human terms. Vast state farms were set up and the rest of the farmlands were collectivised. The individual holdings of the peasants were brought together and collective farms, called *kolkhozes*, were set up. By the end of the 1930s, almost all land was brought under collective farming. The peasants worked on these farms collectively, without owning any piece of land. This was often done by adopting measures of extreme coercion. The class of rich peasants was eliminated. Many million peasants are believed to have perished during the period of collectivisation.

Formation of the USSR

According to a new constitution proclaimed in 1924, all the Soviet republics such as the Russian (RSFSR), Georgian, Armenian, Turkmen, Ukrainian, Azerbaijan, Caucasian, etc., were brought under one union—the Union of Soviet Socialist Republics (USSR). In 1936, when another constitution came into force, there were eleven republics constituting the USSR. These republics were formed on the basis of the principle of nationality and the equality of all nationalities. According to the constitution, they were given the right to secede from the Union. The constitution gave each nationality of the former Russian empire the right to promote its own language and culture. The cultural and economic development of the Asian republics of the USSR was very impressive, particularly to the peoples of other countries of Asia who were struggling to liberate themselves from colonial rule, and for them the USSR became an ideal model to be imitated.

From One Party Rule to Dictatorship

The political development of the Soviet Union was accompanied by gross violation of individual liberty and the principles of democracy. The Soviets, which had been formed during the struggle for revolution, had been acclaimed as the true and authentic form of democracy. They involved vast masses of people in the process of decision-making, which affected their lives and brought millions of common people into direct political activity. A number of political parties and groups—such as the Mensheviks, the Socialist

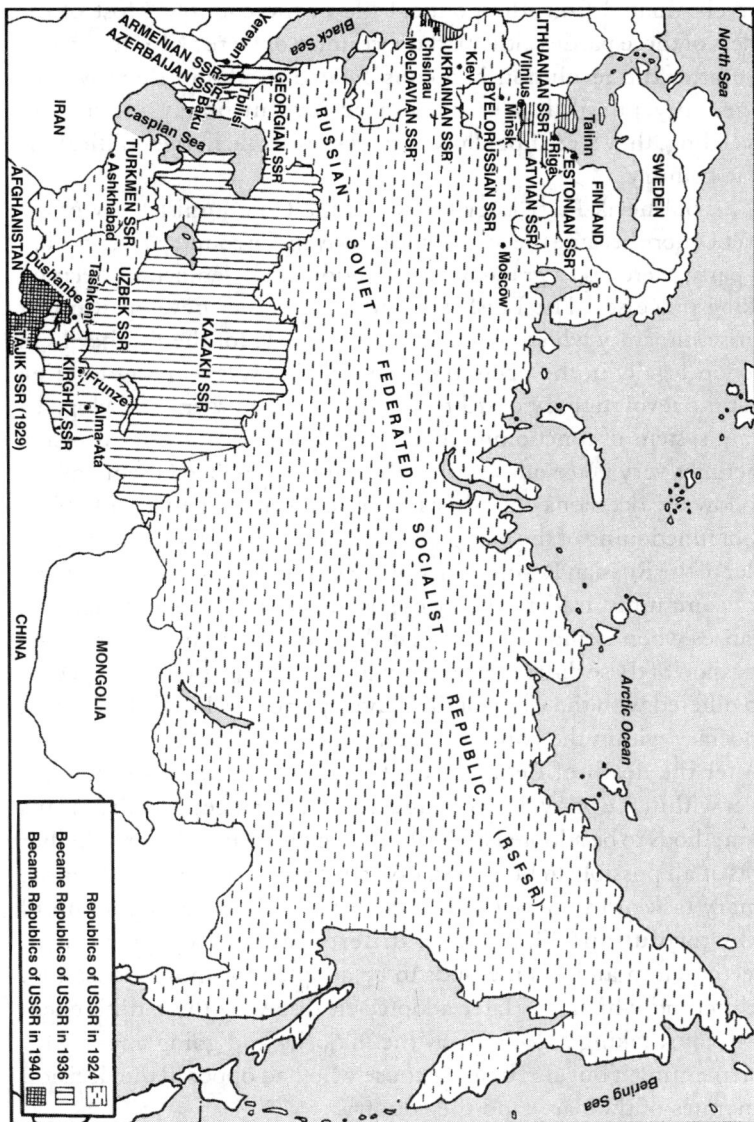

UNION OF SOVIET SOCIALIST REPUBLIC (Before its break-up in 1991)

Revolutionaries—had their members in the Soviets. During the civil war and later, when there were attempts to organise uprisings, they were eliminated from the political life of the country. Most of the leaders of these parties either left the country or were exiled to Siberia. Even after the revolution had consolidated itself and there was no longer any possibility of a counter-revolutionary movement succeeding, they were not allowed to play any role in the political life of the country.

The Bolshevik Party, later known as the Communist Party of the Soviet Union, became the sole political party in the country. Even within this party, there was a gradually elimination of all democratic decision making processes. The Bolshevik Party had earlier developed under Czarist autocracy which had made it impossible for the Bolsheviks to function legally in the open. As a party which was working to bring about the revolutionary overthrow of the existing order, it developed a certain system of functioning that allowed debates and controversies, sometimes very fierce ones, within the party, but obliged the members to follow the decisions once they had been taken by the majority. This way of functioning of the party continued as long as Lenin, the greatest leader of the Russian Revolution, was alive. There were occasions when other communist leaders openly opposed Lenin's views and there are instances when Lenin was left isolated within the party. However, the expression of these differences did not lead to suppression of the people who differed with the views of the majority or of the leadership. Thus, democracy within the party was maintained.

After the death of Lenin in 1924, there was a fierce struggle for power within the party. There were serious differences over the means and methods to be adopted for building socialism and also on whether it was at all possible to build socialism in one country or whether the primary task of the Soviet government should be the promotion of world revolution. There were differences on the question of collectivisation and the methods to be adopted for industrialisation. The method which was later adopted in resolving these differences was not just taking a decision by the majority and going ahead with implementing it but also treating those who had opposed the decision as enemies of the party and the country.

The first major struggle inside the party took place between Stalin and Trotsky. Stalin had become the general secretary of the party.

Trotsky's role in the revolution and subsequently as foreign minister and still later as war minister is considered to be second only to Lenin's. In 1927, however, Stalin emerged victorious, and Trotsky was expelled from the Party and, in 1929, he was exiled. In 1940, Stalin, got him assassinated in Mexico where he had been living for some years. Later, many other leaders were accused of being Trotskyites and they were arrested and executed. Two other leaders of the party—Zinoviev and Bukharin—who disagreed with Stalin's policies on different occasions, were eliminated.

Gradually, in the 1930s, in a country which professed building a new type of society and a higher type of civilisation, dictatorship of one man took shape. All power was concentrated in the hands of Stalin, who was supposed to be the source of all wisdom. His decision could not be questioned. In the writings of some socialist thinkers and leaders, "Dictatorship of the Proletariat" was envisaged as a stage in the building up of socialism. All capitalist countries were viewed as having dictatorships of the bourgeoisie, even when they had democratic political institutions, because the state in these countries was seen as the instrument for the maintenance of bourgeois predominance. The "Dictatorship of the Proletariat", in the same way, was viewed as a state which would use its power to maintain the domination of the working class. This "Dictatorship" did not meant the abolition of political freedom, elimination of all other political parties, and rule by one single party. However, the way the Soviet Union's political system developed, it came to mean, first, the dictatorship of the party and, by virtue of Stalin's domination of the party, the dictatorship of Stalin. After Stalin's death in 1953, this phenomenon was described by the Soviet communist leaders as Stalin's "cult of personality".

The dictatorship or the "cult of personality" of Stalin led to grave distortions in the building of socialism in the Soviet Union. In 1934, Kirov, the leader of the Communist Party in Leningrad (now St Petersburg) was assassinated. It is now generally believed that Stalin got him assassinated. The assassination was, however, utilised by Stalin to launch repression against everyone who was suspected of the slightest disloyalty. It soon developed into what has come to be known as the Great Purge. The number of people who perished in the Great Purge is only now beginning to be fully estimated. Their number was enormous. They included some of the most prominent communist leaders, veterans of the revolution, writers, artists, scientists, military and civil officers as well as some leaders of the communist parties of other countries.

For a long time, the people outside the Soviet Union, who were sympathetic to socialism and in their own countries were involved in the struggle against colonial rule or capitalist exploitation, did not realise the enormity of the crimes that were being committed in the name of socialism. One reason for this was that the Soviet Union was surrounded by countries which were hostile to her and to socialism. Some of these countries made no secret of their aggressive designs against the Soviet Union and declared that they would destroy communism. Many of these countries held many other people under colonial subjugation. The economic system of these countries bred inequality, and resulted in mass unemployment, misery and poverty. Repression inside the Soviet Union came to be seen in the context of the Soviet Union's efforts at preserving her independence as well as the socialist system in an extremely hostile world.

Foreign Policy of the Soviet State

The international role of the Soviet Union demarcated her from all other great powers of the time. She had been kept out of the peace conference held in Paris after the war to prepare treaties of peace with the Central Powers. In 1921, she entered into treaties with Iran and Afghanistan which strengthened the independence and sovereignty of these countries. A treaty was signed in the same year with the government of Mustafa Kemal, which was engaged in a war to restore the territorial integrity of Turkey. She participated in various disarmament conferences and made proposals for general and complete disarmament. In the 1930s, she took a forthright stand against the fascist countries' acts of aggression and strove for united action with other countries to check fascist aggression. Most Western countries, however, chose to appease fascism in the hope that fascism would destroy communism. In 1934, the Soviet Union joined the League of Nations and made efforts in the direction of making the League take resolute action for the maintenance of peace and for the liberation and independence of subjugated nations. The Soviet Union was also the only major power at that time which opposed the continuance of colonialism and imperialism. She came to be looked upon as a friend of the people who were fighting for their independence.

It may be appropriate to mention here the formation of the Communist International. With the outbreak of the war, the Second International had collapsed. During the war, some efforts were made to bring together some sections of the socialist parties of various countries. After the revolution in Russia, the left-wing sections of socialist parties in many countries were formed into one communist parties. A move to bring all communist parties into one international organisation was initiated. In March 1919, a conference was held in Moscow, which was attended by representatives of the communist parties of thirty countries. The Communist International (Comintern, for short), or the Third International, was formed at this conference. By the mid-1930s, there were communist parties in more than sixty countries. Some of these were very strong, such as the Communist Party of Germany before Hitler captured power and launched a systematic campaign to exterminate it, and the Communist Party of France. The Communist Party of China had also emerged as a powerful party.

The communist parties built a strong support for themselves among the workers of the capitalist countries as well as in the colonies. In almost all countries, they played a leading role in organising the workers against their miserable condition, particularly during the period of the Great Depression. In some countries that were under colonial rule, they became the leading force in the struggle for independence. Formed under the impact of the Russian Revolution, most communist parties looked upon the Communist Party of the Soviet Union as their model and as the leading force of the world communist movement. The Russian Revolution was also looked upon as the model of a socialist revolution. Because of their close association with the Communist Party of the Soviet Union, all communist parties were often viewed by others with suspicion. The Comintern with its headquarters in Moscow was often seen by others as an instrument of Soviet foreign policy.

While the formation of the communist parties on the pattern of the Soviet Communist Party and the Comintern were claimed to strengthen the revolutionary movement for socialism, it, in fact, led to a permanent division of the socialist movement. The communist parties and the various socialist and social democratic parties had many differences and they began to view each other as enemies, instead of trying to find common points of agreement or evolving a common agenda. The opponents of socialism took advantage from these internal differences. For example the cleavage between the Communist Party and the Social Democratic Party of Germany made it easier for the Nazis to capture power, which proved disastrous not only for socialism and democracy but also for the peace of the world. In 1935, the Comintern, at its seventh congress, held under the leadership of Georgi Dimitrov, a communist leader from Bulgaria, called for a united popular front against fascism and a united anti-imperialist front in the colonies. This was a significant development which helped unite vast masses of people—communists, socialists and others—for the achievement of common aims. The popular fronts that came up as a result of this policy prevented fascists from taking over power in some countries.

Japan

Expansionist Policy

The drive for expansion had been a marked feature of Japanese history since the beginning of her modernisation in the second half of the nineteenth century. At the end of the First World War she made major colonial gains in the Pacific and over a large part of China. The treaty she signed in Washington, though restricted the growth of her navy, had still left her as the greatest naval power in the Pacific. For a time, she pursued 'peaceful' ways of extending her domination over China as well as South-East Asia through economic means. However, the growth of the movement for Chinese national unification, as well as the influence of the Chinese Communist Party created major hurdles for extending her control over China. One of her major objectives was to prevent Chinese national unification. One of the first major acts of aggression after the First World War was committed by Japan when she occupied Manchuria in 1931 and later set up a puppet government there. This was followed by a massive invasion of China in 1937. In 1936 she had signed the Anti-Comintern Pact with Germany. She planned to establish her hegemony over the entire

Asian continent and the Pacific, as Germany along with Italy had planned to do it over the rest of the world.

The Japanese economy continued to grow after the war and she became the biggest exporter of cotton textiles, rayon and raw silk. However her dependence on other countries for raw materials, machinery and foodstuffs had made the economy somewhat fragile. In order to overcome some of these problems, she underwent extensive industrial expansion particularly in iron and steel and heavy engineering industries. But direct control over the resources and markets of China and other countries was considered essential by Japanese industrialists and political and military leaders.

Political Repression

The Japanese industrial expansion had taken place under conditions of extreme exploitation of the workers. The industry and the banks were under the domination of the *zaibatsu*, a small group of money-cliques. The zaibatsu had close links with the Japanese government and politicians. The living condition of the workers was miserable. The condition of farmers was no better. Most of the pesasants had extremely small holdings, a little more than an acre, and a large number of them worked as tenants. The Japanese agriculture was unable to absorb Japan's growing population or meet its food requirements. There was widespread unrest in the country. In 1919, there were disturbances throughout the country over the high price of rice which most people—the general level of their wages being low—could not afford to pay. These are generally referred to as 'rice mutinies'. Factories, the houses of the rich, and the shops of rice traders were attacked and burnt. In the 1920s, there was a wave of strikes, and trade unions began to gain strength. Communist and Social Democratic Parties were also formed and they tried to organise workers and peasants against the oppressive economic system. These parties also aroused the people of Japan against the policy of imperialism and war. However, they were suppressed ruthlessly as were the trade unions and the peasants' organisations. In 1925, the Peace Preservation Law was passed to suppress 'dangerous thoughts'. According to this law, anyone forming or joining an organisation which advocated change in the form of government or the abolition of private property could be arrested. Even academic discussions on these questions or other political problems were banned.

'Military Fascism' in Japan

Japan seemed to be making some progress in having a parliamentary form of government in the 1920s. In 1924, the franchise was extended to all males—women continued to be denied the right to vote. For sometime the government seemed to work under the control of the civilians. However, the military continued to be a major force in the political life of the country and from the early 1930s increasingly dominated the government. Even before the military had established its domination over the government, it would openly defy the government, and the government could do nothing to control it. The Japanese military was the most aggressive force in the Japanese society. It had close links with a number of secret societies, which had been formed. All these societies attacked ideas of liberalism, pacifism and democracy, and advocated ideas of national chauvinism, the superiority of the Japanese culture and preservation of the purity of Japanese culture from foreign influences. Ideas of peace, socialism and democracy were considered foreign ideas from which Japan had to be protected. These societies had their own notions of what constituted the 'national essence' of Japan. Emperor-worship was an idea common to most of them. They advocated the belief that "[t]o die for the Emperor is to live forever". They had their armed gangs, and resorted to political assassinations. The ideology of the armed forces and of many political leaders of Japan was largely shaped by these secret societies. The imperialist expansion of Japan was considered a desirable aim by all political forces except the Communists and the Social Democrats. The latter had been reduced to a position of insignificance by the repressive policies followed by the Japanese government during the inter-war period. The political system which emerged in Japan may be called 'military fascism'. Its growing affinity with the fascist governments of Germany and Italy was natural.

In 1926 Emperor Hirohito succeeded to the throne of Japan. The reign of the emperor under whom modernisation of Japan had begun in 1868 was known as Meiji, meaning "enlightened government". Emperor Hirohito took the title of Showa for his reign, which means "enlightened peace".

ASIA

India

The inter-war years saw the growth of the nationalist movement in every country of Asia. The freedom movement in India entered a new phase—the phase of a mass anti-imperialist upsurge—soon after the First World War was over. On 13 April 1919, British imperialism committed the barbarous massacre at Jallianwala Bagh in Amritsar. The Non-Cooperation Movement launched soon after drew millions of common people—peasants, workers, students, women, and almost every other sections of the Indian society—into the struggle for freedom and open defiance of British authority became the creed of millions of Indians. At the end of 1929, Poorna Swaraj (Complete Independence) became the objective of the Congress, which led India's struggle for independence. In 1980, a great mass movement was launched and hundreds of thousands of Indians broke British laws and went to prison. As a part of the nationalist struggle, there also grew the vision of a new India—free, democratic, secular and egalitarian. The struggle also extended to areas which were, with British support, under Indian princes.

The Indian freedom movement also developed close contacts with the freedom movements in other colonies as well as with the anti-fascist democratic movements in the European countries. The attainment of political independence came to be increasingly viewed as an essential pre-requisite for the reconstruction of Indian society. The basic features of the role which independent India would play in world affairs also were formed during the period of the struggle for independence. The nationalist movement in every country, while uniting the people for the immediate task of overthrowing foreign rule, also increasingly thought in terms of social and economic reconstruction and building of a modern nation.

China

Anti-Imperialist Upsurge

The role of Dr Sun Yat-sen in the revolution of 1911, which resulted in the proclamation of China as a republic, and the usurpation of power by Yuan Shih-kai, who dreamed of becoming the emperor, have already been referred. China was ruled by warlords who controlled different regions of China and fought among themselves for supremacy. Various foreign powers supported them in their hope for concessions later. At the end of the First World War, there were two main governments in China. One of these was controlled by the Guomindang and had its headquarters at Canton. Dr Sun Yat-sen became the president of this government. The other government was headed by a military general and had its headquarters at Beijing. The decision of the Paris Peace Conference to hand over Shantung to Japan led to an anti-imperialist upsurge in 1919. It began with a protest demonstration by the students of the Beijing University on 4 May 1919 and the movement that started with it came to be known as the May Fourth Movement. It soon spread to various parts of China.

The Russian Revolution had a deep impact on the Chinese nationalists, and radical tendencies began to grow. In 1921, the Communist Party of China was formed, and it soon became a major force. In the meantime, Dr Sun Yat-sen, having failed to secure Western countries' help to unify China, sought the support of the Soviet Union. In 1924, the Guomindang and the Chinese Communist Party came together. While the Communist Party continued as a separate party, several communists also joined the Guomindang. It was decided to form a national revolutionary army and for this purpose a military academy was set up with the help of Soviet military and political advisers. In 1925, the Chinese national revolutionary army launched its operations against the warlords. However, in about two years after the death of Dr Sun Yat-sen, in March 1925, the situation in China underwent a drastic change. The alliance between the Guomindang and the Communist Party broke up, and soon conditions were created for a civil war in China.

Civil War in China

The operations of the national revolutionary army for the political unification of China were accompanied by workers' and peasants' movements. In 1925, there were strikes and demonstrations throughout Shanghai against the killings of workers' leaders. These killing were organised by the Japanese industrialists and the demonstrators were shot at by the British police. In many areas, the peasants started seizing the lands of the big landlords. In March 1927, when the national revolutionary army reached Nanjing, the British and the US warships opened fire, killing hundreds of people. At this moment, there occurred a split in the Guomindang, and General Chiang Kai-shek, who was chief of staff of the national revolutionary army, set up his government at Nanjing. The growth of the peasants' and workers' movement and the increasing strength of the left-wing elements within the Guomindang had alarmed him. General Shek was now less concerned with putting an end to the foreign domination of China and her political unification than with the suppression of the left-wing and the communists. His troops raided workers' quarters in Shanghai, killing thousands of workers along with a number of communists. In December 1927, the communists led an uprising in Canton, and set up a Soviet government there. However, the uprising was suppressed and over five thousand workers were killed. This marked the split in the nationalist movement in China. The Soviet advisers were expelled, and many leaders of the Guomindang, including the widow of Dr Sun Yat-sen, went into exile. After the suppression of the Canton uprising, the communists were scattered in different parts of the country and brought some areas under their control. China now entered a long period of civil war between the armies of Chiang Kai-shek and the Chinese Communist Party.

After the Japanese occupation of Manchuria, a wave of anti-Japanese feelings swept the country and there was a nation-wide movement to boycott Japanese goods. However, the Guomindang led by Chiang Kai-shek and the Communist Party failed to unite themselves against the Japanese aggression. The communists gave a call for anti-Japanese resistance but were not willing to ally with Chiang Kai-shek. Chiang Kai-shek's army launched operations against the communist strongholds but not against the Japanese. In the meantime, the Communist Party's influence started growing, particularly in the countryside. The most important leader of the Communist Party to emerge during this period was Mao Zedong (Mao Tse-tung). He advocated the view that in China the peasantry was the main revolutionary force, and he built up the strategy of bringing about socialist revolution with the help of the peasantry.

In 1934, Chiang Kai-shek launched an attack on the communist-held areas in southern China with the help of a million strong army. The communists were forced to give up their base and, to escape annihilation, about 100,000 of them moved to Yenan in north-western

China. This movement, known as the Long March in which they covered a distance of about 12,000 km, added to the nation-wide popularity of the communists. During the Long March, they seized the lands of the landlords and distributed them among the peasants, thus continuously strengthening support for themselves against Chiang Kai-shek's government. The latter was by now associated in the minds of the people as the government of big landlords, merchants and bankers. The communists also called for a national war against the Japanese aggression, while Chiang Kai-shek's army continued to target only the communists.

In 1937, the massive Japanese invasion of China began. The armies of Chiang Kai-shek retreated in the face of the Japanese attack, and his government moved from Nanjing to Chungking. However, by this time, a united front to resist the Japanese aggression had come into being. In December 1936, a dramatic incident had taken place. Chiang Kai-shek had gone to Sian to persuade his troops to fight the communists. His troops arrested him and released him only when he agreed to end the civil war and form a joint front with the communists to fight the Japanese. From that time on, the semblance of a national war of resistance against the Japanese aggression was maintained though each side—Chiang Kai-shek's Guomindang and the communists under Mao Zedong's leadership—remained suspicious of the other and tried to increase their own strength against the other. The communists, during this period, emerged as the genuine representatives of China's national struggle against the Japanese aggression.

Korea

The movement for the independence of Korea from Japan's colonial rule became powerful soon after the First World War was over. The Russian Revolution also helped the spread of anti-imperialist ideas in Korea. In 1918, the Korean nationalists drafted a Declaration of Independence. In March 1919, the Declaration was read out at a public meeting in Seoul, and there were demonstrations in which thousands of people participated. Soon the demonstrations took the form of a country-wide uprising in which over 150,000 people participated. The uprising was suppressed by the Japanese army, killing about 8,000 and seriously wounding 16,000 people. About

50,000 people were arrested. However, the peasants' revolts and workers' strikes continued. The Koreans settled in China, Japan, the Soviet Union and other countries also played an important role in strengthening the anti-Japanese struggle in Korea. After 1931, following the Japanese seizure of Manchuria, the Koreans began organising anti-Japanese armed actions in Manchuria as well as in Korea. The Japanese made use of Korea as a base for launching military operations against China and, later, other countries of Asia as well as against the Soviet Union. They also tried to set up organisations of Koreans who were loyal to them, and to use the Korean people in their aggressive wars against other countries.

SOUTH-EAST ASIAN COUNTRIES

The Philippines

During the period of US colonial rule, the Philippines had been reduced to an economic appendage of the US. She exported about 80 per cent of all her exports, mainly sugar, coconuts and tobacco, to the US, and was dependent on the US for about 70 per cent of her imports. The pattern of her economic development under US patronage was similar to the one that existed in most Latin American countries, that is, production of a few export oriented crops mainly for bartering against essential imports. Also, as in most Latin American countries, the land was owned by big landlords. The peasant unrest had given rise to radical political movements which aimed at ending the colonial rule as well as the exploitation of landlords. A peasant uprising took place in the early 1930s but it was suppressed. There were other political movements for the independence of the country. In 1935, autonomy was granted to the Philippines with the promise of independence after ten years.

Indo-China

The most outstanding leader of the freedom movement in Indo-China, comprising Vietnam, Laos and Cambodia, was Nguyen Ai Quoc who, later, became known as Ho Chi Minh. During the First World War, about 100,000 Vietnamese had been sent to France, some as soldiers and many as labourers. They came into contact with the socialist and other radical movements in France. Ho Chi Minh was actively associated with the formation of the Communist Party of France. In 1925, he set up the Revolutionary Youth League of Vietnam. In 1930, the various communist groups came together to form the Vietnamese Communist Party, which was later renamed as the Communist Party of Indo-China. This party became the leading force in the struggle for independence against French rule. There was another parry, the Vietnam National Party, which was modelled on the Guomindang. This party organised a rebellion in 1930, which was suppressed.

Indonesia

In Indonesia—or the Dutch East Indies, as the colonial rulers called her—political movements for freedom from Dutch rule and workers' and peasants' organisations had emerged during the early years of the twentieth century. These included the Islamic Alliance and the Indies' Social-Democratic Association. In 1920, the Communist Party of Indonesia was formed, which organised uprisings in Java and Sumatra. The uprisings were suppressed by the Dutch authorities. In 1927, the Nationalist Party was formed under the leadership of Ahmed Sukarno, who later became the president of independent Indonesia. This party brought together various other organisations and parties for launching a united struggle for freedom. It also adopted the objective of establishing socialism once the country had won her independence. Alarmed at the growing strength of the nationalist movement, the Dutch authorities banned the Nationalist Party and arrested many of its leaders, including Sukarno. The repression continued for many years, and even political discussions on the demand for independence were banned.

Burma

After her annexation by the British, Burma (present Myanmar) had been made a part of Britain's Indian empire. She was separated from India in 1937. The nationalist movement had started emerging in Burma in the early years of the twentieth century with the formation of the Young Men's Buddhist Association in 1906. The growth of the anti-imperialist struggle in India was an important influence on the

Burmese nationalist movement, and the leaders of the freedom movements in the two countries developed close contacts with each other. In 1921, the General Council of Burmese Association was set up and, like the Indian National Congress at the time, raised the demand for self-government for Burma. In the 1930s, an organisation of the youth who called themselves Thakins, or owners of their country, was set up. It demanded complete independence. The most prominent leader of this organisation was Aung San who later became the leader of the Burmese Communist Party. After her separation from India, constitutional reforms similar to the Government of India Act of 1935 were introduced in Burma but these failed to satisfy the aspirations of the Burmese nationalists. There was a mass anti-British upsurge and protest marches and strikes all over the country.

Malaya

The British colony of Malaya comprised a number of states some of which were under direct British administration while others enjoyed some measure of autonomy under local rulers. The country was exploited by the British mainly for her rubber and tin. The plantations and mines were owned by the British and the workers included many of Indian origin. Singapore was crucial to British imperialism in Asia because of its commercial and strategic importance. Besides, the Malays and the people of Indian origin, Malaya had a large population of Chinese origin who were mostly engaged in trade and commerce. The different ethnic groups had formed their own political associations, and the British authorities exploited the differences among them to prevent the rise of a united nationalist movement in Malaya.

Sri Lanka

The population of Sri Lanka (Ceylon) comprised mainly the Sinhalese, the Tamils and plantation workers of Indian origin. The British authorities introduced constitutional changes which gave the upper sections of the Sri Lankan society a share in the administration of the country. In 1931, under a new constitution, adult franchise was introduced and an assembly was created. The members of the assembly along with the British secretaries ran the government. A number of political parties were formed and a number of leaders, who later were at the forefront of the political life of independent Sri Lanka, rose to prominence in the 1930s.

COUNTRIES OF WEST ASIA

Afghanistan

Soon after capturing power, Amanullah Khan declared the independence of Afghanistan. The Soviet Union signed a treaty with the new government of Afghanistan, which helped Afghanistan in consolidating her independence. Amanullah Khan took some steps to modernise the country. In 1929, he was overthrown and Muhammad Nadir Shah became the king. During Nadir Shah's reign, a new constitution was introduced, which aimed at making Afghanistan a constitutional monarchy.

Iran

After the Revolution, Russia had renounced the Anglo-Russian agreement of 1907 under which northern Iran had become a Russian sphere of influence. The British—worried over the spread of revolutionary ideas and the danger to their oil interests in Iran—threatened to occupy the entire country. In 1919, they signed an agreement with the government of Iran, which established British control over the army and the economy of Iran. There were uprisings in different parts of Iran against the British occupation and the agreement which the government had signed with Britain. The Iranian communists tried to use these uprisings to establish a soviet styled republic but failed. However, in 1921, the pro-British government of Iran was overthrown with the help of Reza Khan, an army officer. The new government, while it ruthlessly put down the revolutionary uprisings, also annulled the 1919 agreement with Britain, which had made Iran more or less a protectorate of Britain. Many Iranians looked up to Reza Khan as the Mustafa Kemal of Iran and supported him in his quest for absolute power. In 1925, the Iranian Constituent Assembly called the Majlis, deposed the ruler of

Iran, and made Reza Khan the Shah of Iran. The dynasty of Reza Khan is known as the Pahlavi dynasty. The new ruler took many steps for the modernisation of Iran. Industry and transport were developed, and efforts were made to introduce modern education and curb the influence of the *mullah*s. Many reforms were made in the legal system. While the Anglo Iranian Oil Company continued to remain important, a larger share of its profits now went to Iranian government. However, in spite of these measures, the Shah's rule was tyrannical and brought few benefits to the common people.

Iraq

After the end of the First World War, Iraq, Palestine and Transjordan had been given to Britain as mandates. The decision to hand over Iraq to Britain provoked a rebellion there, which was suppressed by the British troops. In 1921, the British installed Faisal, who had been deposed in Syria by the French, as the King of Iraq, but they retained with them the ultimate military, political and economic control of the country. Iraq's rich oil resources were also brought under British control. In 1930, Iraq was granted full independence, and soon after it became a member of the League of Nations. Iraq had become a constitutional monarchy with a pro-British government. The British troops continued to remain in Iraq, and the British also maintained its hold on the economy of Iraq. In 1936, the National Reform Party, with the help of a section of the army, overthrew the pro-British government, and tried to introduce agrarian reforms and re-build Iraq's economy. In 1937, however, this government was overthrown and replaced by one headed by the pro-British Nuri Said.

Palestine

The British followed the same policy in Transjordan. They installed Faisal's brother Abdullah as the king and, in 1928, granted independence to that country while retaining military and financial control. In Palestine, however, the British policy ran into serious difficulties, and the region became a source of tension and conflict.

In the late nineteenth century, a movement to secure for the Jews a home in Palestine was started in Europe. The movement was called Zionism. The Jews in Europe and USA had been fighting for equal

BRITISH AND FRENCH MANDATES IN WEST ASIA

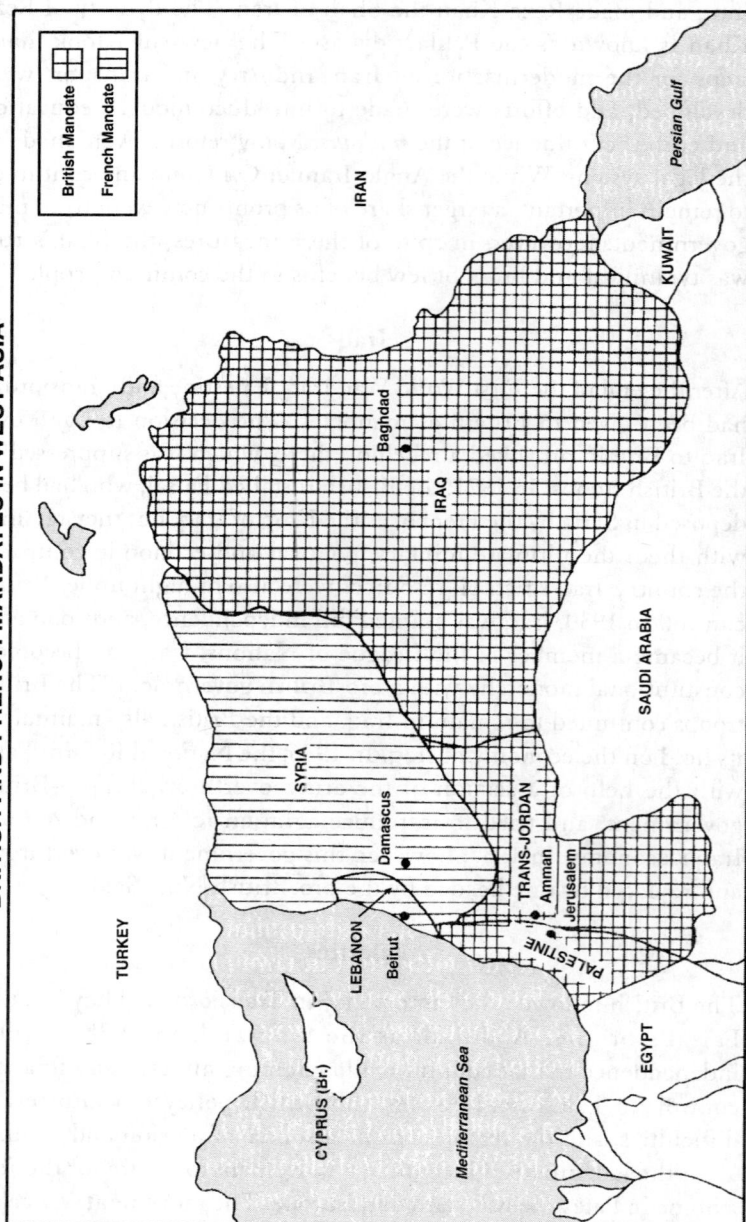

British Mandate

French Mandate

TURKEY

IRAN

Persian Gulf

KUWAIT

Baghdad

IRAQ

SAUDI ARABIA

SYRIA

Damascus

TRANS-JORDAN

Amman

Jerusalem

PALESTINE

LEBANON

Beirut

CYPRUS (Br.)

Mediterranean Sea

EGYPT

rights and for an end to discrimination which was commonly practised against them. Many of them had joined radical political movements. Zionism, however, proclaimed that all Jews, irrespective of the countries to which they belonged, constituted a single nation and that they should have a state of their own in Palestine where they had a kingdom over 2,500 years ago. The influence of Zionism among the Jews was limited as many Jews viewed it as a divisive force which would isolate them from the people of the countries in which they had been living for centuries. During the First World War, as mentioned earlier, the British government, under the influence of Zionist leaders, had promised the setting up of a "national home for the Jewish people" in Palestine.

During the war, Arab nationalism had grown, and as soon as the British mandate in Palestine was set up, serious disturbances broke out. However, while the nationalist aspirations of the Palestinians were suppressed, there was a massive migration of Jews from the West. The Jews took over some of the best lands from the Palestinians, who were rendered landless. In 1919, the population of Jews in Palestine was 58,000. In 1934, it had gone up to 960,000. In 1929, there was an Arab rebellion for the independence of Palestine and an end to Jewish migration to Palestine. The rebellion was crushed, and hundreds of Arabs were killed by the British police and army. The nationalist struggle, led by the Arab Palestinian Congress, however, continued. In 1937, a British Royal Commission recommended the partition of Palestine into three states, one of which would be under Arab control, another under Jewish control, and the third under British control. This recommendation was rejected by everyone, and there were strong protests by the Arabs of Palestine and by other Arab countries. In 1939, the British government issued a White Paper in which independence was promised to Palestine after ten years, with guarantees for the rights of both Jews and Arabs. In the meantime, the Jewish migration was to be restricted and then completely stopped. Restrictions were also placed on the sale of land. However, the issue took a serious turn after the Second World War was over with dangerous consequences for the peace and stability of West Asia.

Syria and Lebanon

Syria and Lebanon had become French mandates, and the French troops occupied these countries in the face of fierce resistance. Faisal, who, earlier, had been made king of Syria, with French support, was later deposed by the French. The people of these two countries resisted the imposition of French rule from the very beginning. In 1925, a rebellion broke out in Syria and the rebels occupied almost the entire country, including the capital city of Damascus. The rebellion also spread to parts of Lebanon. It took the French two years to suppress the rebellion. During this rebellion, Damascus was subjected to heavy bombing, which killed about 25,000 people. However, strikes, demonstrations and armed uprisings for ending the French mandate continued. In 1936, when the Popular Front came to power in France, the French government signed agreements with representatives of Syria and Lebanon, promising independence after three years. However, later, the French government went back on its promise, and both Syria and Lebanon failed to win their independence.

AFRICA

By the end of the First World War, there were about fifty states in Africa and, with the exception of Liberia and Ethiopia, they all were under the rule of one European colonial country or the other. While stirrings of nationalism were felt everywhere, the level of political struggles varied from country to country. During the inter-war years, generally speaking, the resistance and revolts of the type that had occurred during the early period of colonial rule, were no longer the form of struggle waged by the African people. On the surface, colonialism seemed to have established itself, and the stability of colonial rule led some people to refer to this period as the 'golden age' of colonialism in Africa. However, the stability was more apparent than real as new anti-colonial forces had already begun to take shape. In some countries of North Africa, this period saw the emergence of powerful nationalist movements and struggles. In others, including most countries of southern Africa, this period marked the beginning of the rise of modern nationalism and of nationalist political movements.

Egypt

One of the most powerful nationalist movements in North Africa arose in Egypt. In 1918, an organisation, called the Wafd, was set up, which led the Egyptian struggle for independence. A delegation of Egyptian nationalists prepared to go to Paris during the Peace Conference to demand independence for Egypt but the members of the delegation were arrested by the British and the Wafd leader Saad Zaghlut Pasha was deported. This provoked a rebellion in Egypt which was suppressed. However, anti-British disturbances continued and, in 1922, the British government was forced to end her protectorate over Egypt. Ahamd Fuad was made king of the independent Egyptian kingdom.

In 1923, a constitution came in force, which gave Egypt a parliamentary system of government. The British forces, however, continued to remain in Egypt in the name of providing "defence of Egypt and the Canal" and for continuing British rule over Sudan which, nominally, was under joint Anglo-Egyptian control. In the elections to the parliament, Zaghlul Pasha's Wafd party swept the polls and formed the government. The government demanded complete independence. The Egyptian king dissolved the parliament. The Wafd party swept the polls in subsequent elections that were conducted, with the king, instigated by the British, dissolving the parliament four times in a period of six years. After the death of Zaghlul Pasha, Nahas Pasha became the leader of the Wafd party, which continued to pursue an anti-British policy. In 1930, a new constitution was proclaimed, which increased the powers of the king and reduced those of the parliament. There were widespread popular protests and, in 1935, the constitution of 1923 was restored. In the elections held in 1936, the Wafd party again came to power. This marked a victory for the nationalist forces. The new government signed a treaty with Britain which ended the British occupation of Egypt but Britain was allowed to keep 10,000 soldiers in the Suez Canal zone. The continuation of the British troops in Egypt was to become a major source of conflict between Britain and Egypt after some years.

Morocco

Powerful nationalist movements also arose in Tunisia, Libya, Algeria and Morocco. In 1921, the Rif tribes of Spanish Morocco rose in rebellion under the leadership of Abdel Karim. They inflicted a crushing defeat on the Spanish troops and established the Rifian Republican Nation. Soon after, the French sent their troops against the Rifian Republic but they were repulsed. Finally, in a war which continued for two years, Spain and France launched joint military operations with a disproportionately large army of 400,000 soldiers. In May 1926, Abdel Karim surrendered and, by 1927, Spain and France were again masters of their respective parts in Morocco. The Rif Rebellion became a source of inspiration to anti-imperialist movements all over Africa. During the French war against the Rifian Republic, many people in France, notably the Communist Party and various other trade unions, extended their support to the Riffs. On 12 October 1925, the French workers went on strike and held demonstrations against the French policy in Morocco. They also extended support to the cause of Algerian and Tunisian independence.

Southern Africa

In the countries of southern Africa, the growth of nationalist movements was uneven. The states which the colonial rulers created in southern Africa, were mostly new entities and the people inhabiting most of these states did not necessarily share a common past. Therefore, the people in these states took time to develop a sense of national identity. This situation was different from the one in the Asian countries or, earlier, in the countries of Europe. The growing sense of national identity among the people of these states was a major development during the inter-war years.

In every country, the grievances of the peasants, workers, the intelligentsia and other sections of society led to the formation of trade unions and various other types of organisations. These organisations inevitably had an anti-colonial political character as the source of all grievances was the existing colonial regime. The intelligentsia played a leading role in arousing political consciousness and setting up nationalist political organisations.

Educational facilities in southern Africa had been extremely limited and even secondary education was considered dangerous for the continuance of the colonial rule. Many African historians are of the view that the European colonial rulers of Africa deliberately kept the level and facilities of education in the African colonies extremely low because of the experience of the British colonial rule in India. However, some Africans did receive education and were absorbed in the administration as it is impossible to run any colonial administration solely with the help of people from the mother countries. Those who were absorbed in the administration experienced the discrimination against them practised by the colonial rulers and were increasingly made aware of the exploitation of their people. Many of them went to other countries, particularly Britain, France and USA, for higher studies, and thus came into contact with the revolutionary and democratic ideas and movements. Some of the future leaders of Africa who rose into prominence during their stay in other countries were Jomo Kenyatta of Kenya, Nnamdi Azikiwe who became the first president of the Republic of Nigeria, Kwame Nkrumah of Gold Coast (Ghana) and Leopold Senghor of Senegal.

A number of organisations were set up in different countries of southern Africa in the 1920s. In the countries where some representative institutions had been introduced, regular political parties came into being. For example, the National Democratic Party of Nigeria was formed with the introduction of constitutional reforms in that country. Some of the organisations which were formed during this period were the Young Kikuyu Association, the Gold Coast Youth Conference, the League of the Rights of Man and Citizenship, and the Liga African in Angola.

Pan-African Congress

During this period, many international organisations and movements played an important role in the emergence of anti-colonial movements in Africa. Many of these movements were initiated by the leaders of the Black people's struggle for equality in America. Some had their origin among the Black people in the French and British colonies in the Caribbean. A common feature of these movements was the advocacy of the unity and solidarity of all the Black peoples. The most important among these were the Pan-African Congresses organised by W.E.B. Du Bois who placed an important role in setting up the National Association for the Advancement of Colored People. Du Bois convened the first Pan-African Congress in Paris in 1919, during the Paris Peace Conference. The Congress passed resolutions demanding equal political rights for the Black people in the US and other parts of the world and the right of self-determination for the African people. In 1921, 1923 and 1927, Pan-African Congresses were held in different capital cities of Europe and brought together Black intellectuals from Africa, USA and the Caribbean. Another Pan-Africanist movement was initiated by Marcus Garvey, who was, by birth, a Jamaican. In 1914, he had set up an organisation, called the Universal Negro Improvement Association. He organised a campaign to encourage Black Americans to emigrate to Africa, and played an important role in developing a sense of pride among the Black people everywhere.

Negritude Movement

In the 1920s and 1930s, there also emerged a cultural movement which promoted a sense of identity and pride among the Black people and a rejection of White and colonial domination. This is known as the negritude movement. It was based on an affirmation of Black culture, the beauty of African art and music, and "a belief in a common cultural heritage among all African and African-descended peoples". Some of the prominent figures in this movement were Aime Cesaire of Martinique, a French colony in the Caribbean, Leopold Sedar Senghor of Senegal, who later became the president of Senegal, and Langston Hughes of USA. All the three were poets of great eminence, the first two of French and the last of English. Another poet, of Jamaican origin, who inspired Black people to "protest against their common suffering and assert their dignity" was Claude McKay.

The anti-imperialist movements which had their origin in Europe also promoted nationalist movements in Africa. In 1927, an International Congress was held in Brussels at which the League Against Imperialism was formed. This Congress was attended by leaders of left-wing movements and radical intellectuals from Europe and representatives of Asian and African countries that were under colonial rule. They included delegates from Egypt, Kenya and South Africa. Among them were Jomo Kenyatta and La Guma. Jawaharlal Nehru represented the Indian National Congress at this Congress. The Italian invasion of Ethiopia and world-wide protests against it also strengthened anti-imperialist feelings in Africa.

Racial Oppression in South Africa

The inter-war years saw the further strengthening of the system of racial oppression in South Africa as well as of the struggle against it. In 1910, the British colonies, Natal and Cape Colony, and the Boer states, the Orange Free State and Transvaal, had been brought together as a self-governing state—called the Union of South Africa—of the British empire. After the First World War, the White population of South Africa was about 1,800,000, which was about 20 per cent of the total population. The Whites comprised people of British origin and Boers, who were of Dutch origin. The majority of the population was African. There were about 200,000 people who were of Asian, mainly Indian, origin. The government was completely in the hands of the Whites. During the last quarter of the nineteenth and early part of the twentieth century Gandhiji had initiated a struggle in South Africa against racial discrimination to which Indians were subjected. In 1912, the African National Congress was formed. It was to play a leading role in the struggle against racial oppression in South Africa. In 1921 the Communist Party of South Africa was formed.

The Nationalist Party, which was mainly a party of the Boers (or Afrikaners), was dominated by ideas of extreme White racism. It advocated a policy of colour bar to maintain the social and political supremacy of the Whites who, it said, were threatened by the Blacks. From the mid-1920s onwards, the White rulers, influenced by racist ideas, passed laws to exclude the Black people from getting skilled jobs or getting training for skilled jobs, or living in areas where the Whites lived. All the best lands had already been taken away from them. They were asked to move to areas called 'tribal reserves', and were required to seek permission to work in the cities or on farms owned by the Whites. They had to carry identity cards and passes in the cities to prove that they had been permitted to be there, and were arrested if found without them. They were forced to live under horrible conditions and in specific areas of the towns or cities. The average wage of a White worker was about ten times that of his African counterpart. The Blacks were debarred from forming trade unions or joining unions of White workers. They had no right to vote, and were completely debarred from having any say in the political life of their country. In the 1930s, the White racists organised fascist movements on the model of the Nazi party of Germany. There was widespread discontent against the racist policies, and a united struggle to overthrow the vicious system began to be built up.

LATIN AMERICA

Most of the countries of Latin America continued to have regimes dominated by big landlords and the army. However, in almost every country, democratic and left-wing political movements and workers' and peasants' organisations gained in strength. In most Latin American countries, communist parties were also formed during this period. There was a popular uprising led by Augusto Cesar Sandino against the puppet government in Nicaragua, which had been installed with the help of the US troops. The uprising continued for many years and, in 1933, the US troops were withdrawn. However, Sandino was assassinated and power was captured by Anastasio Somoza, who established his dictatorship in Nicaragua. The popular uprising led by Sandino had won the sympathy and support of people in all Latin American countries and, because of this, the US policy of sending troops to intervene in the internal affairs of Latin American countries had changed. The economic crisis of 1929 had affected the economy of all Latin American countries. Most of the economies were heavily dependent on exports and they faced a serious crisis when USA and other countries imposed severe restrictions on imports. This resulted in a vast increase in the number of unemployed in industry. The impact on the people engaged in agriculture was even worse, and they constituted an overwhelming majority of the population in these countries.

Mexico

Significant devélopments took place in Mexico during the inter-war period. Mexico had been one of the first countries in Latin America to assert her independence from the US as well as to adopt social and economic policies in the interests of the peasants. She was the first country in the Americas to establish diplomatic relations with the Soviet Union. Between 1934 and 1940, Lazaro Cardenas was the president of Mexico. He introduced many radical steps to end the power of big landowners and to build up the economy. Many landed estates were confiscated and lands distributed to the peasants. Initially he nationalised the railways along with some other industries, but later the entire petroleum industry, which had been owned by the British and American oil companies, was nationalised. The nationalisation of the petroleum industry had a far-reaching significance as it meant an assertion by the people of their right over the wealth and resources of their country. In course of time, the example of Mexico was followed by many other Latin American countries.

Changes in US Policy

A major feature of this period was the assertion by the Latin American countries of their independence from foreign interference as well as their independent role in world affairs. This was the major objective behind their joining the League of Nations. An all-American Anti-Imperialist League was formed, and its representatives attended the Brussels Conference in 1927 where the League Against Imperialism was set up. All Latin American countries were united in their opposition to the US domination of the Pan-American Union which had been set up on US initiative. They also opposed the claims by the US of her right to interfere in the affairs of other countries in the Americas. At a conference of the Pan-American Union in 1933, the US had to formally affirm its support to the declaration, with the statement that "no state has the right to interfere in the internal or foreign affairs of another".

There were some important changes in the US policy towards Latin America. From the 1920s, she relied more on what is called 'dollar diplomacy' by increasing investments in Latin American countries and controlling their economy rather than on direct military interference. The US policy towards Latin American countries during the period of Franklin D. Roosevelt's presidency is described as the "Good Neighbour Policy". In some respects, the changes in policy were significant. The US annulled what is known as the Platt Amendment which gave her the self-assumed right to send troops to Cuba. The US withdrew her troops from Nicaragua and Panama, but kept some troops in the Panama Canal Zone which continued to remain under US control. These steps, however, did not end the hegemony of the US over Latin America, and the policy of non-interference was not adhered to in the subsequent years.

After the rise of fascism in Europe, fascist groups and parties began to be set up in some Latin American countries, some of whom had many immigrants from Germany, Italy and Spain. The peoples of Latin America were awakened to the danger of fascism, and efforts were made to set up united fronts to curb the activities of fascist groups and parties, and the aggressive acts of fascist countries and Japan were condemned. Mexico consistently followed an anti-fascist policy. She condemned the Japanese aggression in Manchuria, the Italian invasion and occupation of Ethiopia, and Germany's annexation of Austria. She also provided shelter to thousands of Spanish Republicans who had to leave their country after Franco, with Italian and German support, had destroyed the Spanish Republic.

Europe From 1919 to 1923

New States in Europe

The end of the First World War was accompanied by the emergence of a number of European nations as independent states. These included Estonia, Latvia, Lithuania, Finland, Poland and Czechoslovakia. Some new states were formed such as Yugoslavia by merging new territories with an already existing state. By 1922, Ireland, which had been fighting for independence from Britain, was partitioned. An Irish Free State was given the Dominion status while Northern Ireland (Ulster) comprising six counties retained her connection with Britain. A few years later, the Irish Free State proclaimed herself a sovereign state with the Eire (subsequently the

Republic of Ireland). Hungary and Austria became separate states with the end of the Austro-Hungarian empire.

The settlements of the boundaries of various states in Europe as a result of the peace treaties became a source of tension and conflicts. Most countries of central, southern and eastern Europe were dissatisfied with the boundary settlements and many of them continued to feel insecure. Many ententes, alliances and treaties of friendship and non-aggression pacts were signed between different countries during this period and, later, many shifts in alliances and friendships took place. Some of the territorial disputes within Europe were to provide the immediate causes of the Second World War twenty years later.

Rise of Authoritarian Regimes

In almost every country of Europe, the immediate post-war years were a period of unrest. The dislocation of the economy during the war years, the problem of reorganising it to meet the requirements of peace, the misery caused by the war in terms of the millions who had been killed and the millions who had survived but were crippled, the problem of survivors who had to return now to civilian occupations, the unemployment—all these had given rise to widespread discontent. There were strikes in every country of Europe and attempts at revolutionary overthrow of the existing order in some countries. The example of the Russian Revolution was a source of inspiration to the working class of many countries, and the communist parties and some sections of the Social Democrats tried to organise Soviet-type revolutions. The most serious revolutionary outbreaks took place in Germany. In Hungary, a revolutionary government, under the leadership of Bela Kun, came to power in 1919. However, by 1923, the prospect of a socialist revolution succeeding in other parts of Europe had receded—the Hungarian revolution having lasted barely five months.

The collapse of revolutionary expectations, often due to lack of unity among various socialist parties and radical groups, led to the strengthening of anti-democratic and authoritarian forces in many countries, and by the early 1930s, only a few countries of Europe had succeeded in maintaining the democratic institutions and the

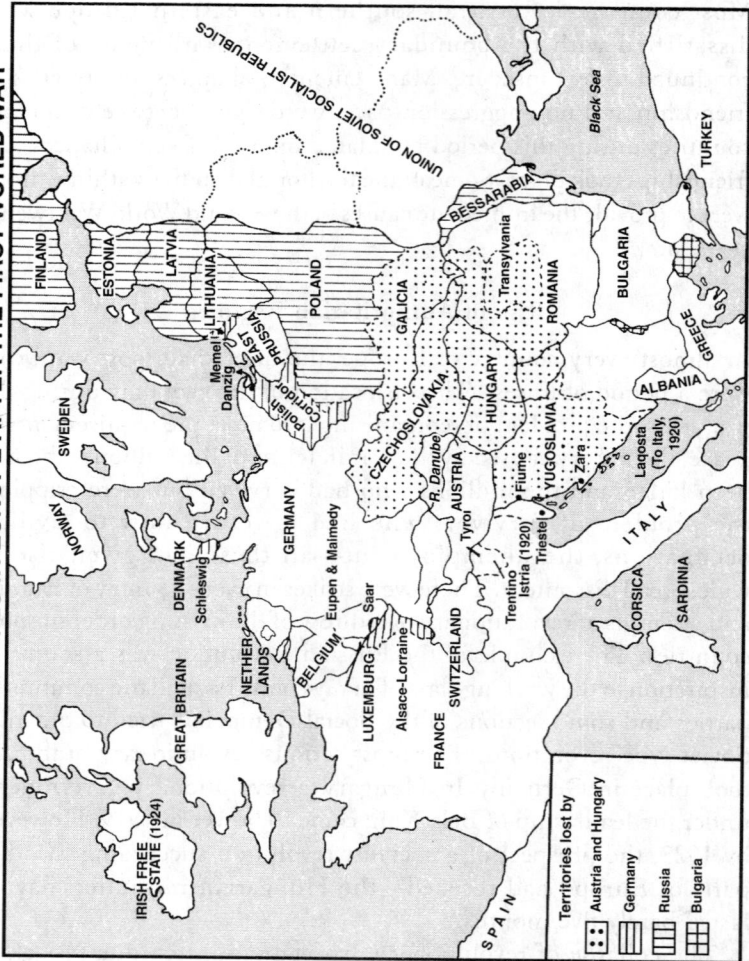

TERRITORIAL CHANGES IN EUROPE AFTER THE FIRST WORLD WAR

Territories lost by

:: Austria and Hungary

||| Germany

▦ Russia

▦ Bulgaria

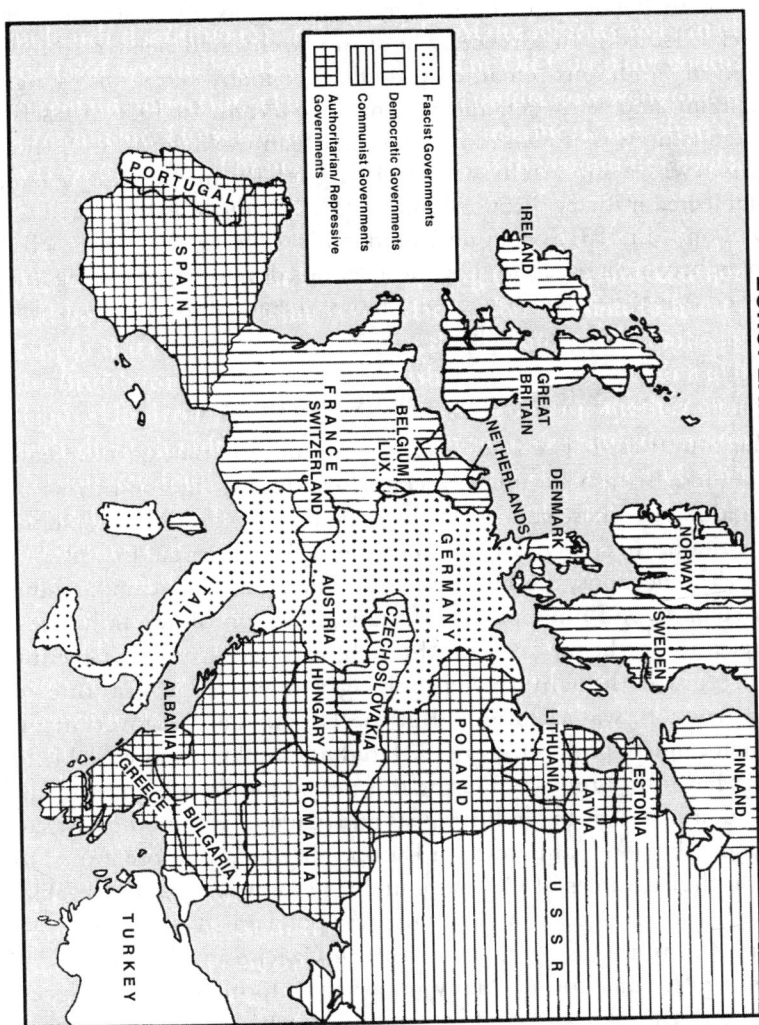

EUROPEAN GOVERNMENTS IN 1930s

Fascist Governments

Democratic Governments

Communist Governments

Authoritarian/Repressive
Governments

democratic forms of their governments. In Hungary, an authoritarian government came to power under Horthy as Regent. In Romania and Yugoslavia, authoritarian monarchical governments came to power. In Poland, a dictatorial government was established under Josef Pilsudski. In Greece, where monarchy had been restored, political conditions remained unsettled for many years, with kings changing and army generals staging *coup d'etats*. In 1936, a fascist dictatorship was established there under Joannes Metaxas. In Spain, which was a monarchy, General Miguel Primo de Rivera had established military dictatorship in 1923. The dictatorship lasted till 1930 and, in 1931, when anti-monarchical forces swept the polls, Spain became a republic. The most serious development during this period was the establishment of a fascist dictatorship in Italy, which will be described separately.

Britain, France and Czechoslovakia

The countries that did not give way to authoritarian governments included Britain, France, Czechoslovakia and the countries of Scandinavia. These countries, however, also faced serious problems. In Britain, there were two million unemployed people in 1921. In the 1923 elections, the Labour Party, which had been campaigning for steps to end unemployment, nationalisation of key industries, imposition of heavy taxes on the rich, increase in wages, meeting shortages of housing by launching a massive programme of construction, was victorious. But the Labour Party's government, which came to power in early 1924, did not last long and was able to fulfil few of its promises. During this period the French government was dominated by big industrialists and bankers. Its ambition was to become the dominant power in Europe for which purpose it tried to bring the resources of Germany under its control. Czechoslovakia, which had emerged as a new state, was proclaimed a republic with Tomas Masaryk as president. In 1919, Czechoslovakia adopted a democratic constitution. Many important reforms were introduced in Czechoslovakia and while most countries of eastern and southern Europe remained economically backward throughout the inter-war period, Czechoslovakia saw a period of rapid industrial growth.

Weimar Republic

In Germany, in 1919, a parliamentary republic was proclaimed. This is known as the Weimar Republic, after the name of the town where the constituent assembly had met and framed the new constitution. The constitution provided for a president enjoying many special powers, a chancellor responsible to the parliament, called the Reichstag, which was elected on the basis of universal adult franchise, and safeguards for the rights and liberties of the people.

There was much discontent in Germany against the "dictated peace" and many provisions of the Versailles Treaty were almost universally considered unjust. In spite of this, the Social Democratic Party and the Communist Party which were opposed to aggressive nationalism had emerged as powerful parties. The Social Democratic Party was one of the ruling parties in Germany till 1930. The Communist Party had made another attempt at revolution in 1923 but had failed.

In the meantime, authoritarian groups and parties had begun to emerge. They denounced democracy, advocated repudiation of the Versailles Treaty, extolled war, organised conspiracies to overthrow the democratically elected government, and aimed for the establishment of a dictatorship. Big business and a large section of the German army supported them. They blamed the Jews and the communists for the defeat of Germany in the war and organised assassinations and terror to rid the country of their influence. In 1920, a *putsch* to capture power was organised. Berlin was occupied by the volunteers of a conspiratorial organisation and their supporters in the army. The government of the Social Democratic Party was dissolved and a new government was installed under Kapp. This event brought together all the socialist and democratic parties. There was a general strike and the workers armed themselves to fight against the conspirators. Soon the putschists were overthrown. In 1919, the National Socialist German Workers' Party (for short, Nazi Party) had been formed. This party, led by Adolf Hitler, also attempted a putsch in 1923 but it was suppressed.

Economic Problems of the Weimar Republic

The Weimar Republic, although it succeeded in establishing a democratic form of government in Germany, was faced with grave economic problems. These problems were aggravated by certain provisions of the Versailles Treaty and the attitude of some European powers. The amount of reparations to be paid by Germany to the Allied Powers had been fixed at £ 6,600 million. She had paid the first instalment of £ 50 million in 1921 but was incapable of fully making further payments. She simply did not have the resources to meet this obligation. In the meantime, German economy came to a near collapse because of unimaginable inflation. By the end of 1921, the value of the deutsche mark, the German currency, fell by over 50 times. It had been 20 deutsche marks to the British pound; now it was over 1,000. In 1922, it fell further. In January 1923, Belgian and French troops occupied the Ruhr valley, which was the centre of Germany's coal and metallurgy industry, to recover from Germany the reparations by taking over her coal and steel. The German workers, however, refused to cooperate with them and went on strike. They resorted to passive resistance and were supported by their government. The German government started printing enormous amounts of paper money, which led to a catastrophe. The German currency became utterly worthless by November 1923. One British pound was now valued at 50,000 milliard deutsche marks (one milliard = 1,000 million). By the end of 1923, a currency reform was introduced, which was essential under the circumstances, but it had disastrous consequences for many sections of the German population. A new currency was introduced. This meant that the savings of millions of people were wiped out. The worst affected were the people of the middle class and the lower middle class—the salaried people. Millions of people were suddenly impoverished. The Nazi Party gained most from this disaster. Many people turned, in despair, to this Party for their salvation. In 1924, the German economy began to recover with the help of loans from the US and other countries. The loans helped Germany to start building her economy again and she started paying the reparations. The payments were finally stopped when the world-wide economic crisis again brought the economy of Germany and other countries to a state of ruin.

Fascism in Italy

The immediate post-war years in Italy, as in other countries of Europe, were years of widespread unemployment and popular unrest. The socialist movement had emerged as a powerful movement though its effectiveness was weakened by many internal divisions. In the meantime, a violent anti-democratic movement—the fascist movement—had emerged in Italy. Armed bands, called the *fasces*, were formed to create terror among the people who were considered enemies of the nation—mainly the socialists, the communists, and the leaders of workers' and peasants' movements. They were inspired by the glory of the ancient Roman Empire and preached the cult of violence and war to revive Italy's greatness.

The ruling classes of Italy had led their country to war on the side of the Allies. At the end of the war, they felt cheated. The Allies failed to satisfy the colonial and great power ambitions of Italy and though she gained territories in Europe at the cost of Austria, she was denied the gains in the colonies she had aspired to. The ruling classes found in the fascist movement an instrument to satisfy their ambitions. Within the country, the fascist movement was seen as the only force that could save them from a social revolution.

The National Fascist Party was formed in November 1921 under the leadership of Benito Mussolini. Thousands of 'Blackshirts' were recruited to break up strikes and assassinate socialist and communist leaders. The popularity of the fascist movement did not extend much beyond these armed gangs and the ruling classes—the industrialists and the big landlords. But they succeeded in smashing the strikes and demonstrations which were held to protest against the growing fascist menace. The government chose to remain a silent spectator to the increasing fascist violence. In 1919, the fascists had failed to win even a single seat in the parliament. In 1921, they won thirty-five seats. However, the fascists' failure to make much headway in winning popular support did not prevent the ruling classes of Italy from conniving with them. The fascists seized the cities of Bologna and Milan by force. On 24 October 1922, they organised a march on Rome. The government, instead of crushing the armed marchers, surrendered. The King of Italy invited Mussolini, who had not even taken part in the march, to form the government. He soon assumed dictatorial powers and, in the midst of a reign of terror unleashed by the Blackshirt gangsters, held elections in 1924. When a socialist member of parliament, Giacomo Matteotti, spoke in the parliament against the violence by the fascists during the elections, he was assassinated. Shortly after, organised murders of socialists, communists and other political opponents took place and, in 1926, all non-fascist parties and organisations were declared illegal and dissolved. The methods adopted by Italian fascists were emulated in other countries, in some countries with success.

EUROPE FROM 1924 TO 1936

Impact of the Great Depression on Europe

The period beginning from 1924 to the Great Depression was generally a period of economic recovery and growth. Though the danger of a revolutionary overthrow of the existing order had passed, the governments of many countries as well as the opponents of socialism continued to raise the scare of a revolution for pursuing conservative policies; in some countries fascist movements, with the backing of big industrialists and connivance of the army and the government, openly advocated the establishment of authoritarian rule. By 1929, the period of economic recovery, which had started in the mid-1920s, came to an end. The year 1929–30 has been described as the "beginning of a nightmare", which continued till 1933 when again a period of recovery began. The crisis in European economies was the direct consequence of the Great Depression which had hit the US in 1929. It showed how dependent European economy had become on the US. The American loans to Europe were completely stopped and the economies of the countries that had grown as a result of the continuing supply of loans, such as Germany, were the worst affected. As was happening in the US at that time, industrial enterprises began to close down and millions were thrown out of employment. In Germany, there were six million unemployed in 1932 and about half the population impoverished; in Britain the unemployed numbered three million. The European countries that had remained basically agricultural were also badly affected. They depended entirely on the export of their agricultural products. The sharp fall in agricultural prices badly affected their economies. Each country imposed restrictions on imports from other countries, which further worsened the situation. The political effects of the economic crisis in Europe were disastrous for democracy. Before this period ended, authoritarian, semi-fascist and fascist regimes had been established in most countries of Europe and even in the countries where democracy survived, fascist forces were gaining strength. In Germany, the most barbarous regime of modern times was established. Towards the end of this period, Europe and the rest of the world were relapsing into war.

Developments in Britain

In January 1924, the first Labour Party government came to power in Britain on the basis of the promise of radical changes in the economy. It accomplished little and its rule came to an end within ten months. A forged letter meant to create scare played some part in the defeat of the Labour Party. The letter was forged in the name of Zinoviev, who was chairman of the Comintern at that time. It instructed the communists in Britain to start uprisings in Britain and take steps to subvert the British army and navy. In October, the Conservative Party, which had used the forged letter to attack the Labour Party for being friendly to the communists, came to power and remained the ruling party till 1929.

The biggest strike in British history took place during this period although it ended in failure. In May 1926, the British coal miners went on strike against the threatened cut in wages and increased hours of work. The British government fully sided with the owners of the collieries. On 4 May 1926, three million workers struck work in support of the miners. They included railwaymen, transport workers, steel workers, and workers from other industries. This is known as the "general strike". The strike alarmed the government and the industrialists of Britain, and every effort was made to subvert it. In the face of the total hostility of the government and the massive propaganda campaign launched by it to rouse the general population against the strikers, the strike was called off on 12 May. The miners' strike, however, continued for many months but it ended in total failure, and workers were forced to go back to work at reduced wages and for longer hours of work. Soon after, the government declared general strikes illegal.

In 1929, the Labour Party again returned to power. When the economic crisis hit Britain, the Labour prime minister wanted to cope with the crisis by imposing cuts in wages and salaries as well as in unemployment relief and other social welfare programmes. Most of the other ministers refused to go along with him and he resigned, only to form a new government, called the National Government, in which the majority of the ministers were from the Conservative Party. The parties supporting the National Government remained in power after the 1935 elections, though with a reduced majority. A fascist movement had also emerged in Britain, which advocated violence against the Jews and created disorder and riots.

Britain began to recover from the economic crisis after 1933, though the number of the unemployed remained at about one and a half million. The international position of Britain was further diminished during this period as a result of the growing strength of the nationalist movements in the colonies. In 1931, the 'White' dominions of the British Empire became virtually free. They remained as members of what was later called the British Commonwealth of Nations, but British laws were no longer applicable to them and they pursued their own policies. By 1936, the fascist countries had started their wars of aggression, which led to the catastrophe of another world war. The British government, however, like other Western countries, followed a policy of appeasement of fascism though efforts were made by anti-fascist parties and groups to rouse the people against the dangerous consequences of this policy.

Political Instability in France

In France, this period was one of instability. France had ambitions of becoming the dominant power in Europe and had launched a massive armament programme. When Germany was unable to pay the reparation as agreed by the Treaty of Versailles, France occupied the Ruhr Valley in order to take over Germany's coal and steel industry. After 1924, France had to withdraw from the Ruhr Valley. There were frequent changes in the government which was generally dominated by influential business interests and corrupt politicians. During the economic crisis, when the number of unemployed rose to about one and a half million and industrial and agricultural production fell by over 30 per cent, the socialist and communist parties gained in strength. At the same time, however, a strong fascist movement also arose and took to methods of violence and terror to capture power. In

1933, a major scandal rocked France. Alexander Stavisky, a speculator, had amassed six hundred million francs through fraudulent means and by cheating people. When the scandal unearthed, it was found that many politicians, including those holding positions in the government, were also involved and were the beneficiaries of Stavisky's corrupt dealings. Making use of this scandal, the fascists tried to occupy Paris, dissolve the government and take over power. However, the communists and the socialists mobilised workers to prevent the fascist from taking over the reigns of the government. There were violent clashes between them and the fascists, and the fascists' attempt to seize power was foiled.

In 1936, a significant development took place. This was the formation of the Popular Front comprising Communist, Socialist and Radical Socialist parties to counter the danger of fascism and bring about long-needed economic reforms, particularly relating to the promotion of workers' welfare. The Popular Front swept the polls and the Socialist and the Radical Socialist parties formed the Popular Front government. The government lasted for a little over two years. During the first one year of its rule when Leon Blum was the prime minister, the Popular Front government took many important steps— the armament industry was nationalised, the cuts in wages and salaries were withdrawn, and forty-hour week was introduced for the workers.

The foreign policy of France aimed at the realisation of her great power ambitions as well as to safeguard herself against any possible German aggression. She had encouraged what is known as the Little Entente comprising Romania, Yugoslavia and Czechoslovakia and provided it with arms in the hope that these countries would help divert any future German aggression to be concentrated against her. In the 1920s, she had also started constructing strong defences to prevent a quick German advance into France, as had happened at the beginning of the First World War. This defence system is known as the Maginot Line. In 1935 she signed a mutual aid agreement with the Soviet Union and the Soviet Union signed a similar treaty with France's ally, Czechoslovakia. Thus, in a sense, a tripartite mutual aid pact was signed. When the Popular Front government was formed, it was hoped that France would take a forthright stand against fascist aggression. However, the Popular Front came to an end in 1938. The government headed by Edouard Daladier followed the British government in appeasing fascist countries, and she was to betray her ally, Czechoslovakia, soon.

Portugal and Spain

Similar to the other authoritarian and semi-fascist governments in Hungary, Poland, Romania, Yugoslavia and other countries other countries of Europe, in Portugal too, Salazar had established a fascist dictatorship, with the help of the army. He was sympathetic to the fascist regimes in Italy and Germany and helped in the overthrow of the Republicans in Spain even while maintaining friendly relations with Britain. After proclaiming herself a republic, Spain underwent many serious difficulties. In 1932, there was a revolt led by an army general but it was crushed. In the meantime, a fascist movement, called *Falange*, had started growing in strength. The movement was supported by the Catholic Church. The Spanish fascists committed political murders and won many supporters in the army. The fascists and the monarchists were promised aid by Mussolini and there was an uprising with the objective of uniting anti-fascist forces but it was crushed. In October 1935, the miners in Asturia rose in revolt and General Francisco Franco was asked to crush the rebellion against the unpopular government. In 1936, elections were held in Spain. The Popular Front, which was formed to resist the fascist danger, was victorious in the elections. It comprised all the socialist parties— the Communist Party, the Anarchists and the Republican Left. Thousands of political prisoners were released by the Popular Front government and major economic and political reforms were initiated. However, soon Spain was plunged into a civil war when the Spanish fascists—the *Falange*—joined together with the army generals, and with the active support of fascist countries, to overthrow the Republican government.

Triumph of Nazism in Germany

The most serious development during this period was the triumph of fascism in Germany. The Nazis came together during a time of crisis in Germany. The nation was defeated in the First World War and was imposed a humiliating Treaty of Versailles, with reparations huge enough for the economy to collapse. The impact of the post-war inflation and the terrible misery caused by the economic crisis of 1929 dealt a further blow to the German attempts at economic recovery. The Nazis made use of these crises for strengthening their position. Nazis also attempted a putsch similar to the one that had brought Mussolini to power in Italy.

Nazism, as the German version of fascism is called, was the most barbarous form of fascism. Like the Italian fascism, Nazism also held political democracy and civil liberties in contempt and glorified war, and like the Italian fascists' slogan of reviving the Roman Empire, the Nazis wanted to revive the greatness of the Teutonic empire. The Nazis aroused anti-Semitism—hatred of the Jews—among the non-Jewish Germans, holding the Jews responsible for the defeat of Germany and for all other miseries that the German people faced after the war. The Nazis extolled the purity of the German race—"pure blond Aryan"—and considered it superior to other races over whom they thought they had a right to rule. They aimed at uniting all the people of the German 'race' under one state and to form a greater Germany, and further claimed "land and territory for the nourishment of our people" and for settling their surplus population.

The idea of a great leader who would set everything right and would make Germany great was fostered. Communism was viewed by the Nazis as their greatest enemy and its destruction as their main aim. The Nazis made use of the sense of humiliation of the German people for their defeat in the war and the "dictated peace" with its many unjust clauses, including the war guilt and the reparations, and promised to restore their national pride. These ideas also found much support in the army, with its officers drawn mostly from the class of big landlords, who wanted to avenge the humiliation of their defeat. Most of all, they received the full backing of the German industrialists who were alarmed at the growth of the socialist and communist parties and thought of the Nazis as their only saviour.

The Nazis, like the Italian fascists, organised gangs of armed volunteers, called the SA, popularly known as the Brownshirts, who increasingly resorted to beating and murdering anti-fascists and Jews, destroying their property and perpetrating various other acts of public humiliation. By 1930, the Brownshirts numbered about 100,000. There were frequent violent clashes between them and the communists, but the government did little to stop the Nazi brutalities. Before the 1929 economic crisis, however, the Nazis' popular support was limited. In 1928, they had won only 12 seats in the Reichstag. They had polled about 800,000 votes as against nine million polled by the Social Democrats and over three million by the Communists. In the 1930 elections, however, the Nazi vote rose to about 6.5 million while the Social Democrats polled 8.5 million and the Communists over 4.5 million. In the elections for the presidency held in April 1932, Field Marshall Paul von Hindenburg, who had led the German armies in the First World War and was now in his eighties, was elected, polling over 18.5 million votes. He had been supported by the Social Democrats. Hitler polled over 11 million votes in this election while the Communist candidate Ernst Thalmann, polled over 3.7 million votes. In the elections to the Reichstag in July 1932, the Nazi Party emerged as the single largest party, polling over 13.7 million votes against the Social Democrats' eight million and the Communists' 5.2 million. In November, there was another election to the Reichstag in which the Nazi vote declined by about 2 million while the Communist vote rose to about 6 million.

However, other forces were now at work, which ultimately brought the Nazis to power. On 30 January 1933, Hindenburg appointed Hitler as the Chancellor of Germany. Thus, his coming to power was not the result of a victory in elections nor of a violent overthrow of the existing government but it was part of a "backstage deal" with the politicians of the right-wing parties. These parties along with the bankers, the industrialists and the big landowners had persuaded Hindenburg to make Hitler the chancellor.

After coming to power, Hitler set about consolidating his rule. He persuaded Hindenburg to dissolve the Reichstag and call for another election on 5 March 1933. On 27 February 1933, five days before the elections, the Reichstag building was set on fire. It was widely believed, though it has not been established, that the Nazis themselves had set the building on fire in order to create terror and to intimidate voters. The government blamed the Communists for the fire. Thousands of people were immediately arrested, including Georgi Dimitrov who was a leader of the Bulgarian Communist Party and was in Germany at that time. The elections were held in the midst of these developments but even then Hitler failed to secure a majority. Within a few months, however, Hitler consolidated his dictatorial rule by the use of terror and assassination against Social Democrats, Communists, trade union leaders, and other anti-Nazis. The Social Democratic Party and the Communist Party were banned. Over 60,000 people were imprisoned or sent to concentration camps. By mid-1933, all other parties were also dissolved. In 1934, Hitler became President of Germany. Within a few months of coming to power, Hitler perfected his machinery of terror and had begun to command the absolute obedience of the German people. The entire country was soon transformed into an armed camp.

Soon after coming to power, Hitler secretly began, the rearmament of the country and took a whole series of steps in violation of the Treaty of Versailles. In October 1933, Germany withdrew from the League of Nations. The building of an air force was taken up, which had been specifically prohibited by the treaty. In March 1935, Hitler announced that Germany was no longer bound by the restrictions which the treaty had imposed on the strength of the German military, and along with the army and the air force started building a navy. In March 1936, the Rhineland, which had been demilitarised, was occupied by German troops. All these moves, which were in total defiance of the treaty, met with no resistance from the Western powers. By 1936, Germany had built her military strength and the stage was set for acts of aggression which later led to the Second World War.

The League of Nations

The members of the League of Nations included countries from all continents. However, the League was dominate by major European powers and thus its fate was ultimately decided by them. At the time of its formation, it had forty-four members. They included most of the countries of Europe, except Russia and Germany; most of the countries of Latin America; Iran, Japan, China, Thailand and India (which was then still a colony) represented Asia; the Union of South Africa, Ethiopia and Liberia were from Africa; and Australia and New Zealand. The League had an Assembly, a Council and a Secretariat. In the Assembly, all the member-countries were represented, and each country had one vote. The Council initially had nine members out of whom five—Britain, France, Italy, Japan and USA—were to be permanent and four non-permanent members. The US did not join the League and her place on the Council was taken by Germany when she was admitted in 1926. Germany's admission came after a conference held in October 1925 at Locarno, Switzerland, and attended by seven European nations, including Germany, but excluding the Soviet Union. At this conference, a pact was signed guaranteeing the existing frontiers between Germany and France, and Germany and Belgium. These three countries undertook not to commit aggression against each other. By 1928, all countries of Europe had become members of the League of Nations. The Soviet Union was admitted as a member in 1934. By then both Japan and Germany had walked out of the League of Nations.

The League was dominated by the major European powers, notably Britain and France. It was able to resolve minor disputes between small states but it proved a dismal failure when disputes between big power were involved. Some of the main functions the League performed were to prevent aggression, maintain the independence and territorial integrity of member-states, and preserve peace. The League's dismal record in this regard was a reflection of the policy of appeasement which the big powers had adopted towards aggression by fascist and militarist powers. The Covenant of the League provided for effective means to prevent aggression. These means were, however, not applied.

The Japanese occupation of Manchuria and the subsequent setting up by her of a puppet government, called the Manchukuo, were the first major acts of naked aggression after the First World War. The League refused to recognise the Manchukuo government but it did not ask Japan to restore the pre-1931 position in Manchuria and end her aggression. Japan left the League of Nations and nothing further was heard of the matter. A few years later, Japan launched a massive attack on China.

In October 1935, Italy invaded Ethiopia with an army of 600,000 soldiers. In November, the League announced limited economic sanctions against Italy, but in May 1936, despite stiff resistance by the Ethiopians, Ethiopia, a member of the League of Nations, was annexed by Italy. In July 1936, even the limited sanctions applied earlier were withdrawn. The countries dominating the League showed total unwillingness to resist acts of aggression. USA, which was not a member of the League, followed the same policy.

The only country which advocated the use of sanctions to stop aggression and the formation of an anti-fascist front comprising Britain, France and herself, was the Soviet Union. The position adopted by the Soviet Union was supported by anti-fascist opinion the world over. However, the Western countries' appeasement of fascism and aggression was based on the belief that fascist countries' aggression would be directed against the Soviet Union. During the next three years, the world slowly relapsed into another world war. In October 1936, Italy and Germany signed an agreement on political cooperation. This is known as the Rome-Berlin Axis. In November 1937, Italy joined the Anti-Comintern Pact which Germany and Japan had signed in November 1936. In 1937, Italy left the League of Nations. Even before the Rome-Berlin Axis came into being, Germany and Italy had already started cooperating with a view to installing a fascist dictatorship in Spain.

Aggression and Appeasement

During 1936–37, the bloc of aggressive powers—Germany, Italy and Japan—had emerged. It had been strengthened by the policy of appeasement followed by major Western powers, notably Britain and France. The US also remained indifferent to the various acts of aggression committed by these countries. The policy of appeasement continued, and Hitler was convinced that his invasion of Poland which precipitated the war in September 1939, would not provoke Britain and France into action. The basic cause of the war was the imperialist ambitions of these three countries—German design conquer Europe and establish world supremacy, Italian ambition to conquer the Balkans, the Arab countries and large parts of Africa, and the Japanese desire to become master of Asia and the Pacific.

The Spanish Civil War

The first victim of joint German-Italian aggression in Europe was Spain. In the elections held in February 1936 the Popular Front, formed in order to resist the fascist forces in Spain, won convincingly. The new government started introducing reforms by restoring political liberties, meeting the peasants' demand for land by breaking up big estates, and improving the lot of miners and other industrial workers. A programme of educational development was taken up.

The Falange and other right-wing parties and groups, representing interests which had kept Spain a backward country, and their allies—the army generals—now made plans to overthrow the government of the Popular Front and establish a fascist rule. In July 1936, the fascists organised mutinies, supported by most of the Spanish army, both within the country and in Spanish colonies. The main leader of the mutineers was General Franco, who led his army from Spanish Morocco to join the rebels in Spain. Three years of brutal war followed. The Nationalists, as the anti-Republican fascist forces and their allies were called, had in the meantime secured the help of Italy and Germany to overthrow the Republican government. In fact, the civil war in Spain brought the two fascist countries of Europe together and they poured in vast quantities of arms and ammunition and aeroplanes as well as troops to support the Spanish fascists.

The rebels, with foreign support, captured many parts of the country and unleashed a reign of terror against the peasants and all those who were suspected of being supporters of the Republic. At this time, Britain, France and USA adopted a policy of non-intervention. This policy meant that no aid could reach the Republicans while the German and Italian military support to Franco continued unchecked. The only country that came to the support of the Republicans was the Soviet Union. The Republicans organised the defence of the Republic with the help of the citizens, who formed their militia and fought many fierce battles. In November 1936, they heroically defended Madrid, the capital city, and prevented its capture by Franco's troops.

The Spanish Civil War had aroused the conscience of the world. Anti-fascists from over fifty countries enrolled themselves as volunteers to fight in defence of the Spanish Republic. An International Brigade with over 40,000 volunteers was formed and fought in Spain and thousands of them died on Spanish soil. The volunteers included anti-fascist Italians and Germans. The battalion of the German volunteers was named after Thalmann, the German

Communist leader who had been put in a concentration camp by the Nazis and later murdered. The American battalion was named after Abraham Lincoln, the US President who had abolished slavery in USA. The international solidarity with the Spanish Republic reflected the growing concern all over the world at the rise of fascism.

The civil war in Spain was not viewed as merely a Spanish affair but one in which the entire world, threatened by fascism and aggression, was involved. Jawaharlal Nehru went to Spain to express the solidarity of the Indian freedom movement with the cause of the Republicans. Many writers, poets and artists from different parts of the world fought in the Spanish Civil War and mobilised world public opinion in support of the Republic. Pablo Picasso, the greatest artist of the twentieth century, painted *Guernica*, a great work of art. Guernica was a Spanish town which was destroyed by aerial bombing by fascist planes. The painting, named after the town, was a powerful protest against the brute force which fascism represented.

By February 1939, most parts of Spain had fallen to the fascists and Franco's government was recognised by Britain and France, and, a little later, by USA. The city of Madrid continued to resist till about the end of March and after the fall of that city the fascist take-over of Spain was complete.

The Spanish Civil War is often described as the "Dress rehearsal" of the Second World War in which the fascist countries tested their new weapons on the battlefields of Spain.

Japanese Aggression on China

Japan consolidated her conquest of Manchuria and in July 1937 launched a massive invasion of China. Within a few months, large parts of northern China, including the cities of Beijing, Nanjing and Shanghai, were occupied by the Japanese troops. The Japanese bombed the Chinese cities, which had no military significance, and committed atrocities on the Chinese population. In 1938, they proclaimed what they called a "New Order in East Asia" which would bring Japan, China and Manchuria into a political union. By this time, united Chinese national resistance to Japan had emerged. The League of Nations condemned the Japanese aggression but nothing was done to put an end to it.

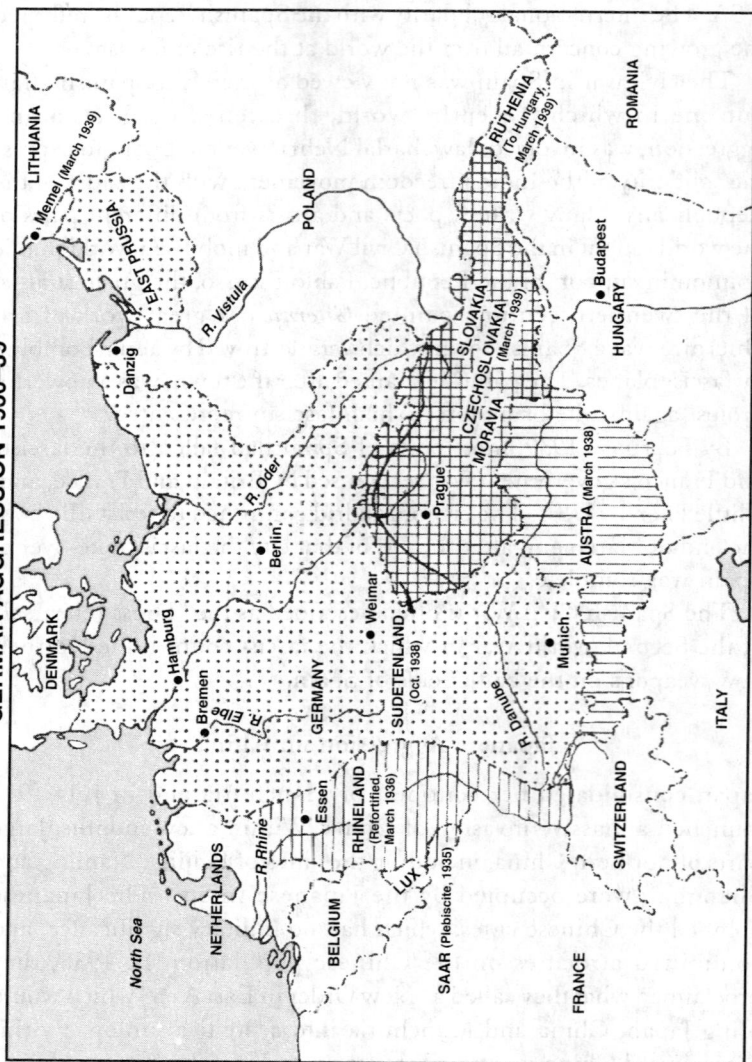

GERMAN AGGRESSION 1936-39

Annexation of Austria

The treaties with Germany and Austria had prohibited the political union of the two countries. With the rise of Hitler to power, however, the danger of Germany annexing Austria had emerged. A Nazi movement had also begun to grow in Austria with the aim of bringing about an *anschluss* (union with Germany). During the early 1930s, Engelburt Dollfuss had established his dictatorship in Austria. He suppressed the socialist and communist parties in Austria but he was also opposed to the union with Germany. He was supported by Mussolini, who till then was not allied to Germany and was pursuing his own independent great power ambitions. In 1934, Dollfuss was assassinated, and Austrian Nazis tried to capture power through a putsch. There were violent clashes between the Nazis and the communists and other anti-Nazis. The attempt at putsch failed Mussolini also moved his troops to the border with Austria, and Hitler, who was still not confident of Germany's strength, decided not to intervene in Austria. By 1938, however, the situation had changed. After the Italian conquest of Ethiopia and during the civil war in Spain, Italy and Germany had been drawn together through the Berlin-Rome Axis and the Anti-Comintern Pact. Hitler, with Mussolini's connivance, marched his troops into Austria on 11 March 1938, and the Austrian Nazis captured power. Hitler announced that German troops had been sent to Austria "to the help of these brother Germans in distress" who had been suffering under the misrule and oppression of the Austrian government. The anschluss was achieved without any opposition from the Western powers, even though it was in total violation of the peace treaties. Britain's Prime Minister Neville Chamberlain was of the view that Germany's eastward expansion and the satisfaction of Germany's "just territorial demands" would save Western Europe and help in safeguarding peace.

The Munich Pact

The worst act of appeasement and shameful betrayal took place when Czechoslovakia's Western allies handed her over to Germany. Czechoslovakia had emerged as an independent state after the First World War. She was one of the few states in Europe which had maintained her democratic political system while most other parts of eastern, southern and central Europe had fallen victims to authoritarian rule. She was also then the most industrialised country in eastern Europe. A part of Czechoslovakia, called Sudetenland, had a large German population. It was also the centre of some of Czechoslovakia's most important industries. After the annexation of Austria, the next target of Hitler's aggressive designs was Czechoslovakia. The initial German demand was the handing over of Sudetenland to her. France had been allied to Czechoslovakia since the 1920s. The rejection by Czechoslovakia of Germany's demand to cede Sudetenland was supported by the Soviet Union, which had signed a treaty with that country in 1935. The Soviet Union offered to immediately come to the aid of Czechoslovakia if she decided to resist German aggression. However, on 29 and 30 September 1938, a meeting was held in Munich, which was attended by Hitler, Mussolini, Chamberlain, and the Prime Minister of France, Daladier. Neither Czechoslovakia, the fate of which was being decided, nor the Soviet Union, which had a treaty with Czechoslovakia, was invited to the meeting. At this meeting it was decided to hand over Czechoslovakia to Germany. Czechoslovakia was made to surrender Sudetenland to Germany by Britain and France. She surrendered without opting for Soviet help. Sudetenland was occupied by German troops and parts of the Czech territory were also handed over to Hungary and Poland. In March 1939 Germany marched her troops into the remaining parts of Czechoslovakia and occupied them. Around the same time, Lithuania was forced to surrender the town of Memel on the borders of East Prussia to Germany.

Jawaharlal Nehru was in Europe at the time and went to Czechoslovakia and "watched at close quarters the difficult and intricate game of how to betray your friend". In an article, entitled 'On the Brink', which he wrote a week before the Munich Pact was signed, he said that Nazi aggression could have been stopped "if England and France and Russia had stood together". But Britain and France preferred Hitler.

The Polish Question and Negotiations with USSR

The next threat from Germany came to Poland. Germany demanded the return of the corridor and the city of Danzig which separated East Prussia from the rest of Germany. After the First World War, the corridor had been given to Poland and Danzig had been turned into a "free city". The British and French governments declared that "in the event of any action which clearly threatened Polish independence", they would extend to Poland "all support in their power". Germany did not seem to have taken these promises of support to Poland seriously.

For the first time, however, since the aggression by the fascist powers began, Britain and France started negotiations with the Soviet Union for an alliance against Germany. Both Britain and France had no border with Poland and could not directly come to the aid of Poland in case she was attacked by Germany. Poland had a long frontier with the Soviet Union and an alliance between France, Britain and the Soviet Union alone could effectively check German aggression against Poland. However, Poland, which had been consistently following anti-Soviet policies, was not prepared to let Soviet troops enter Poland even when her existence was in danger. This hampered the talks which were held in Moscow by the military missions of Britain, France and the Soviet Union from 12–21 August 1939. The talks finally broke down when the British and French military missions made it known that they had not been given the necessary powers by their respective governments to conclude any effective alliance with the Soviet Union. On 23 August 1939, Germany and the Soviet Union signed a non-aggression pact. On 1 September, Germany invaded Poland. On 3 September, Britain, followed by France, declared war on Germany.

THREE

The Second World War

THE BEGINNING OF THE WAR

On 23 August 1939, the Soviet-German Non-Aggression Pact was signed. The stage was now set for the invasion of Poland. Hitler was convinced that the Western powers would acquiesce in the aggression. He had told his commanders, "Our opponents are little worms. I saw them in Munich". On 1 September 1939, Hitler's armies invaded Poland. On 3 September 1939, Britain and France declared war on Germany. Poland, completely unaided by Britain and France in spite of the declaration of war, was defeated in about three weeks' time. Britain and France neither directly came to the aid of Poland nor launched any military operation against Germany in the West. The Second World War had begun but it was confined to a small part of Europe in the east. For about seven months after the declaration of war, there was no active war between Britain and France, and Germany, except for a few minor naval clashes. This period in the history of the Second World War is known as the 'phoney war'.

Soviets Occupy Eastern Poland and Baltic States

A few days after the German invasion of Poland, the Soviet Union occupied the eastern part of Poland comprising the territories which had earlier been part of the Russian empire's Ukraine and Byelorussia provinces. These territories were merged with the Ukrainian and Byelorussian republics of the Soviet Union. The occupation of these territories was justified by the Soviet Union on the ground that they had been seized from her by Poland after the First World War and that the advance of Germany in Poland threatened her security. Most historians are of the opinion that the Soviet occupation of the eastern parts of Poland was part of the German-Soviet plan to partition Poland between them. In November 1939, war broke out between the Soviet Union and Finland. It ended in March 1940 with the signing of the

Soviet-Finnish peace treaty. According to this treaty, the Soviet Union gained a naval base in the north of Finland, and the two countries decided not to join any other country hostile to either of them. During this period, the Soviet Union had established her military bases in the Baltic states of Latvia, Lithuania and Estonia, which had been part of the Russian empire and had become independent after the First World War. By August 1940, Soviet Republics had been set up in these countries and they had become part of the Soviet Union.

Conquest of Denmark and Norway

In early April 1940, the British Prime Minister, Chamberlain, had declared that "Hitler had missed the bus" because he had failed to launch an attack on the West when the West was not prepared for it. He was to be proved wrong a few days later and to lose his Prime Ministership after a month. Sweden was a major supplier of iron ore to Germany, and the occupation of Norway was important for Germany to protect the supplies from Sweden. In the meantime, a fascist movement had arisen in Norway and its leader, Vidkun Quisling, was in touch with Germany to facilitate her conquest of Norway. On 9 April 1940, Germany launched an invasion of Denmark and Norway. Denmark surrendered without any fight, and by early June, Norway was defeated, with the active support of Norwegian fascists. The British and French forces sent to the aid of Norway had left Norway even earlier. With the conquest of Denmark and Norway, Germany acquired important air and naval bases in northern Europe.

Capitulation of Belgium, the Netherlands and France

On 10 May 1940, Germany invaded the Netherlands (Holland), Belgium, Luxemburg and France. Within a few hours Luxemburg surrendered and the Netherlands, surrendered within five days of the attach. The Belgian King ordered the surrender of his troops on 28 May, seventeen days after the invasion. The 'phoney war' had come to an end. On 26 May, evacuation of about 350,000 British, French and Belgian troops (the Belgian troops being those who had refused to surrender) who had retreated to Dunkirk, began, and by 4 June they were transported to Britain. They left behind at Dunkirk all their heavy equipment. In the meantime, there had been political changes in Britain and France. On 10 May, Chamberlain had resigned and was replaced by Winston Churchill as the prime minister of a coalition government, with the Labour Party's Clement Attlee as the deputy prime minister.

In March 1940, the French Prime Minister Daladier had been ousted. He was replaced by Paul Reynaud. Most of the French cabinet at this time comprised 'defeatists', that is, those who wanted to surrender to Germany. On 9 June, the French government left Paris which, on 14 June, was occupied by German troops. Now the head of the French government was Marshal Henri Philippe Petain, who appealed to Germany for peace. So far, Italy had kept herself aloof. Now that the defeat of France as well as of Britain seemed imminent, she entered the war on 10 June on the side of Germany. On 22 June, Petain's government signed an agreement according to which Alsace-Lorraine was annexed by Germany, northern France was occupied by the German troops and Petain's government was allowed to retain control of about half of France. Petain's puppet government, which moved to Vichy, was also allowed to retain control of the French colonies, and collaborated with the Nazis. Charles de Gaulle, who had been a colonel in the French army at the time of the German invasion of France, had escaped to Britain after the surrender by the French government. Under the leadership of de Gaulle (who was given the title of General de Gaulle), the Free France movement was started and a French army was organised in Britain to fight against Nazi Germany. That part of France which was ruled over by Petain's government and collaborated with the Nazis is known as Vichy France.

The Battle of Britain

After having conquered about the whole of Western Europe, Germany now planned the invasion of Britain. This plan was given the code name of 'Sea-Lion'. The invasion of Britain was possible only if Germany could gain control over the English Channel which the German armies would have to cross to reach Britain. This required the British air force and navy to be made ineffective for preventing the crossing of the Channel. German bombers and fighters started the bombing of British ports, airfields and aircraft factories. There were dogfights between the aircrafts of the two countries over the Channel and over the ports and cities of Britain. The German air force suffered heavier losses than the British air force. Because of the stiff resistance by the British air force, Germany started raiding Britain's big cities, particularly London, at night in the hope of destroying the morale of the people. Britain, in return, conducted air raids on Germany. This aerial battle between Britain and Germany is known as the Battle of Britain.

In order to keep the moral of the British people high, the British Prime Minister broadcast a number of speeches. Some of these speeches are among the most famous examples of oratory in the world. Offering his countrymen nothing but "blood, toil, tears and sweat", in one of his speeches, he said,

> Even though many old and famous states have fallen, or may fall, into the grip of the Gestapo and all the odious apparatus of Nazi rule, we shall go on to the end; we shall fight in France, we shall fight on the seas and oceans, we shall fight with growing strength and confidence in the air, we shall defend our island whatever the cost may be, we shall fight on the beaches, we shall fight on the landing grounds, we shall fight in the fields and in the streets, we shall fight in the hills; we shall never surrender.

The British were also able to save their airfields from any serious damages and increased the production of aircraft, so that the losses in the Battle of Britain were more than made up for. As a result of the British resistance, operation 'Sea-Lion' was indefinitely put off and, by November 1940, the German air raids on London had more or less ceased.

Other Theatres of War

In the meantime, the war had spread to some other parts of Europe and to Africa. On 27 September 1940, Germany, Italy and Japan signed a Tripartite Pact. According to this Pact, each country pledged to give full support to the others in the event of an attack by any other power. Germany and Italy recognised Japan's claims to create what was called the Greater East Asia Co-Prosperity Sphere, which implied

AXIS CONQUESTS IN EUROPE (up to November 1942)

Index

| Allied Areas |
| Allied Countries |
| Neutral Countries |
| Areas occupied by Axis Countries |

① SUDETENLAND   ② SWITZERLAND   ③ NETHERLANDS   ④ LUXEMBURG

that both Germany and Italy will not object to any of the Japanese conquests of China, Manchuria and of the entire East and South-East Asia. Japan, in turn, recognised German and Italian supremacy over Europe. In October 1940, Italy invaded Greece but she faced stiff resistance and appealed to Germany for help. Between November 1940 and March 1941, Germany got Hungary, Romania, Slovakia and Bulgaria to join the Tripartite Pact and sent her troops to these countries. These countries thus became the allies of Germany, Italy and Japan.

By this time, Hitler had decided to invade Soviet Union. The sending of German troops to these countries was part of the preparation for the invasion of the Soviet Union. In April, the German troops were sent to Yugoslavia and Greece, which had repelled the Italian invasion, and these countries were subjugated. By June 1941, Germany and Italy had conquered all of Europe, except Britain and the Soviet Union.

In the meantime, Italy had invaded British Somaliland and Sudan and had started advancing towards Egypt. However, by December 1940, the British succeeded in not only recovering all their colonies in Africa which Italy had taken, but also in driving the Italian troops out of the African, with the exception of Libya. In February 1941, German troops were sent to Libya, and Germany and Italy launched another drive against the British in Africa. The war in Africa, between these European powers continues for two years.

German Invasion of the Soviet Union

We have already discussed Hitler's hatred of communism and the Soviet Union, the Western countries' appeasement of Hitler, the Soviet Union's efforts to build a coalition to check fascist aggression, and the signing of the Soviet-German Non-Aggression Pact. Hitler had always held the view that the 'real' war to be waged by him would be against the Soviet Union. The conquest of the Soviet Union with her vast resources would, he believed, make Germany 'invulnerable' and give her the power to "wage wars against whole continents".

The objective of the conquest of the Soviet Union was also very different from the objective of Germany's other military campaigns. This was to be a total war of extermination, and not only of communism. Hitler dreamed of settling 100 million people of 'pure Aryan blood'—Germans—in the territories west of the Urals and as so many Germans did not exist, the privilege was to be extended to others—the North Europeans, the Dutch and the English—who were considered "racially approximate to Germans". During the war, he described the new 'civilisation' that he planned to build up in this area in the following words:

> The area must lose the character of the Asian steppe. It must be Europeanized!... The 'Reich peasant' (the German peasant) is to live in outstandingly beautiful settlements. The German agencies and authorities are to have wonderful buildings, the governors palaces. Around each city, a ring of lovely villages will be placed to within 30 or 40

kilometres ... the German cities will be placed, like pearls on a string, and around the cities the settlements will lie. For we will not open *Lebensraum* (the term used by the Nazis for the territory of other countries which they considered necessary for Germany's national existence) for ourselves by entering the old, godforsaken Russian holes! The German settlements must be on an altogether higher level!.

The extermination of the Jews and the enslavement of the Slavs were integral parts of this plan.

The planning of the invasion of the Soviet Union had started in early 1940. It was given the code name of "Operation Barbarossa". Hitler had a low opinion of the Red Army, as the Soviet Union's army was called, and called it "no more than a joke". According to the plan, the Soviet Union was to be defeated within nine weeks or, at the most, in seventeen weeks. As it turned out, the invasion led to the destruction of the Nazi regime and of Hitler himself.

After the German invasion had started, the Soviet government justified the Soviet-German Pact on the ground that it had given the Soviet Union "peace for a year and a half and the opportunity of preparing our forces" to meet the Nazi aggression. Thus, it was tactics to gain time. When the invasion took place, the Soviet Union was taken totally unaware and suffered terrible reverses and devastation. Some Soviet writers are of the opinion that the Soviet Union did not have much time to prepare against the aggression. However, most historians, blame it on Stalin and are of the view that Stalin had put too much trust in the Non-Aggression Pact and had come to believe that Germany would remain involved in a war exclusively with Western imperialist countries. It is important to note in this context that since the outbreak of the war, Stalin had imposed a ban on the publication of anti-Nazi and anti-German views in the Soviet Union. Until the German invasion of the Soviet Union, the Second World War was presented exclusively as an inter-imperialist war—not a war launched by aggressive fascist powers. The Non-Aggression Pact and the Soviet invasion of Poland and occupation of Baltic states had been a major setback to the popularity of the Soviet Union and the communist parties the world over.

The German invasion began on 22 June 1941 without a formal declaration of war. The German tanks, supported by air attacks, rapidly advanced into the Soviet Union along a front which stretched over more than 3,000 km towards Leningrad, Moscow and Kiev. The Soviet forces steadily retreated, and the German forces occupied Kiev, Smolensk and Odessa. Germany had hoped to end the war with the Soviet Union before the onset of winter. In early October, Moscow was besieged. By then, however, it was too late. Soon, the Russian winter started. By the middle of November, the assault on Moscow' had been halted. By the end of November, the temperature had fallen to – 40° C rendering much of the German heavy equipment useless. The German soldiers were not sufficiently clothed to withstand the winter. In December the Soviet counter-attack started, and by January the German forces were driven back from Moscow. "Operation Barbarossa" had failed but the total rout was to come later. In the meantime, many other significant developments had taken place in the world.

US Entry into the War

When the Second World War broke out, the US announced her neutrality. Since the beginning of the aggressions by fascist powers, the US had followed a policy similar to that of Britain and France. During the Munich talks on Sudetenland, the US President had supported Chamberlain's policy of appeasement. The US had protested against the Japanese aggression in China but did nothing to prevent it. Most Americans were sympathetic to Britain in the war but were opposed to direct US entry into the war. Britain was allowed to buy arms on what is known as the cash-and-carry basis from the US. Gradually, the US support to Britain grew. By early 1941, the British were in no position to pay for the arms and other goods for which they were heavily dependent on the US. In March 1941, the US Congress passed a law under which the US President was given the right to lend or lease armaments to any country whose defence was "vital to the defence of the United States". This was known as the "lend-lease" system, and Britain began to receive massive supplies from the US. Subsequently, US also undertook the protection of her shipments to Britain against German attacks. Simultaneously, US industries began producing enormous quantities of armaments, aircraft and ships. In November 1941, the US "lend-lease" system was extended to the Soviet Union.

The Atlantic Charter

Another important development was a declaration which the British Prime Minister, Churchill, and the US President, Roosevelt, (he had been elected President for the third time in 1940) issued after a meeting in August 1941. This is known as the Atlantic Charter. This was an important document even though it did not imply any direct military commitment on the part of the US to take part in the war. The Charter set out certain common principles for constructing "a better future for the world". The two countries committed themselves to these principles, and they became, in a sense, a statement of war aims. Both Britain and USA declared that they do not seek "aggrandizement, territorial or other" or any territorial changes "which do not accord with the freely expressed wishes of the people concerned". The Charter also stated that the two countries "respect the right of all peoples to choose the form of government under which they will live; they wish to see sovereign rights and self-government restored to those who have been forcibly deprived of them...." The Charter also called for "the final destruction of the Nazi tyranny". Later the Soviet Union also became a party to the Atlantic Charter.

Ironically when the leader from India presented their demand for independence from Britain and quoted the principles set out in the Atlantic Charter, Churchill rebuffed them saying that those principles were applicable only to countries which were under German occupation.

Attack on Pearl Harbor

The US had still not directly entered the war. In July 1941, the Japanese had occupied Vietnam in Indo-China. In October, an even more aggressive government came to power in Japan. It was headed by General Hideki Tojo. The Japanese made preparations for launching another act of aggression, this time in the Pacific. On 7 December 1941, the Japanese bombers attacked the US naval base at Pearl Harbor in Hawaii. The US had expected a Japanese attack on the British and Dutch colonial possessions in the area and was completely taken by surprise. In the bombing, 188 aircraft and many battleships, cruisers and other naval vessels of the US were destroyed and over 2,000 sailors and soldiers killed. The Japanese losses were minor. On 8 December, the US declared war on Japan. On 11 December, Germany and Italy declared war on the US and the US declared war on Germany and Italy.

A Global War

The events of 1941—the German invasion of the Soviet Union, the Japanese attack on Pearl Harbor and the US entry into the war—made the war a truly global war. By the middle of 1942, Japan had occupied many islands in the Pacific, the Philippines, Indonesia, Burma, Malaya, Singapore and Thailand. During this period there emerged the anti-fascist coalition comprising Britain, the Soviet Union and the US. Winston Churchill called it the "Grand Alliance". Britain and US waged the war together under joint commands. Though there was no such joint action with the Soviet Union, all the three countries actively collaborated and on many occasions planned common strategies. Besides, the vast resources of the US, her entire war machinery, which included 300,000 aircraft and 85,000 tanks, were now geared up against Germany and her allies. The US has been described as "the arsenal of victory". The Soviet Union recognised General de Gaulle, who later set up a provisional government, as the leader of all 'Free Frenchmen".

The Battle of Stalingrad

Throughout 1942, the war in Europe was fought almost exclusively between the Soviet troops and the German troops and the forces of countries such as Romania and Bulgaria allied to Germany. After the German attack on Moscow had been repulsed, the German troops advanced deep into the Caucasus. In March 1942, Hitler had asserted that the Red Army would be annihilated in the summer of that year. In July, the German troops launched an offensive on Stalingrad (now Volgograd) and by mid-September they reached the outskirts of that city. Then began what has been called "the greatest single trial of strength" of the Second World War. By the middle of November, the

JAPANESE CONQUESTS (UP TO 1942)

German armies were in and around Stalingrad. Bitter fighting had been going on in the streets of Stalingrad for every inch of the territory. In late November the German armies in and around Stalingrad were encircled by Soviet troops, and they could find no way to escape. No supplies could reach them. General Paulus, who commanded the encircled German army, reported on 24 January 1943 that among the surviving German troops there were 20,000 wounded who were unattended and another 20,000 who were suffering from frostbites; they had no weapons and were starving. On 31 January, he surrendered. The battle of Stalingrad lasted for five months and had reduced that city to rubble. The German defeat in this battle has been described as "the greatest defeat in history that a German army has undergone". Germany and the countries allied to her lost over 300,000 troops in this battle. About 90,000 of them survived the battle and they were taken prisoner.

In July 1941, the Soviet government had appealed to Britain to open a "Second Front" by invading France so that the German strength concentrated against her could be diverted. This request was not agreed by Britain. In May and June 1942, the Soviet Union again appealed to the US and Britain for opening a "Second Front". The US President was willing but finally both Britain and the US decided to send troops to North Africa instead. The reason advanced was that they—Britain and the US—were not yet equal to the task of launching a frontal attack against the German forces in Europe. This led the Soviet Union to believe that Britain and the US "wanted to bleed the Soviet Union white" so that they could preserve their forces and emerge supreme in the later stages of the war. After the German debacle at Stalingrad, however, there was greater coordination among the three powers.

The German and allied troops launched another massive military operation against the Soviet army in the middle of 1943 but they suffered a crushing defeat in August, losing about 500,000 troops. This is known as the Battle of Kursk. After that they were steadily swept back and, by January 1944, they began to retreat from all sectors of the Eastern Front.

The War in North Africa and the Pacific

While the fascist powers had reached the height of their power in 1942, they faced defeats in almost every theatre of war in 1943. After the Italian debacle in North Africa, the German troops under General Rommel had been sent to North Africa for assisting their Italian allies. They had achieved remarkable successes and in August 1942 had launched an offensive against the British forces in Egypt. A battle was fought between the German and British armies, the latter under General Montgomery, at El Alamein, and the German armies were forced to retreat in November. Soon after the battle of El Alamein, the British and the US troops landed on the Atlantic coast of Morocco and in Algeria. Both these countries were French colonies and were under the control of Vichy France, which was allied to Germany. However, after sometime, the French army in these countries joined the Allies. Germany occupied Vichy France, and sent reinforcements to Tunisia, which was also a French colony. By March 1943, Rommel's troops had been driven back to Tunisia. In May 1943, the British and American forces launched an offensive in Tunisia and the German and Italian forces surrendered. This marked the end of Italian and German presence in North Africa. Earlier, in 1941, a pro-German revolt in Iraq had been crushed by the British, and the British and Free French forces had occupied Syria and Lebanon, which had been under the control of Vichy France.

In the Pacific, there were many naval battles between the US and Japan during 1942, and though the Japanese offensive had been halted, the Allied victories were not notable. In 1943, however, the Allies recovered many Pacific islands from the Japanese. In China, the Japanese offensive continued and the Allies failed to land their troops there. They had succeeded in flowing supplies to Chiang Kaishek, but his army was not able to launch any attack against the Japanese.

The Allied Victories in Europe

Early in 1943, Britain and the US decided to postpone the offensive in Western Europe to 1944. In July, when the Battle of Kursk was on, they invaded Sicily. By this time, there was widespread discontent in Italy. There were frequent strikes. The disaffection had also spread to the armed forces, which had suffered defeats everywhere, and they surrendered in large numbers to the Allied forces. On 25 July 1943, Mussolini was dismissed and a new government came to power. Italy now wanted to withdraw from the war. On 3 September, the Allied troops invaded southern Italy, and Italy surrendered unconditionally.

On 10 September, the German troops occupied northern Italy, including Rome. They rescued Mussolini from detention and he, guarded by the Germans, set up his government in northern Italy under German protection. In southern Italy, a new government was formed and it declared war on Germany. Though the Allied troops did not advance to the north for many months, the resistance in northern Italy grew in strength and they fought against the German occupation and against Mussolini with great tenacity.

In 1944, the fascist troops were thrown out of Soviet territory and the Soviet Union defeated Finland, which had become Germany's ally. Most parts of the countries of Eastern Europe—Poland,

Romania, Bulgaria, Hungary and Czechoslovakia were liberated. In some of these countries, fascist governments had come to power and they had joined the war on the side of Germany. Others, such as Poland, were under direct German occupation. The fascist troops were also driven out of Greece, Yugoslavia and Albania.

In June 1944, the Allied troops opened the Second Front in Western Europe. On 6 June 1944, known as D Day, the first Allied troops landed on the beaches of Normandy, on the north coast of France. By the end of July, the number of the Allied troops in France rose up to 1,600,000. They were commanded by General Dwight D. Eisenhower of the US Army, who later became the President of USA. By September 1944, France, Luxemburg and Belgium were liberated by the Allied armies. The last major German counter-offensive was launched in December 1944 in the Ardennes region of Belgium. The battle which followed is known as the Battle of the Bulge. It ended by the middle of January 1945, when the Soviet troops, led by Marshal Zhukov, launched a massive attack along the eastern front, which forced Hitler to shift most of his troops from the Ardennes to the east.

Surrender of Germany

The war in Italy continued for many months after Germany had occupied northern Italy and rescued Mussolini, who had set up his government in German-occupied Italy. However, by June 1944, the Allied troops had liberated many Italian cities, including Rome. In the meantime, the anti-fascist Italian forces had intensified their activities. On 23 April 1945, there was an uprising in those areas of Italy which were still under fascist occupation. On 28 April 1945, Mussolini, who had been captured, was executed, and the Germans in Italy surrendered. This marked the end of fascism in Italy.

By early January 1945, the collapse of Germany was in sight. The Soviet offensive, which was launched in January 1945, swept away the last German resistance in the east. Warsaw was liberated on 17 January, Budapest on 13 February and Vienna on 13 April. The Soviet armies moved into Germany and, by 25 April, Berlin was encircled by them. In the meantime, in March, the Allied troops had started their offensive in the west and by mid-April occupied large parts of West Germany. On 30 April 1945, Hitler committed suicide. The same day the Soviet armies hoisted the Red Flag on the Reichstag building. Sporadic fighting continued for another two days in Berlin. On 7 May 1945, Germany unconditionally surrendered to the representatives of the US, Britain, France and the Soviet Union at the headquarters of General Eisenhower in Rheims. On 8 May 1945 Germany made another unconditional surrender at the Soviet headquarters in Berlin. On 11 May Czechoslovakia was liberated, and the war in Europe was over.

Surrender of Japan

The war in Asia and the Pacific continued even after the German surrender. The Allies had scored victories in this region in 1944 but Japan was still strongly entrenched with a huge army in China, Manchuria, Korea and other places. On 6 August 1945, a US aircraft dropped an atom bomb on Hiroshima and on 9 August on Nagasaki. These bombs killed over 320,000 people in these two cities. Japan capitulated on 15 August. On 8 August, the Soviet Union had declared war on Japan. By the end of August, the Japanese armies in Manchuria had surrendered to the Soviet army, in South-East Asia to the British army, and in China to the armies of Chiang Kai-shek and the Chinese communists. On 2 September 1945, Japan surrendered, and the Second World War was over.

FASCIST BARBARITIES

The fascist aggressions and occupation were accompanied by the most inhuman barbarities against the occupied peoples. The term 'fascism' has been used to describe the system set up by all the three Axis powers namely, Italy, Germany and Japan. Each of them had its own peculiar features. Of the three, the German version, Nazism was the most brutal. With their theories of racial purity and supremacy of the 'Aryan' race, the Nazis considered most of the rest of humanity to be sub-humans deserving extermination, or at least enslavement. They tried to convert Europe into a huge slave camp and a death camp. The aggressions committed by these countries led to the Second World

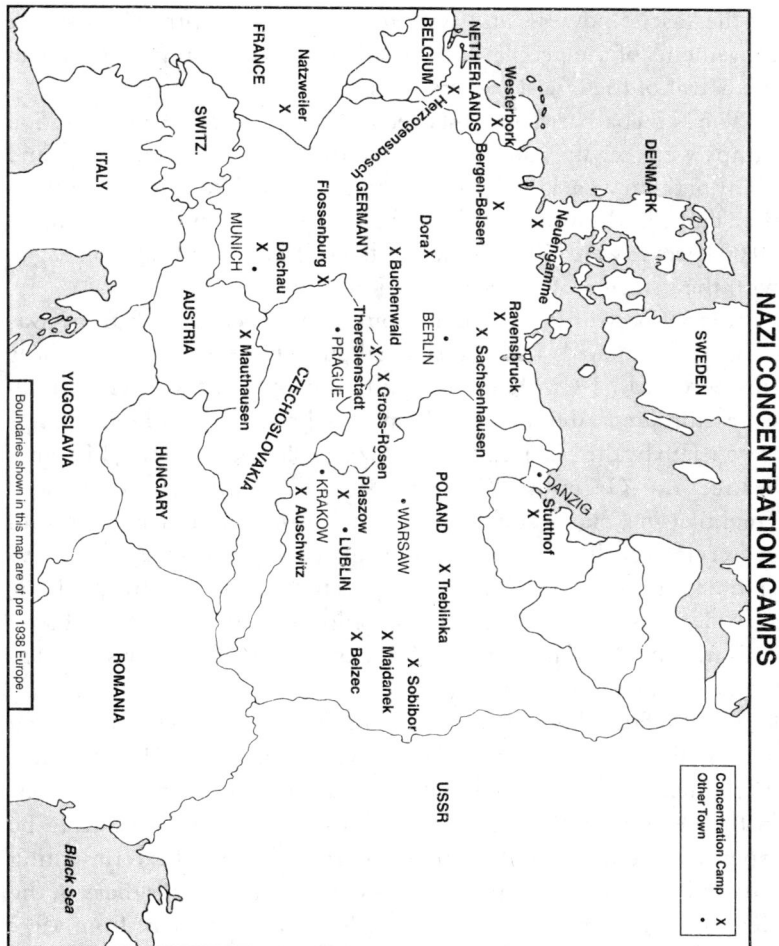

NAZI CONCENTRATION CAMPS

Boundaries shown in this map are of pre 1938 Europe.

| Concentration Camp | X |
| Other Town | • |

DENMARK
SWEDEN
NETHERLANDS
BELGIUM
FRANCE
SWITZ.
ITALY
GERMANY
AUSTRIA
YUGOSLAVIA
HUNGARY
ROMANIA
CZECHOSLOVAKIA
POLAND
USSR
Black Sea

Westerbork X
Herzensbosch X
Natzweiler X
Bergen-Belsen X
Neuengamme X
Ravensbruck X
Dora X
X Buchenwald
X Sachsenhausen
BERLIN •
Flossenburg X
MUNICH •
Dachau X •
X Mauthausen
Theresienstadt X
• PRAGUE
X Gross-Rosen
Plaszow •
• WARSAW
• KRAKOW
X Auschwitz
X Treblinka
X Sobibor
X Majdanek
X Belzec
• LUBLIN
DANZIG •
Stutthof X

War, the most destructive war in history. The war ended with the victory of the anti-fascist alliance, comprising the Soviet Union, the United States and Britain, and their allies. This alliance was the fundamental basis, an essential condition, for the defeat of the fascist powers. Besides, in each country which was invaded and occupied by the fascist powers, and within the fascist countries, resistance movements of the people grew and they played an important role in the defeat of the fascist powers.

The Nazi barbarities had started in Germany itself. Concentration camps were set up and anti-fascists and Jews were sent there and many of them were killed. In 1939, an order was issued to exterminate the "chronically insane and incurable" and within that year about 70,000 people were killed. However, the real war of annihilation began with the invasion of the Soviet Union.

A large part of the civilian population of occupied Europe was either exterminated or used as slave labour. The Jews were particularly singled out. In 1941 alone, one million people of the Soviet Union were murdered. About half of them were Jews. Concentration camps were set up by the Nazis in Poland, Czechoslovakia, Austria, Holland, France and Germany. These included Auschwitz, Belzec and Treblinka in Poland and Dachau, Bergen-Belsen and Buchenwald in Germany. Millions of people from all over Europe were transported to these camps. Some of these were purely death camps. In July 1941, an order was issued on the 'final solution' of the Jewish problem. This meant "the planned biological destruction of the Jewish race in the Eastern territories".

The full facts about these camps came to light only when the Allied troops liberated the territories in which they were located and subsequently when the Nuremberg Trials took place for war crimes. In the beginning, the victims were shot. But this was found to be expensive and messy and, therefore, horrible means of exterminating human beings were invented. A pest control firm, a subsidiary of the German Company I.G. Farben, produced a gas which, from 1942 onwards, was used for the purpose. Its first use began on 17 March 1942 at the Belzec death camp in Poland where 15,000 people could be killed in a day. The victims were marched into cellars which they were told were places for bath. The cellars were actually gas chambers with a gas-proof metal door. Then the crystals of the gas were pushed inside and after twenty-five minutes the gas-laden air was removed through exhaust pumps and the metal door was opened. After removing the gold teeth and hair, the piled-up dead bodies were removed to the furnaces where they were reduced to ash, which was scattered in the nearby streams.

Instead of murdering people straightaway, the Nazis generally let the German industrialists first make full use of their labour. The inmates of the camps began to be leased out to some industrial concerns such as the Krupps, I.G. Farben, Siemens, etc. Some of these industrial concerns set up their industrial units near the camps. As the trains carrying the victims arrived, women, children, the old and the sick were taken straight to the death camps and the healthy to work sites where many of them were worked to death. Those found sick were transferred to the death camps every morning. Some industrial firms manufactured goods from human skins.

Besides extermination in the gas chamber, the inmates of the camps were also used for conducting biological experiments by the Nazi doctors. Various kinds of disease were induced in the victims and vaccines tried. Some were slowly frozen to death and biological changes taking place in their bodies studied. These experiments are too horrible to be described. In recent years, information about similar experiments conducted by the Japanese has come to light.

The total number of the civilian population killed by the Nazis is estimated to be over ten million. These included killings through mass murders—for example, the entire male population of the village Lidice in Czechoslovakia was wiped out in retaliation for the murder of the Nazi governor of Czechoslovakia, Heydrich—and other brutalities, but most of all by the systematic extermination in the camps. The number of victims in the Auschwitz camp is estimated to be four million. A majority of the murdered were Jews—about six million of them, that is, 75 per cent of the total Jewish population of Europe. This mass murder of the Jews has come to be known as the "holocaust". Besides the millions of Europeans who were brought to the camps to perform slave labour and to be exterminated, another 7,500,000 people from various parts of Europe were brought to Germany to work as slave labourers in German factories. They included about two million prisoners of war.

Allied Air Raids and the Use of Atom Bombs

About 1,500,000 civilians were killed in air raids during the Second World War. Although air raids on the civilian population were started by Germany, the Allied countries also resorted to raids on the civilian population on a massive scale. The British dropped over 650,000 incendiaries on the German city of Dresden on 13–14 February 1945, killing about 135,000 people. The two atom bombs used by the US, as stated earlier, killed about 320,000 Japanese men, women and children.

The use of atom bombs by the US is considered by many people an abominable act, not only because of the number of people that the two bombs killed but also because of the very use of the new weapons of mass destruction. The argument that without the use of the atom bombs, the war with Japan would have been a protracted war with many more casualties on both sides than those caused by the atom bombs is not accepted by many scholars. They point out that after the collapse of Germany, Japan was in no position to conduct a protracted war. Around this time, the Soviet Union was also about to enter the war against Japan. The atomic weapons were developed in the US during the war by pooling the scientific skills and resources of many countries. Many scientists, of the US and other countries, had worked on the project to develop atomic weapons because of the fear in the scientific community that Nazi Germany might develop these weapons first and use them to terrorise the world into submission. However, at the end of the war in Europe, it had become clear that no other country had made much progress in developing them. Some scholars hold the view that the US, the only country then possessing these weapons, used them to demonstrate her military supremacy in the post-war world.

The Soviet Union, which suffered the heaviest casualties, both civilian and military, is held guilty of murdering 10,000 Polish soldiers and burying them in mass graves in the Katyn forest in 1940.

Resistance Movements

Popular resistance movements grew in every country that were invaded and occupied by the fascist powers and also within the fascist and the countries allied to them. These movements grew in strength and intensified their activities particularly after the entry of the Soviet Union and, subsequently, of the US into the war. The creation of the anti-fascist alliance facilitated the coming together of all anti-fascist forces in occupied countries and within the fascist countries.

Czechoslovakia

Many leaders of Czechoslovakia had escaped when the Nazi troops marched into their country and set up a puppet government in Slovakia. In 1940, a Czechoslovak government-in-exile headed by Eduard Benes, was set up. The partisans of the Czechoslovak resistance movement which included communists, social democrats and others carried on guerrilla activities against the Germans throughout the war. The assassination of the Nazi governor has already been mentioned. In August 1944, an uprising was organised in Slovakia and the soldiers of the puppet government there also joined the partisans. The uprising of 5 May 1945 in Prague led to the complete and final ending of the German occupation of Czechoslovakia.

Poland

The Second World War had started with the invasion of Poland, and she was the worst sufferer in the war. About 6,500,000 Poles—20 per cent of the total population of Poland—were killed in the war. About half of them were Jews. From the beginning of the German invasion, a powerful resistance movement was built up in Poland. A Polish government-in-exile, headed by General Sikorski, with its headquarters first in France and then in London, guided the Polish resistance. In 1942, the Polish communists formed their own organisation for carrying on anti-German operations. The two organisations, however, did not always see eye to eye. The relations between the Soviet government and the Polish government-in-exile also worsened as a result of the latter's insistence that Poland's pre-war frontiers, including the territories which the Soviet Union claimed as hers, be recognised. This led to some tragic consequences. On 1 August 1944, a mass uprising took place in Warsaw. By this time the Soviet forces had liberated many parts of Poland. However, the organisers of the uprising, who supported the government-in-exile and, apparently, wanted to hand over liberated Warsaw to that government, made no efforts to coordinate their plans for the uprising with the Soviet forces. The people of Warsaw fought most heroically against the German occupation troops but no help reached them from outside, and the uprising was brutally suppressed. About 250,000 Poles perished in the uprising.

Yugoslavia

In Yugoslavia the resistance against the fascist occupation and its local supporters was led by the Communist Party, which was headed by Josip Broz Tito. The various partisan groups were united to form the People's Liberation Army. The partisans of this army organised uprisings as a result of which many parts of Yugoslavia were liberated by the end of 1944. The Yugoslav government-in-exile had little support within the country and a government headed by Tito was set up there.

France

It has been mentioned earlier that the French government capitulated to Germany when the latter invaded France. General de Gaulle formed the Free France movement with its headquarters in London. In July 1942, on the initiative of the French communists, a National Front, which brought together all anti-fascist forces, was formed. The French Resistance grew into a powerful movement and in early 1944 formed the French Forces of the Interior with a membership of 500,000. The members of the resistance movement carried out sabotages against the Germans and their French collaborators. They played a crucial role in the successful landing of the Allied troops in France, and with their own forces liberated many parts of France from German occupation. Under General de Gaulle's leadership, a provisional government had been set up on which various anti-fascist forces of France, including the communists, were represented. On 19 and 20 August 1944, the French Resistance organised an uprising in Paris, and the German commandant, who had refused to obey Hitler's order to destroy the city, surrendered. Soon after this incident, the provisional government headed by de Gaulle entered Paris.

The Soviet Union

In terms of the total number of people killed in the war, the Soviet Union was the worst sufferer. The number of soldiers of the Soviet Union's Red Army who had been taken prisoner and killed by the Germans, is estimated to be 4,000,000. Another 6,000,000 civilians, including about 750,000 Jews, were slaughtered by the Germans. According to the Soviet estimates, the total number of the Soviet people who perished in the war was about 20 million, or 10 per cent of the total population. Some Western historians hold the view that there was widespread discontent against Stalin's regime in the Soviet Union and that people, at least in some parts of the country, would have welcomed the German invasion in the hope that it would lead to the ending of Stalin's rule. However, the unparalleled German brutalities against the Soviet people in the initial stages of the war itself showed them what Hitler had in store for them. Thus, German brutalities united them and they built up the most powerful and effective resistance against the invaders. Large-scale guerrilla warfare developed in every part of the Soviet Union which had fallen to the German army. The guerrilla operations, which were carried on in close collaboration with the Soviet army, played a vital role in the debacle which the Germans suffered in the Soviet Union. More than a million partisans took part in the guerrilla warfare against the German army in the territories of the Soviet Union.

Greece

After the debacle which the Italians suffered in Greece in 1940, Greece was occupied by German troops. The Greek government and the King of Greece fled to Cairo. The resistance against Germany was led by the Greek communists who had formed a National Liberation Front and the ELAS (National Popular Liberation Army). The various anti-fascist groups were brought together and many parts of Greece were liberated. Soon, however, there was a conflict between the Greek government-in-exile and the resistance movement within the country. After Greece had been freed from the fascists in late 1944, the government-in-exile with the support of British troops was sought to be installed in Greece. A civil war followed and it continued for some time even after the end of the Second World War.

Italy

The leading role in the defeat of fascism in Italy, the first country where fascism had been victorious, was played by the Resistance Movement. The Italian fascists had suffered debacles in all their military adventures, both in Europe and Africa. In 1942, the communists and the socialists of Italy had joined together to overthrow the fascist regime. After the overthrow of Mussolini and the German occupation of northern Italy, a powerful resistance movement emerged in the German-occupied area. The role of the Italian communists led by Palmiro Togliatti was particularly notable in the Italian Resistance. The final blow to the German occupation and Italian fascism came from the Italian Resistance in April 1945 when Genoa, Milan and Turin were liberated, and Mussolini was captured and shot.

Germany

All dissent in Germany had been ruthlessly suppressed long before the war started. The anti-Nazi Germans who had escaped, carried on anti-Nazi propaganda and helped to mobilise world opinion against the Nazi regime and its aggressive designs. The greatest literary figures of Germany—their works were burnt in bonfires by the Nazis—and the German communists played a leading role in resistance movement. The anti-Nazi Germans had fought in the Spanish Civil War in defence of the Republic. During the war, small groups of anti-Nazi Germans were able to organise some acts of sabotage inside Germany. The Free Germany National Committee set up by the German emigrés and some from among the German prisoners-of-war conducted anti-Nazi propaganda within and outside Germany. In 1944, some German army officers, who was convinced that Hitler was leading the country to total disaster, organised a conspiracy to assassinate Hitler. On 20 July 1944, Colonel Claus Schenk von Stauffenberg placed a bomb in Hitler's headquarters at Rastenburg from where Hitler was conducting the war in the east. The bomb exploded but it had not been placed close enough to where Hitler sat. Thus, Hitler survived the explosion, suffering only minor burns. Stauffenberg and other conspirators were captured and shot. One of the most brilliant officers of the German army, Rommel, who had led the German troops in North Africa, and had joined the conspiracy was not shot but allowed to commit suicide.

Asian Countries

The resistance movements grew in all countries of Asia which had come under Japanese rule. The most powerful of these was the war of resistance that had been going on in China since long before the Second World War started. After the Sian incident resistance to the Japanese had gained primacy over the civil war between the communists and the Guomindang although the two sides did not really join together. In other countries where Japanese rule replaced British, Dutch or the French rule, the anti-colonial nationalist movements which had emerged earlier, now organised armed resistance against Japanese occupation. Japanese atrocities in these countries were also responsible for the growing intensity of the armed resistance against Japanese occupation. Communists were generally the leading force in the anti-Japanese resistance in almost all Asian countries such as the Philippines, Indo-China, Indonesia, Burma, Malaya, etc. The only exception was Thailand. In 1941, the Vietnamese communists led by Ho Chi Minh set up the Vietminh League, which fought against the supporters of Vichy France and the Japanese. On 2 September 1945, they proclaimed the Democratic Republic of Vietnam. In Burma, the Anti-Fascist People's Freedom League was formed under the leadership of Aung San. In the Philippines, the Anti-Japanese People's Army organised armed actions against the Japanese. All these movements played a crucial role in the final collapse of Japanese imperialism in Asia. In these, countries, the Japanese had displaced the old European colonial rule. In the French colonies they had allowed the rule by Vichy France to formally continue. However, the people of the occupied countries of Asia did not view the Japanese as their liberators. In India, which had escaped Japanese occupation, the Indian National Congress, while fighting for India's independence, extended its full support to the peoples struggling against Nazi occupation in Europe and Japanese occupation in Asia.

ALLIED WAR AIMS

A number of meetings and conferences took place during the war to discuss common strategies for pursuing the war and to arrive at agreements on the aims for which they were fighting the war. Some of these meetings and conferences were attended by many countries. However, the most important decisions were taken by the leaders of the three main Allied Powers—Churchill of Britain, Stalin of the Soviet Union and Roosevelt (till his death on 12 April 1945 and subsequently his successor Truman) of the United States.

The Atlantic Charter issued by Churchill and Roosevelt in August 1941 has already been mentioned. The Soviet Union became a party to this Charter soon after it was issued.

On 1 January 1942, representatives of 26 countries issued the Declaration of the United Nations. With this declaration, the anti-fascist Allied Coalition, which had already come into being, was formally constituted. The signatories to this declaration pledged themselves to make every effort to defeat the common enemy and cooperate with one another for the purpose. They also agreed not to hold separate talks with the enemy countries or conclude separate truce or peace treaties with them.

A major development took place in January 1943 when Roosevelt and Churchill met at Casablanca on the Atlantic coast of Morocco. There had been some differences within Britain and the US and between the two countries regarding the terms of armistice to be offered to the fascist powers. Roosevelt put an end to these controversies by demanding "unconditional surrender" by the fascist powers. This became the standpoint of all Allied nations, or what were now called the United Nations.

The anti-fascist coalition was further consolidated at the meeting of the foreign ministers of Britain, the Soviet Union and USA held in Moscow from 19 to 30 October 1943. The main purpose of the meeting was to prepare for the forthcoming summit meeting. At this meeting, the question of opening the Second Front was discussed and declarations were adopted on Italy and Austria. It was decided to set up Advisory Councils to discuss various questions relating to European states, including the terms of surrender of the fascist states and their allies. The meeting also issued a Four Nation Declaration (the fourth nation being China) which called for the establishment "at the earliest possible date" of "a general international organisation, based on the principle of the sovereign equality of all nations, and open to membership by all nations, large and small, for the maintenance of international peace and security". This Declaration may be said to mark the beginning of the United Nations Charter..

On 1 December 1943, the Cairo Declaration signed by the representatives of Britain, USA and China was issued. This Declaration was mainly concerned with Japan and the countries occupied by her. It called for Japan's unconditional surrender and return by her of all conquests made after 1894. Surprisingly, this Declaration made no reference to the principle of self-determination by the peoples of European colonies in Asia which had come under Japanese occupation.

Teheran Meeting

The first summit meeting of the three Allied powers was held at Teheran, in Iran, from 28 November to 2 December 1943. The meeting was attended by Churchill, Stalin and Roosevelt. By this time, the Soviet Union had emerged as the decisive factor in the war in Europe. At this meeting, Churchill and Roosevelt agreed to the landing of a million Anglo-American troops in France in May 1944— the long-awaited Second Front. The Soviet Union agreed to join the war against Japan once Germany was defeated. The question of Poland's post-war frontiers was also discussed at this meeting. When the Polish government in London did not agree to the terms on which there was broad consensus at the Teheran meeting, a Polish National Council dominated by communists was set up with the support of the Soviet government. This marked a split in the Polish Resistance and a rift between the Soviet Union and Poland's government-in-exile in London.

Dumbarton Oaks Conference

From 21 August to 28 September 1944, representatives of Britain, the Soviet Union and the US held a conference at Dumbarton Oaks, near Washington in USA, to discuss the formation of the United Nations Organisation. The conference was also attended later by a representative of China. This was a major step in the formation of the United Nations Organisation. It was also decided to hold a meeting of the United Nations at San Francisco in May–June 1945 to draft the United Nations Charter.

Yalta Conference

By early 1945, when the defeat of Germany was in sight, Churchill, Stalin and Roosevelt held a conference at Yalta, in the Soviet Union, from 4 to 11 February 1945. A number of important decisions were taken at this conference. The securing of Germany's unconditional surrender was declared the common aim of the three countries. Agreement was reached on various steps regarding the future of Germany after her surrender. The meeting declared that the "inflexible purpose" of the three Allied countries was "to destroy German militarism and Nazism and to ensure that Germany will never again be able to disturb the peace of the world". It was decided that after Germany surrendered, she would be divided into four zones, one each under Britain, the Soviet Union, the US and France. Agreement was reached on the frontiers of Poland, to include non-communist Poles from London in the Polish provisional government which had been set up and to hold free elections there as soon as possible. Through a "Declaration on Liberated Europe", the three countries pledged themselves to assist the countries of Europe in establishing democratic institutions. The Soviet Union agreed to enter the war against Japan, within three months of Germany's defeat. Important decisions were also taken regarding the setting up of the United Nations. On 1 March 1945, it was decided to open to all the states at war with Germany the membership of the United Nations, so that they could attend the San Francisco meeting to draft the Charter. The meeting was fixed for 25 April 1945. Agreement was also reached on the structure of the Security Council of the United Nations, on the Permanent Members of the Security Council and the principle of unanimity of these members regarding decisions affecting peace and security.

The United Nations Charter

As decided at the Yalta meeting, a conference of the United Nations was held at San Francisco from 25 April to 26 June 1945. The conference started discussions on the United Nations Charter even before the surrender of Germany. The Charter was signed by fifty participating nations on 26 June, before even Japan surrendered. The United Nations Charter became effective on 24 October 1945. The Charter defines the purposes and structure of the United Nations. It begins with the following words.

WE THE PEOPLES OF THE UNITED NATIONS DETERMINED to save succeeding generations from the scourge of war which twice in our lifetime has brought untold sorrow to mankind, and to reaffirm faith in fundamental human rights, in the dignity and worth of the human person, in the equal rights of men and women and of nations large and small, and to establish conditions under which justice and respect for the obligations arising from treaties and other sources of international law can be maintained, and to promote social progress and better standards of life in larger freedom,

AND FOR THESE ENDS
to practise tolerance and live together in peace with one another as good neighbours, and to unite our strength to maintain international peace and security, and to ensure by the acceptance of principles and the institution of methods, that armed force shall not be used, save in the common interest, and to employ international machinery for the promotion of the economic and social advancement of all peoples,

HAVE RESOLVED TO COMBINE OUR EFFORTS TO ACCOMPLISH THESE AIMS
Accordingly, our respective Governments ... have agreed to the present Charter of the United Nations and do hereby establish an international organisation to be known as the United Nations.

The purposes of the United Nations were defined in Article 1 of the Charter as:

1. To maintain international peace and security, and to that end: to take effective collective measures for the prevention and removal of threats to the peace, and for the suppression of acts of aggression or other breaches of the peace, and to bring about by peaceful means, and in conformity with the principles of justice and international law, adjustment or settlement of international disputes or situations which might lead to a breach of the peace;

2. To develop friendly relations among nations based on respect for the principle of equal rights and self-determination of peoples, and to take other appropriate measures to strengthen universal peace;

3. To achieve international cooperation in solving international problems of an economic, social, cultural, or humanitarian character, and in promoting and encouraging respect for human rights and for fundamental freedoms for all without distinction as to race, sex, language, or religion; and

4. To be a centre for harmonising the actions of nations in the attainment of these common ends.

The charter also defined the structure and the principal organs of the United Nations. The principal organs are: (1) a General Assembly composed of representatives of all the member states; (2) a Security Council composed of representatives of the United States, Britain, USSR, China and France as permanent members, and of six other states chosen by the General Assembly for a term of two years (their number was subsequently raised to ten and, after the collapse of the Soviet Union, Russia became one of the permanent members); (3) an Economic and Social Council composed of 18 members elected by the General Assembly (their number was subsequently raised to 27); (4) a Trusteeship Council with members drawn, in equal number, from those administering trust territories and others; (5) an International Court of Justice, and (6) a Secretariat. The Charter also included a "Declaration Regarding Non-Self-Governing Territories" which recognised "the principle that the interests of the inhabitants of these territories are paramount" and the obligation "to develop self-government, to take due account of the political aspirations of the peoples, and to assist them in the progressive development of their free political institutions". The Charter also envisaged commissions and specialised agencies and institutions. Two important specialised agencies under the jurisdiction of the Economic and Social Council are the United Nations Educational, Scientific and Cultural Organisation (UNESCO) and the World Health Organisation (WHO).

The creation of the United Nations was a significant and lasting achievement of the countries which had taken part in the war against the fascist countries.

The Potsdam Conference

After the surrender of Germany, the three leading Allied powers held a conference at Potsdam, in Germany. The conference was held from 17 July to 2 August 1945 and was attended by Churchill, Stalin, and Harry S. Truman (who had become the US President after Roosevelt's death). From 28 July, the conference was attended, in place of Churchill, by Clement Attlee who had become Prime Minister of Britain when the Labour Party came to power. The main subject of discussion at the Potsdam Conference was Germany. The Declaration issued by the Conference said that

German militarism and Nazism will be extirpated, and the Allies will take in agreement together, now and in the future, the other measures necessary to assure that Germany never again will threaten her neighbours or the peace of the world.

At this Conference agreement was reached on Poland's western border and the transfer of the northern part of East Prussia to the Soviet Union and the southern part to Poland. Agreement was also reached on the banning of fascist organisations, destruction of the military power of Germany, reorganisation of German economy by abolishing cartels and controlling industries used for production of armaments, payment of reparations by Germany, and division of Germany into four occupation zones. It was also decided to bring the Nazi war criminals to trial. The trials took place subsequently at Nuremberg, in Germany, and lasted for about one year. Twelve of the accused were sentenced to death. Others, including some German industrialists, were sentenced to imprisonment.

The Second World War was the most destructive war in human history. It had taken a toll of more than fifty million human lives. The total cost of the war has been estimated to be about 14 million million dollars. The statistics of destruction cannot really convey the terrible catastrophe that it caused.

FOUR

The World Since 1945

Almost sixty years since the end of the Second World War, the world has changed dramatically. The political shape of the world had been completely transformed. The period witnessed the total disintegration of the imperialist domination and a near total collapse of European hegemony of the world. In 1945, fifty nations had joined together in founding the United Nations. After Namibia's emergence as an independent nation in March 1990 and, later, the collapse of the Soviet Union, the number of member-countries of the United Nations has gone up to 192. Most of the new members are countries, mostly of Asia and Africa, which have won their independence after the Second World War.

USA and the Soviet Union established themselves as the greatest powers of the world for over four decades after the defeat of Germany, Japan and Italy, and the loss of the colonial empires of Britain and France. These two countries exercised a dominant role in world affairs and headed the two power blocs that came into being soon after the war. USA headed the Western bloc, comprising countries of Western Europe, North America and the Pacific. These countries chose to describe themselves as constituting the 'Free World'. The Soviet Union was the dominant power in the Socialist bloc which, came into being as a result of the capture of power by Communist parties in countries of Eastern Europe and, later, in China and North Korea. Many changes took place within and between these two blocs, or groups of countries, but the position of USA and the Soviet Union as pre-eminent military powers in the world remained unchanged till the end of the 1980s.

There have been vast political, economic and social changes in every part of the world. The direction and extent of changes vary from country to country but the United Nations Universal Declaration of Human Rights with its stress on civil and political, and economic and social rights may be regarded as a symbol of the main direction of change. Almost every country in the world attained independence and the people, at least in principle, everywhere have become masters of their own destiny. Though the main direction of change has been in the growth of political freedom and establishment of universal franchise and representative institutions, many countries are still ruled by military dictators, autocrats and oligarchies.

For about 45 years since the end of the Second World War, until the dramatic changes which began to take place around 1990, the two main political, economic and social systems in the world were described as capitalist and socialist. Each of them underwent many important changes. In countries with an advanced capitalist system, there was a general recognition of economic and social rights. This came about, at least partly, as a result of the struggles by workers' unions and labour and socialist movements. Most of the advanced capitalist countries have followed welfare policies which have mitigated the worst miseries associated with capitalism before the Second World War. The kind of socialist system which was built in the Soviet Union and, after the Second World War, in Eastern Europe was for some years seen as an alternative to the capitalist system. This system, often referred to as 'actual existing socialism', also underwent many changes until it collapsed. The newly independent countries have been engaged in the task of building their social, economic and political systems. The backwardness which they inherited from the colonial rule, however, continues to characterise most of these countries. The world economic system continues to be inequitable and is a major factor in the continuing backwardness of these countries which, together, are referred to as the Third World. Some countries of the Third World witnessed very high rate of economic growth. The most spectacular has been the rise of China as a great economic power during the past 20 years. India is also beginning to emerge as a major economic power.

There have been technological changes of a dramatic nature during the past fifty years. These technological changes have particularly transformed the economies of the advanced capitalist countries. Besides USA, Japan and Germany have emerged as major economic powers. The advances in technology have tended to further widen the gap between the economically developed countries and the countries of the Third World which are called developing countries.

The division of the world into developed and developing countries has become a major feature of the post-Second World War world.

The period after the Second World War has been a period of tensions and conflicts. The alliance which had come into being during the war to defeat fascism came to an end soon after the war was over. Then followed a period of confrontation between what came to be known as the Western and the Soviet blocs. This confrontation which continued for fifty years after the end of the Second World War is known as the Cold War. It was accompanied by a race for more and more, destructive weapons which threatened the very survival of the human race. Many wars broke out in different parts of the world, and although in many of these wars the countries of the two antagonistic blocs were directly or indirectly involved, these wars remained localised. There were many occasions during this period when the world was brought on the brink of disaster but a general war was averted.

The emergence of independent nations in Asia and Africa has been a distinctive feature of the world after the Second World War. The independent countries of Asia and Africa along with many countries of Latin America pushed for an independent role in world affairs. During the period of the Cold War, their refusal to align with any of the military blocs helped in creating an atmosphere of peace. The coming together of these countries led to the rise of the Non-Aligned Movement which played an important role in lessening tensions around the world, in ending colonialism, imperialism and racialism and in bringing to the fore the issue of development as an international concern.

There were periods of thaw and the lessening of tensions since the 1960s, but now it can be said with certainty that the world since the 1990s is a post-Cold War world. The end of the Cold War marks the end of an era which began with the end of the Second World War. Whether it also marks the beginning of a genuinely peaceful world cannot be said with certainty. The post-Cold War world is not without tensions and conflicts. It should be remembered that the hunt for more destructive armaments during and even after the Cold War was a more puzzling question for world peace efforts. Only a genuine concern for disarmament and international cooperation, and not merely the avoidance of war, can guarantee world peace.

Since the end of the 1980s, some of the changes that have taken place in the world are so far-reaching that they may be said to mark the beginning of a new phase in world history. The Soviet Union as a state—as a Union of Soviet Socialist Republics—collapsed. The 15 republics which constituted USSR have become independent states. The rule of the communist parties in these states, as well as in the countries of Eastern Europe, has ended. With the ending of the communist rule, the kind of socialist political and economic system which was built in these countries has collapsed. The Soviet Union had been a major factor in world politics since the Russian Revolution. After the Second World War, it headed a mighty military bloc and, along with countries of Eastern Europe, was seen as representing a powerful challenge to the military might and the political and economic system of USA and Western Europe. There is hardly any major event in world history since the Second World War which can be fully understood without reference to the direct or indirect role, or the sheer existence, of USSR. The most obvious consequence of the collapse of USSR has been the end of the Cold War.

THE COLD WAR

At the Teheran, Yalta and Potsdam conferences, agreements had been reached by the leaders of Britain, USA and the Soviet Union on many questions relating to the future of the liberated countries of Europe. The council of foreign ministers set up at the Potsdam Conference discussed the terms of the peace treaties with the Axis Powers and their allies. By 1947, agreements were reached and treaties were signed with Italy, Romania, Bulgaria, Hungary and Finland. The Allied occupation of Austria was ended in 1955 when a treaty was signed with Austria. On the question of Germany and Japan, however, no agreement could be arrived at. While the Western countries signed a treaty with Japan in spite of Soviet objections, the differences over Germany became a major source of conflict between the West bloc led by USA, and the Soviet Union. Soon after the war, the wartime alliances had begun to wear out and a period of Cold War, or armed truce, had set in.

THE BEGINNING OF THE COLD WAR

Origins

Many historians trace the origins of the Cold War to the year 1917, when the Bolshevik Revolution took place. As has been stated before, many Western countries had sent their troops to Russia to destroy the new Soviet government that had been set up after the revolution. The foreign interventions had, however, failed and had ended by 1920. After that the Soviet Union was ostracised by most Western countries and it had taken them many years to recognise the Soviet government and establish diplomatic relations with the Soviet Union. After the triumph of fascism in Germany, the Western countries had hoped that Germany's aggression would be directed against the Soviet Union. They had, therefore, followed a policy of appeasement of the Axis powers and had refused to have any alliance with the Soviet Union to resist aggression.

During the war, and particularly after the German invasion of the Soviet Union, the Soviet-British-US alliance was formed which led to the defeat of Germany and other Axis Powers. This alliance, however, even during the war, had not been free of tensions. The US and Britain conducted their military operations jointly under a unified command and they took their own independent decisions. This was particularly clear on the question of the opening of the 'Second Front' which, the Soviet Union felt, was being deliberately delayed. Differences over the future of Europe, for example on Poland, had emerged early during the war. Though most of these differences had been sorted out at the conferences at Teheran, Yalta and Potsdam, the Western suspicions of the Soviet Union had persisted. The Soviet victories against Germany in Eastern Europe had created a feeling of unease among the Western countries. The British were particularly alarmed at the Soviet army's advance towards Berlin, although Berlin fell within that part of Germany which, by common agreement, had been allocated to the Soviet Union to liberate. Churchill tried hard to pressurise the US President to direct General Eisenhower, Commander of the Allied troops, to march towards Berlin rather than Leibzig.

Communist Governments in Eastern Europe

The developments in Eastern Europe revived the pre-war Western fears of communism. At Yalta, Britain, USA and the Soviet Union had issued a "Declaration on Liberated Europe". According to this Declaration, the three Allied Powers were to assist the liberated countries of Europe to create democratic institutions through free elections. To begin with, in the countries liberated by Soviet armies, coalition governments were set up which included communists as well as others. Within three years, however, other parties were eliminated from the governments of all these countries which came under the exclusive control of Communist parties and their close allies.

The communist domination of the governments in Poland and Czechoslovakia particularly aroused British and US indignation at what they considered was a Soviet betrayal of promises regarding democratic institutions and free elections. In 1946, the provisional government of Poland, which included Polish leaders who had been associated with the anti-Soviet Polish government based in London, was split. In the elections which were held later, the two parties which later merged to form the Communist Party (called the Polish United Workers' Party) won about 90 per cent of the seats. The leaders of the main opposition party alleged that the elections had not been free and that thousands of their workers had been arrested. In Czechoslovakia, a coalition government had been formed in May 1946. The government included communists as well as leaders of other parties. In February 1948, the communists demanded that the government should be reconstituted as some of the government parties were alleged to be harbouring fascists. The President of Czechoslovakia, Eduard Benes, reconstituted the government under immense pressure, it was alleged, of the Soviet Union. A communist-dominated government then came to power.

Similar developments took place in Bulgaria, Romania and Hungary. In Yugoslavia and Albania, communists who had led the national resistance, had come to power. Thus, seven countries in Europe had governments dominated by communist parties and the Soviet Union was no longer the only country in the world to be ruled by a communist party. Britain and USA were particularly concerned at these developments which, they viewed as a danger to what they called the "Free World".

EUROPEAN COUNTRIES RULED BY
COMMUNIST PARTIES – 1950

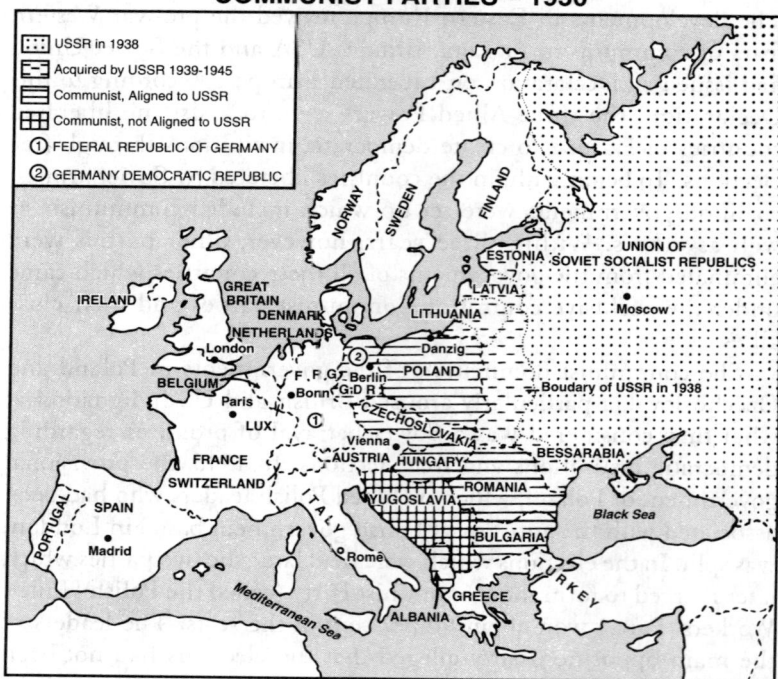

Developments in Germany

The developments in Germany further aggravated the differences between the Soviet Union and the Western countries. Germany had been divided into four occupation zones, each under the supervision of the Soviet Union, USA, Britain and France. At the Potsdam Conference, Germany had been visualised as a single economic zone with a common currency. Gradually, however, Germany became divided into two parts —the three zones under USA, Britain and France becoming one, the western part, and the Soviet occupation zone becoming another, the eastern part. The economic unity of Germany was broken with the western part stopping the despatch of industrial machinery to the eastern part and the latter ending the supply of agricultural goods to the former. Each part now had a separate currency. The political and economic policies followed in each part became different. In the eastern part large landholdings were confiscated and redistributed among peasants, many industries and mines were nationalised, and German communists, who had been living in exile since the fascist takeover, and other parties and groups who were willing to form an alliance with them were encouraged. In the western part, a capitalist economy developed with massive US aid and political parties and groups which were hostile to communists and the Soviet Union became dominant there. The policies followed in the western part were now based on the fear of communism and the Soviet Union.

By 1947, Germany had been divided into two distinct economic and political parts. Later this division was formalised with the setting up of two independent states.

Civil War in Greece

Another development which brought about the Cold War was the civil war in Greece. It has been mentioned in the previous chapter that communists had been a major force in the resistance movement against the fascist occupation of Greece. However, the British troops which had been sent to Greece wanted to restore the rule of the king who was brought back. This led to a civil war. There were 10,000 British troops who fought against the Greek communists in the civil war. Early in 1947, however, Britain decided to withdraw from Greece. She informed the United States that she could no longer bear the burden of supporting the Greek government in the civil war. The British withdrawal of military and financial support to the Greek government would have almost certainly led to communist victory in the civil war. The US government decided to take the "burden" of supporting the Greek government in the civil war upon itself. She also supported Turkey which, it was thought, was threatened by the Soviet Union.

THE TRUMAN DOCTRINE

The years 1945–47 are generally taken to mark the beginning of the Cold War. The first 'shot' in the Cold War was fired by Winston

Churchill. No longer the Prime Minister of Britain, he made a speech at the University of Fulton, Missourie, in the US, in the presence of the US President, Truman, in which he said, "From the Stettin in the Baltic to Trieste in the Adriatic an Iron Curtain has descended across the continent". The "Iron Curtain" referred to the division of Europe into the Soviet Union and the countries under Soviet control, and the rest of Europe. This division meant that the countries behind the iron curtain—the Soviet Union and communist-ruled states of Eastern Europe—were isolated from the rest of the world and lived under strict censorship and rigid control. Churchill also appealed for British-US political and military alliance to confront the Soviet Union

The US decision to intervene in the Greek civil war may be considered as formally ushering in the Cold War. President Truman, while asking the Congress for $ 400 million as military and economic aid to the Greek government, made a policy statement which has been called the Truman Doctrine. In his speech, he said, "I believe that it must be the policy of the United States to support free peoples who are resisting attempted subjugation by armed minorities or by outside pressure".

The Truman Doctrine proclaimed communism as the threat to the 'Free World' which the United States, as the head of the 'Free World', would not allow to succeed anywhere in the world. Every revolution was seen as being the result of Soviet expansionism which had to be crushed by all the might of the United States. This Doctrine became the basis of the foreign policy of the United States for about four decades and every conflict in the world was seen in terms of a struggle between the United States and the Soviet Union.

THE CRISIS OVER BERLIN AND THE DIVISION OF GERMANY

The Berlin Crisis

By early 1948, the Western powers had started the process of the creation of a separate state of West Germany by merging the occupation zones of Britain, France and the United States. These zones were also being brought under the European Recovery Programme under which the United States was to provide massive

GERMANY AFTER THE SECOND WORLD WAR

aid for the building of the economies of Western Europe devastated by the war. The city of Berlin which came within the Soviet zone had also been divided into four zones, like the rest of Germany. The three Western powers treated West Berlin as a part of West Germany which was being created as a separate state. The Soviet Union was opposed to this development. In June 1948, she closed the road which passed through the Soviet zone connecting West Germany with West Berlin.

The blockade of West Berlin was intended to force the Western powers to accept the Soviet position on Berlin. This created the danger of war because the Western countries were not willing to budge from West Berlin but they could not hold West Berlin without continuing supplies from outside. The Western allies responded to this situation by conducting a massive airlift of supplies to West Berlin. The blockade continued for about 11 months during which period over 275,000 plane-loads of supplies of food and fuel were sent to West Berlin by the Western allies. Thus, the danger of hostilities was averted. The Soviet Union ended the blockade in May 1949.

In the meantime, a new Western military alliance had come into being. In April 1949, the United States, most countries of Western Europe—Britain, France, Belgium, Luxemburg, Holland, Norway, Denmark, Portugal and Italy—and Iceland and Canada formed the North Atlantic Treaty Organisation (NATO). Through this alliance the Western countries launched a massive programme of rearmament to check what they called "Russian expansion" in Europe and to "contain" communism. During the next six years, the United States gave massive military aid to the NATO countries of Europe. In 1952, Greece and Turkey were also made members of NATO.

Two states in Germany

In May 1949, the Federal Republic of Germany (West Germany) was formed with her capital at Bonn. The rearmament of West Germany also began although West Germany was made a formal member of NATO only in 1955. The formation of a military alliance by Western countries within four years after the end of the Second World War was a major development which further increased the confrontation between the Western bloc and the Soviet Union. A few months after the formation of West Germany, the Soviet zone of Germany became an independent state—the German Democratic Republic. Thus, by the end of 1949, the division of Germany had been formalised and two separate states emerged, each confronting the other. This division of Germany continued for over forty years. It ended on 3 October 1990 when Germany was reunited.

In 1955, when West Germany was admitted as a member of NATO, the Soviet Union and the East European countries ruled by Communist parties formed their military alliance which is known as the Warsaw Pact. The Warsaw Pact countries, like the NATO countries, had a joint military command. In the meantime, the Cold War which initially had been confined to Europe had spread to other parts of the world and, besides NATO, other US-sponsored military alliances had been set up in other parts of the world.

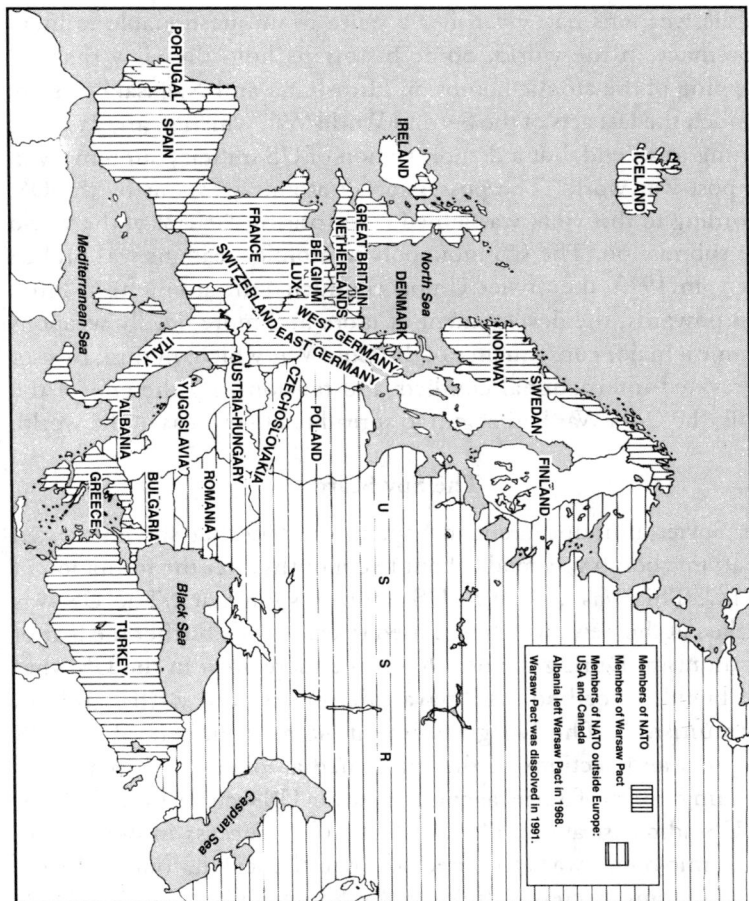

MILITARY BLOCS IN EUROPE

Members of NATO

Members of Warsaw Pact

Members of NATO outside Europe:
USA and Canada

Albania left Warsaw Pact in 1968.
Warsaw Pact was dissolved in 1991.

The Soviet Union Becomes a Nuclear Power

The United States had emerged as the mightiest military power at the end of the Second World War. For four years, she was the only country in the world to have atomic weapons. The monopoly in atomic weapons had given her a sense of unquestionable military supremacy in the world. Some historians hold the view that the dropping of the atomic bombs on Hiroshima and Nagasaki was not so much the last acts of the Second World War, which in any case was coming to an end, but a demonstration of US military supremacy in the post-war world. The possession of atomic weapons by the US, according to this view, was aimed at terrorising the rest of the world into submission. The US monopoly in atomic weapons was broken when, in 1949, the Soviet Union conducted an atomic test. From then onwards, the development of more and more deadly weapons became a major consequence of the Cold War which, in turn, further aggravated international conflicts and tensions. By the end of the 1940s, the Cold War had begun to spread to other areas of the world.

The Spy Scare

The Soviet announcement in September 1949 that she had tested the atomic bomb was made about five months after the formation of NATO. This was a blow to US military supremacy. The US was shocked at the news which was used to exacerbate further the fear of communism. During the next few years there grew in the US what has been described as "paranoic obsession with 'godless communism'". The US government, some members of the US Congress and sections of the mass media added to the panic by spreading stories of Soviet agents subverting US security by infiltrating the US administration. The Soviet Union's success in developing the atomic bomb was attributed solely to the leaking out of British and US atomic secrets by spies to the Soviet Union. The loyalty of many scientists and others who had been associated with the atomic bomb project was suspected and some of them were tried and sentenced to long terms of imprisonment and even death. Some of the leading scientists of the time held the view that even though there was truth in the charges of espionage and some atomic secrets were leaked out to the Soviet Union, this would have made little material difference to Soviet scientific and technological capability in making the atomic bomb as Soviet scientists had started working towards it almost at the same time as the scientists in the US. It was also pointed out by many public figures that the US, the Soviet Union and Britain had been allies during the war and sharing of secrets with allies could not be held treasonable. The spy scare was, however, whipped up and used to further worsen the climate of fear and hostility towards the Soviet Union.

COMMUNIST VICTORY IN CHINA

Soon after, the United States and her allies received another shock. On 1 October 1949, the People's Republic of China was established. During the Second World War, massive quantities of armaments had been made available by the US to Chiang Kai-shek's government in China for the war against the Japanese. China was under the grip of a civil war. The civil war in China was suspended when Chiang Kai-shek was forced to give primacy to the war against Japan instead of fighting the communists. However, the two—Chiang Kai-shek's government and the Chinese communists—did not really fight against the Japanese unitedly, but some semblance of not fighting against each other was maintained during the war. In July 1946, the civil war was resumed. With three years, Chiang Kai-shek's forces were completely routed, in spite of the US supply of sophisticated weaponry. Chiang Kai-shek, along with the remnants of his forces, fled to Taiwan (Formosa) which had been freed from Japan after the Japanese defeat in the Second World War.

The communist victory in the most populous country further aggravated the fear of communism with the Western bloc. The overthrow of the communist rule in China and the restoration of Chiang Kai-shek's government on mainland China became a major objective of the US policy. For over two decades, the US refused to recognise the government of China. The US, with the support of her allies, also kept China out of the United Nations. China's seat in the United Nations, including the one in the Security Council as a permanent member, was occupied by Chiang Kai-shek's government which, with US military support, was in occupation of only a Chinese island. Chiang Kai-shek's army continued to be armed and prepared by the US to launch an invasion into mainland China.

The fear of communism led the US to intervene in the affairs of Asian countries and the Cold War was brought to Asia. The US was also involved in many military conflicts and wars in Asia. Seeing every issue in terms of the Cold War, the United States also came in conflict with anti-colonial nationalist struggles for freedom and with many independent nations which were trying to strengthen their national independence and to assert their independent role in world affairs.

THE WAR IN KOREA

The first war in which the US got directly involved was the war in Korea which broke out in 1950. After the Japanese occupation of Korea was ended as a result of the Japanese defeat, Korea had been divided into two occupation zones—the northern zone under the Soviet Union and the southern zone under the United States. The division was along the 38th parallel. In August 1948, the southern zone proclaimed herself as the Republic of Korea and in September 1948, North Korea declared herself the People's Democratic Republic of Korea. The Soviet troops left North Korea in September 1948 and the US troops left South Korea in June 1949. The government of North Korea was headed by Kim Il Sung, leader of the Korean Communist Party, and of South Korea by Syngman Rhee, a right-wing politician. Neither of the government accepted the division of Korea and both claimed reunification of the country as their objective.

In June 1950, war broke out between the two sides, with each side blaming the other for the war. It is, however, generally agreed that the war was started by North Korea. This was the view of the United Nations Security Council which voted to assist South Korea against North Korea. However, it may be remembered that the Security Council's support to South Korea had become possible due to the Soviet Union's decision at the time to boycott the United Nations for its refusal to admit China. Within two months, the North Korean armies had swept across almost the entire South Korea—the South

Korean capital, Seoul, having fallen during the first three days of the war. However, the US army, navy and air force intervened in the war massively and North Korean troops were pushed back. The US forces now carried the war inside North Korea. At this juncture, the Chinese troops moved in and the US troops were forced back. From mid-1951, the war entered a stalemate. There were negotiations for an armistice in which India played an important role. The armistice was signed in July 1953 which restored the position that existed before the war. In this war, 142,000 American soldiers and 17,000 soldiers from other countries who had taken part in the war as United Nations troops were killed. The number of Koreans killed in the war is estimated to be between three and four million.

The Korean war was the first major war after 1945, and the first one in which the US had taken part in a massive way and had suffered heavy casualties. The US casualties during the entire period of the Second World War had been about 300,000. In spite of the heavy casualties, it may be remembered that the Korean war was a localised war. There was every danger that it might turn into a general war. General MacArthur who commanded US troops in the Korean war wanted to invade China. There was also a danger that the US might use atomic weapons in the war.

Further Intensification of the Cold War

Theories of 'Brinkmanship' and 'Deterrence'

Even before the armistice in Korea was signed, the Cold War had begun to intensify resulting in conflicts and wars in other regions. The US foreign policy during this period was dominated by John Foster Dulles who was the US Secretary of State from 1953 to 1959. He considered the US policy of "containment" of communism as inadequate and advocated a more aggressive policy of "rolling back" communism by "liberating" people from what he considered communist tyranny. He advanced some dangerous doctrines. One of these was called "massive retaliation" which meant the use of nuclear weapons. The other was the doctrine of "brinkmanship" which meant pushing the Soviet Union on the brink of war to force her to grant concessions. He claimed that "the ability to get to the verge of war without getting into war" was "the necessary art" for a statesman and that "if you are scared to go to the brink, you are lost".

During this period, the race for armaments had reached a new stage. In November 1952, the US tested her first thermonuclear bomb, popularly known as the Hydrogen Bomb. The Soviet Union followed soon after in August 1953. The destructive power of these weapons was hundreds and thousands of times more than the atom bombs that were dropped on Hiroshima and Nagasaki The doctrine of "brinkmanship", when the two antagonistic powers possessed these weapons, was fraught with danger for the very survival of humanity. However, the development of these weapons was sought to be justified by the doctrines of Mutually Assured Destruction (MAD) and Nuclear Deterrence. The former meant that countries possessing these weapons would not go to war because they knew that even if they succeeded in destroying the enemy country with the use of these weapons, the other side would also succeed in destroying its enemy country. The acronym MAD reflected the true nature of this doctrine. The second doctrine meant that the possession of nuclear weapons by a country was a 'deterrent' to any possible invasion by another. It was the belief in this doctrine that led Britain to develop her "independent deterrent" in 1957. France and China later followed suit.

Military Alliances in Asia

The US also started forming military alliances in every part of the world, and establishing her military bases encircling the Soviet Union and China. In 1954, the South-East Asia Treaty Organisation (SEATO) was set up, comprising Australia, Britain, France, New Zealand, Pakistan, Thailand, the Philippines and the United States. Soon after, the Baghdad Pact was signed which brought Iran, Iraq, Turkey and Pakistan into a military alliance with the United States. When Iraq left the Baghdad Pact after a revolution which overthrew the monarchy, the Baghdad Pact was renamed as the Central Treaty Organisation (CENTO). These military alliances were used to maintain many undemocratic regimes in Asia. The massive inputs of arms in these countries created tensions between the members of these alliances and their neighbouring countries which refused to join these alliances. The latter countries viewed these alliances as sources of tensions in their region and the world and as threats to their independence. It was in this context that the Non-Aligned Movement was born. Countries which wanted to retain their independent role in world affairs and wanted to play an active role in bringing about relaxation of tension became non-aligned, that is, they refused to join these military alliances. Non-alignment was condemned by Dulles as "immoral".

The Role of the CIA

The US was led into conflicts with nationalist forces in Asian countries, particularly where the nationalist forces espoused programmes of radical social changes. All such forces began to be viewed as communists or allies of communists. Attempts were made to bolster unpopular right-wing regimes and even military dictatorships through massive aid, mainly of armaments. The region extending from Iran to North Africa became of vital importance because of its huge oil reserves. The extraction of oil and oil refineries in this region were under the control of Western companies, mainly of Britain and the US. This control was considered vital for the economies of the Western countries and maintaining it a legitimate objective of their foreign policy. The governments which tried to establish their rights over their natural resources for their own development were sought to be subverted. A major instrument of subversion was the US Central Intelligence Agency (CIA) which was set up in 1947. The CIA had huge funds at its disposal which were closed to public scrutiny. It not only collected intelligence through its vast network of spies but also carried out undercover paramilitary operations against the governments of other countries.

In 1951, Iran's Majlis (Parliament) ordered the nationalisation of the Anglo Iranian Oil Company, a British-controlled company. Mohammed Mussadeq was made the Prime Minister of Iran. The United States was convinced that Mussadeq was friendly with the Soviet Union. The government led by Mussadeq was overthrown in a coup in which the CIA played an important part. The Shah of Iran, Mohammed Reza Pahlavi, established his despotic rule with the support of the US. The Shah was closely tied to the US through a military alliance and gave the US oil companies concessions to

VIETNAM

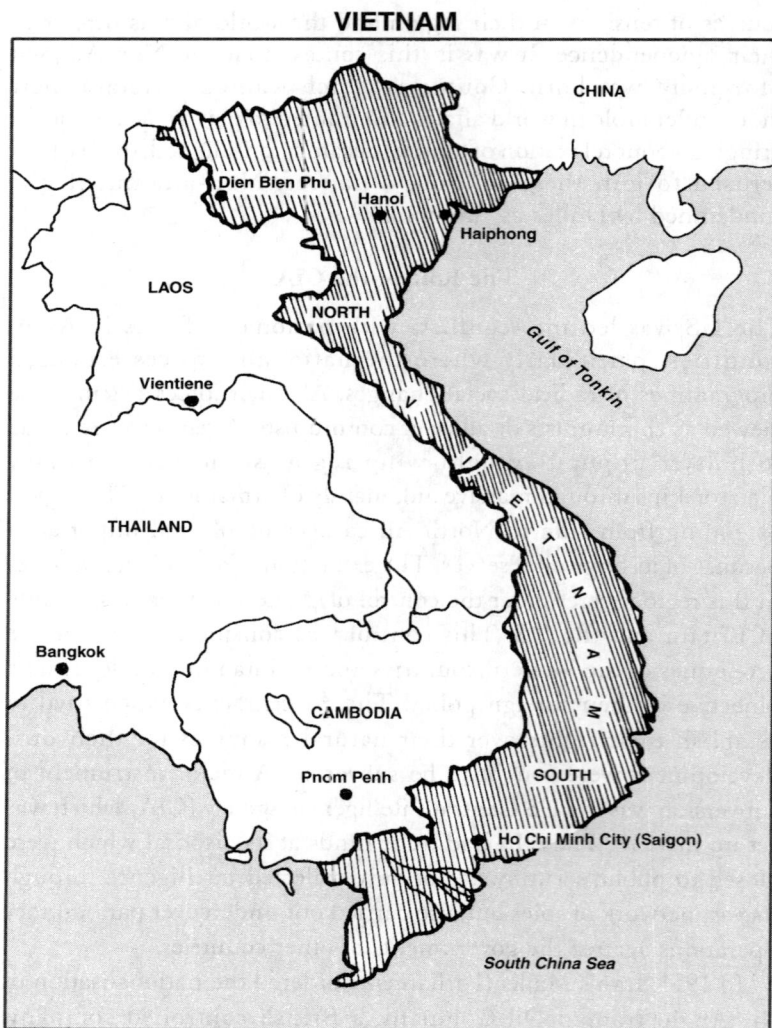

develop the oil reserves of Iran. His despotic rule continued for over twenty-five years, until it was ended in 1979 by the Islamic revolution in Iran.

In recent years the US has started threatening Iran, this time not through a covert operation by CIA but through a military invasion. Iran is alleged to be developing nuclear weapons which would pose a threat to peace in the world and the US consider it its right to prevent this. Israel, the US ally in the region, has also threatened to destroy Iran's nuclear installations through air strikes.

THE VIETNAM WAR

The French Debacle

The policy of 'containment' led to the US involvement in a protracted war in Vietnam. We have seen in the previous chapters the rise and growth of the nationalist movement in Indo-China. On 2 September 1945, Ho Chi Minh had proclaimed the independence of Vietnam and established the Democratic Republic of Vietnam. The French tried to restore their rule there. In this, they were aided by Britain and, later, by the US. Thus, from 1946, France was drawn into a war. Because the nationalist forces in Vietnam were led by the Communist Party, Dulles advocated direct involvement of the US in the Vietnam war and continued to press France to continued the war for which the US provided the funds. The Vietnamese forces led by Ho Chi Minh received help from the Soviet Union and China but they relied mainly on their own strength and the popular support they enjoyed within the country. In 1954 the French forces suffered a debacle. The Vietnamese besieged 12,000 French troops at a place called Dien Bien Phu. President Eisenhower, at this time did not accept the advice of Dulles that the US should send her own troops to Vietnam. In July 1954, an agreement was signed at Geneva according to which French rule in Vietnam was ended. Vietnam was temporarily divided into North Vietnam and South Vietnam, but the country was to be reunited after elections which, it was decided, would be held in 1956.

The US War in Vietnam

The US started building South Vietnam as an independent state under the dictatorial and corrupt rule of Ngo Dinh Diem. It was universally believed that Ho Chi Minh's party was certain to win the elections. Diem's government, on the US advice and support, refused to comply with the decision to hold elections. The US started building the South Vietnamese army to resist the North Vietnamese army and crush the South Vietnamese guerrillas. In spite of US support, Diem's government was on the verge of collapse in 1963 due to its growing unpopularity. It was brought down by a US-supported military coup.

The US government increasingly committed itself to the maintenance of an anti-communist regime in South Vietnam. The US policy makers advocated what was called the 'domino' theory. According to this theory, if South Vietnam fell to the communists, all other South-East Asian countries would also collapse and come under communist rule and this would lead to the expansion of communism over the entire Asia continent. The US started sending her own troops, to begin with, as military advisers, but gradually as regular combat troops. By the end of 1967, the number of US troops fighting in Vietnam had gone up to 500,000. It has been estimated that by 1967 the power of bombs dropped on Vietnamese territory by the US exceeded that of the bombs dropped all over Europe during the entire period of the Second World War.

The US war in Vietnam was the most unpopular US war in history. It was condemned by people all over the world. Even with the United States there was huge opposition to the war. No other single event in the years after 1945 had united people all over the world as the opposition to the war in Vietnam. The US troops withdrew from Vietnam in 1973. By April 1975, the South Vietnamese army was routed and the last of the US advisers also left. In this war, 58,000 US soldiers were killed and about 300,000 wounded. The Vietnamese casualties, both military and civilian, were much higher. The entire country had been ravaged. Vietnam soon emerged as a united country. The defeat of the greatest military power in the world by the people of a small country in Asia was an event of great significance in recent history.

The Arab World

Israel as a Major Factor

The main cause of conflicts in the Arab world during the post-war period was the hostility of the United States and her allies to the spread of Arab nationalism. This was done in the name of preventing the spread of communism and the influence of the Soviet Union in

ISRAEL AND OCCUPIED TERRITORIES

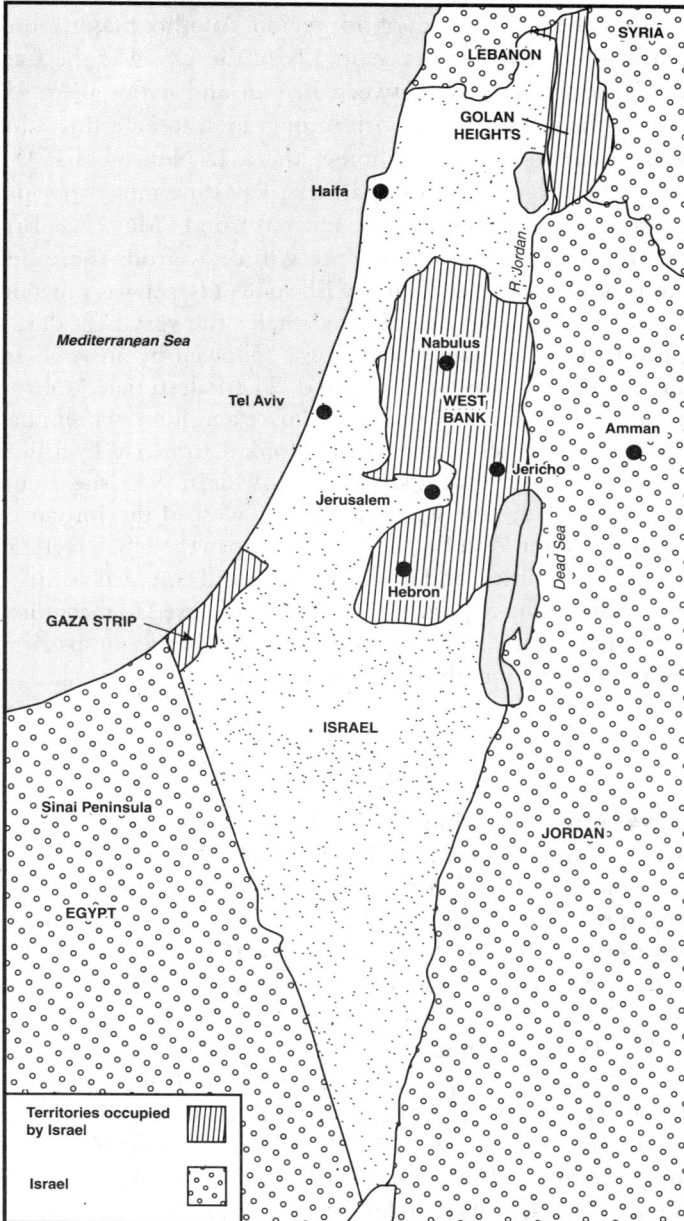

SYRIA

LEBANON

GOLAN
HEIGHTS

Haifa

R. Jordan

Mediterranean Sea

Nabulus

Tel Aviv

WEST
BANK

Amman

Jericho

Jerusalem

Dead Sea

Hebron

GAZA STRIP

ISRAEL

Sinai Peninsula

JORDAN

EGYPT

Territories occupied
by Israel

Israel

the region. The Western countries' were determination to retain their control over the oil resources of this region. Another major source of tension in this area, and the main ally of the US, was the state of Israel. There was conflict between Britain and nationalism of the Arabs over the question of Jewish immigration to Palestine and the creation of a Jewish "national home" there. In November 1947, the United Nations had agreed to partition Palestine into two separate states—an Arab and a Jewish state. However, on 14 May 1948, Britain which held Palestine as a mandate withdrew from there before partition could be effected. The Jewish state of Israel was proclaimed which was recognised by the United States the very next day. The establishment of the state of Israel was followed by an Arab-Israel war in which the Arabs were defeated. The Palestinian Arabs were deprived of their lands and homes and over a million of them had to live as refugees in other Arab countries. Jordan, formerly Transjordan, had become an independent kingdom in 1946. In 1949, she occupied the territory of Palestine which lay to the west of the Jordan river, popularly called the West Bank. With the help of the US, Israel started developing its technical and military power and emerged as the most powerful state in the region. The Arab states refused to recognise the state of Israel and the Arab nationalists viewed her as an instrument to curb the rising strength of Arab nationalism.

The Suez War

Egypt, under the leadership of Gamal Abdel Nasser, represented the forces of nationalism in the 1950s and the 1960s. Britain, in 1954, was asked to withdraw her troops from Egypt. At this time, Egypt also began to build her independent military strength with the help of arms from the Soviet Union. The US had offered to help Egypt build the Aswan Dam across the river Nile. However, when Egypt started receiving Soviet arms, US aid for the Aswan Dam was stopped. On 26 July 1956, the Suez Canal was nationalised. On 29 October 1956, Israel invaded Egypt and on the next day British and French troops were landed there to occupy the Suez Canal. The British-French-Israel invasion of Egypt aroused world-wide protests, including protests in Britain and France. The United Nations, with the support of the US, also condemned the invasion. On 5 November, the Soviet Union issued an ultimatum to the invaders to withdraw from Egypt and threatened to use missiles to defend Egypt. On 7 November 1956, the British-French military operations in Egypt were ended and their troops were withdrawn. Egypt and Israel agreed to a cease-fire.

The Eisenhower Doctrine

The end of the 1956 war in Egypt was acclaimed as a victory of Arab nationalism. It also led to the strengthening of the Soviet influence in the region. Egypt had now turned to the Soviet Union for help in building the Aswan Dam. Nasser also tried to strengthen Arab unity by uniting various Arab states. The US, alarmed at this development, proclaimed what is called the Eisenhower Doctrine, named after the US President. According to this Doctrine, the US decided to give economic and military aid to the countries in this region to protect them from what it called "international communism". In July 1958, however, the pro-Western government in Iraq was overthrown. US and British troops were sent to Lebanon and Jordan to prevent the pro-Western governments of these countries from falling. The US also continued to arm Israel.

The Arab-Israel Wars

In 1967, another war broke out between Israel on one side and Egypt, Jordan and Syria on the other. This is known as the Six Day War. The Arab states were defeated and Israel occupied Egyptian territory in the Sinai peninsula, the Palestinian territory on the West Bank of the river Jordan (from Jordan) and Gaza Strip, and a part of the territory of Syria called Golan Heights. Israel also established her control over the entire city of Jerusalem. In 1973, there was another Arab-Israel war. During this war, the oil-producing Arab states announced that they would stop shipment of oil to countries which were supporting Israel. This meant mainly the United States and her NATO allies. The European members of NATO, however, refused to align themselves with the US in her support to Israel and US herself was compelled to persuade Israel to agree to a cease-fire.

Israel has refused to vacate the many Arab territories that she occupied during the wars in 1956, 1967 and 1973.

THE CRISIS OVER MISSILES IN CUBA

One of the most serious crises in the history of the post-Second World War occurred on the installation of nuclear missiles in Cuba. The development of nuclear weapons had been accompanied by the development of new systems of delivery, that is, of means of transporting and dropping these weapons on enemy targets. For this purpose, missiles were developed. These missiles, or rockets, with nuclear warheads, could be directed to hit targets thousands of kilometres away, anywhere in the world. The US had set up these missiles aimed at Soviet targets at bases which she had set up in different parts of the world. The Soviet Union generally had no bases and her missile sites were within her own territory. Each side also had submarines carrying these nuclear missiles. To begin with, the range of these missiles was limited, say a few hundred kilometres, which had made the setting up of bases near the territory of the enemy countries necessary. New technology for spying on other countries had also been developed. For example, aeroplanes flying at very high speeds and at very high altitudes could take accurate photographs of the enemy country's territory and find out exact location of armies installations, tanks, airports, industries, etc. These can also locate missiles and even take photographs of these missiles.

In January 1959, there was a revolution in Cuba under the leadership of Fidel Castro. The United States turned hostile to Cuba when the new government started adopting radical social and economic measures, introducing agrarian reforms, and nationalising industries. Another reason was the friendly relations which the new government began to develop with the Soviet Union and China. The United States broke off diplomatic relations with Cuba in January 1961 and stopped all economic transactions with her. In April 1961, she landed 2000 Cuban exiles at the Bay of Pigs in Cuba to overthrow the Cuban government. However, the invasion ended in a fiasco and within two days it was crushed. Even though the entire world had condemned the US for the invasion of Cuba, the US government was not willing to give up its intention of overthrowing the Cuban government. John F. Kennedy, the US President at that time, had openly declared after the fiasco of the Bay of Pigs: "We do not intend to abandon Cuba to the communists". This was the background of the crisis which broke out in October 1962.

While the Soviet Union was surrounded by US bases, including those with nuclear missiles, the Soviet Union had no bases anywhere near US territory. In October 1962, the US found, from the pictures taken by her spy planes, that the Soviet Union was building missile sites in Cuba which is less than 150 km from the southernmost part of the US. All through all the wars which the US had fought were in the territories of other countries, with her own territory being completely inviolable. The installation of missiles in Cuba would bring US territory within easy range of attack. This was perceived as a serious threat to the security of the US.

Although the Soviet Union had done for the first time what the US had been doing all along, that is, establishing military bases in other countries, it created the danger of a war between the US and the Soviet Union, something which had not happened in spite of various tensions and conflicts between them. Such a war would have endangered all humanity. On 22 October 1962, President Kennedy announced a naval and air blockade around Cuba which meant that the US would stop any ship or aircraft moving towards Cuba. The US also prepared to launch an attack on the missile sites in Cuba. This crisis which had brought the world close to disaster, however, ended on 26 October. On that day, Khrushchev, the Premier of the Soviet Union, sent a message to President Kennedy that the Soviet Union would remove her missiles from Cuba if the US pledged not to attack Cuba. This was agreed to and the crisis was over. The US also agreed to withdraw the missiles which she had installed in Turkey, close to Soviet territory.

END OF THE COLD WAR

It has been mentioned earlier that the world had, from about the 1990, entered the post-Cold War era. Many efforts had been made since the 1950s to promote relaxation of tensions and on many occasions in the past it appeared that the two power blocs had entered the period of detente. The Non-Aligned Movement played a crucial role in promoting a climate of peace. However, many developments that seemed to mark the beginning of detente were followed by new tensions and conflicts.

One of the factors that played an increasingly important role in changing the policy of confrontation was the realisation that unlike the past events in human history, the practicability of an all-out war simply could not be the basis of conducting international relations. The reports prepared by scientists on the effects of a nuclear war and the voices raised by them against the armaments race and the doctrines of MAD and Nuclear Deterrence, and the popular anti-war movements around the world, played an important role in creating an atmosphere of detente. The Non-Aligned Movement, since its inception, pressed for disarmament so that the vast resources released by it could be utilised for development and for ending misery in the world.

Since the early 1960s, the rigid military alliances showed tendencies of breaking down. From 1956, the Soviet leaders began laying stress on peaceful coexistence. After the split in the communist movement which began in the late 1950s, the theory of the danger of the expansion of communism lost much of its relevance. The hostility between the Soviet Union and China destroyed the fear of communism which had been earlier viewed as a monolithic bloc. Albania went out of the Warsaw Pact in 1961 and Romania began to play an independent role. US relations with China improved in the early 1970s and China was admitted to the United Nations in 1971. There were changes in the US-sponsored military alliances also. France withdrew her military contingents from the NATO forces in 1966 and NATO forces and bases were removed from French territory. In the early 1970s, SEATO also began to be phased out as a military alliance. Pakistan withdrew from SEATO in 1973 and France in 1974.

The process of the end of the Cold War was not an easy one. At a number of occasions the breakout of an all out nuclear war seemed imminent. In 1956, there was an uprising in Hungary and in 1968 a change of government in Czechoslovakia. In both cases, it meant these countries going out of Soviet control and following political and economic policies which deviated from the Soviet sponsored 'socialism'. Both these countries were invaded by Soviet troops. In Czechoslovakia they were joined by troops from some other countries of the Warsaw Pact and a pro-Soviet government was installed there.

In 1961, East Germany built a wall between East and West Berlin to make it impossible for East Germans to escape to West Berlin. This created widespread resentment in the West. In 1979, the Soviet Union sent her troops to Afghanistan to help the Afghan government crush the rebels who had been armed by the United States and were operating in Afghanistan from and with the support of Pakistan. There were also many instances of US overt or covert intervention in many countries, particularly in Latin America. In Africa also, the US aided rebels against regimes which she considered pro-Soviet and pro-communist.

As it has been pointed out earlier that, the elimination of the means of destruction can alone ensure peace. The existence of the weapons whose destructive power is beyond ordinary human imagination is itself a source of tension. The end of confrontation, therefore, must lead to disarmament, to begin with, nuclear disarmament. Though disarmament remains a far cry, some positive steps were taken in this direction. In 1963, a Test Ban Treaty was signed by the US, the Soviet Union and Britain which prohibited the testing of nuclear weapons in the atmosphere, in outer space and underwater. France and China, however, had refused to sign the treaty and continued to carry out nuclear tests in the atmosphere. In 1969, negotiations aimed at the reduction of arms began between the United States and the Soviet Union and in 1972 an agreement was reached on limiting certain categories of missiles. These negotiations were known as Strategic Arms Limitation Talks (SALT).

The negotiations for disarmament were hampered in the 1980s when the US started working on a new system of weaponry called the Strategic Defence Initiative (SDI), popularly known as the "Star Wars" programme. This would mean taking the arms race to a new terrible height by extending it to outer space. However, some progress was made in eliminating some categories of nuclear missiles and in cutting down others. A treaty on the Non-Proliferation of Nuclear Weapons, popularly known as NPT, was also signed by many countries. Its aim is to prevent the countries that do not possess nuclear weapons from acquiring them but does not require that countries already in possession of nuclear weapons should eliminate them. Because it gives the five nuclear powers—the countries that presently possess nuclear weapons—the exclusive monopoly over nuclear weapons, this treaty is considered discriminatory by some countries, including India. India has tested a nuclear device in 1974 and, more recently in 1998, both India and Pakistan conducted nuclear tests. Israel, is believed to be in possession of nuclear weapons; the number of nuclear weapons she is said to possess is estimated to be 50.

Some very important events could be said to have brought the Cold War to an end. In 1989, the Communist parties' monopoly of power in the countries of Eastern Europe came to an end. This can be considered a major consequence of the policies pursued by the new leadership headed by Mikhail Gorbachev which came to power in 1985. The Soviet control over the governments of East European countries was loosened and new governments were formed after free elections were held in these countries. In October 1990, Germany was reunited. In 1991 the Warsaw Pact, the military bloc headed by the Soviet Union, was formally dissolved. It may be noted that NATO was not dissolved; it has in fact, expanded over the years with 26 countries being its members at present. In 1991, the Communist Party's exclusive control over the Soviet Union, which it had exercised soon after the October Revolution in 1917, came to an end. By the end of the year, the Soviet Union broke up into 15 independent republics. With the collapse of the Soviet Union the Cold War fanally came to an end.

The term, Cold War, is used to describe the confrontation and rivalry between the two military blocs—one consisting of West European and North American countries headed by USA, and the other consisting of the Soviet Union and European countries ruled by communist parties. It had its impact on almost every conflict in every part of the world because almost every major conflict in every part of the world was seen in terms of this confrontation and rivalry or, as is often said, in terms of the Cold War. The Cold War was also often seen as confrontation and rivalry for world domination by two opposing political, economic and social systems—capitalist and communist. This 'war' remained 'cold' because even though there were many conflicts and tensions and even wars in which the two military blocs were, directly or indirectly, involved, there was no widespread general war and in none of the wars the two superpoewers—USA and Soviat Union—directly fought against each other. The end of the Cold War means the end of the confrontation and rivalry between the two military blocs. It does not, however, mean that tensions, conflicts and wars have come to an end. The danger of a general conflagration can be said to have certainly come to an end.

After the end of the cold war USA became the sole 'superpower' in the world and often acted as one. The world it was often said, had become 'unipolar'. However, recent developments in the world have eroded the belief in unipolarity. Some experts have already started describing the period up to about the 1990 as the First Cold War and the possibility of another 'cold war' breaking out.

USA

The period after the end of the Second World War saw the emergence of the United States as the pre-eminent military and economic power in the world. Every part of the world came under the purview of US interests. The US also viewed herself as a great "moral force" in the world. Many Americans liked to think that the period in which they were living could quite legitimately be described as the "American Century". With the collapse of the Soviet Union, the US became the only superpower in the world.

Economic Supremacy

The Second World War had done no damage to the US economy. In fact, the problems created by the Great Depression had been overcome during the war. The post-war period was one of unprecedented economic prosperity. From 1940 to 1987, the GNP rose from about $ 100 billion to about $ 5,200 billion while the population rose from about 132 million to about 240 million. The affluence of the American people was reflected in the growth of what is usually described as "consumer culture" or "consumerism". There was an unprecedented growth in the production and consumption of a huge variety of consumption goods. The motor car became a symbol of this consumer culture. Every technological innovation, minor or major, made the existing product obsolete and worthless. The US was able to sustain this "consumerism" because of her own vast natural resources as well as the control she exercised over a variety of natural resources of many other parts of the world.

The growth of economy was, as in the earlier periods, accompanied by the growing centralisation of the economy. Most of the economy was controlled by a relatively small number of companies and corporations. There was tremendous increase in the growth of industries connected with armaments and a huge amount of government funds were spent for procuring defence equipment which benefited a few big corporations. The growing "interfusion" of the military and the industry in peace time alarmed many Americans and Eisenhower, the US President, while laying down office in January 1961, warned the country against "the acquisition of unwarrantable influence ... by the military-industrial complex". In the US, the relationship between political leaders and higher levels of government bureaucracy and the military establishment, and the corporations and big financial institutions has been closer than in most other democratic countries with capitalist economies. Very often, the government, when faced with a deficit, resorted to cuts on expenditure in medical care and other social welfare programmes, rather than increase taxes on the corporations.

During recent years, there has been a decline in the economic supremacy of the United States. From 1948 to 1952, the US had provided about $ 12 billion to the countries of Western Europe under the European Recovery Plan, popularly known as the Marshall Plan after the name of the then US Secretary of State. This plan had helped the European economies to recover to their pre-war levels within a very short period. In the following years, the economies of West European countries developed at a very fast rate. Japan also emerged as a major economic power in the world and Japanese goods began to compete with US goods not only in the world market but also in the US domestic market. The decline in US pre-eminence would be clear from the data on industrial production. In 1950, the US share of world industrial production was more than 60 per cent; in 1980, it was about 45 per cent. Western Europe and Japan have become the major economic rivals to the United States.

The US faith in her world supremacy had been first shaken when in 1957 the Soviet Union launched the Sputnik, its first satellite in space. This was followed three years later by the first Soviet manned flight in space. These 'shocks' led to vigorous efforts in areas in which the US thought she had been surpassed by the Soviet Union. Vast resources were made available to the space research programme. The

US made a great achievement when two US astronauts landed and walked on the surface of the moon in 1969.

Anti-Communist Hysteria

The Cold War had a vitiating influence on life in the US for many years. There emerged in the US a "paranoiac obsession" with "godless communism". The anti-communist and anti-radical hysteria led to branding every opinion which did not conform to the US view of the Cold War as 'un-American" and subversive.

During the presidency of Truman (1945–52), the loyalty of government officials was investigated and thousands of people were thrown out of jobs. Thousands of school, college and university teachers were dismissed from their jobs for teaching what were considered "un-American" ideas. Many film writers and producers were jailed and many blacklisted and debarred from employment in Hollywood for refusing to disclose their past communist connections. The anti-radical hysteria continued for some years during the presidency of Eisenhower who was elected president twice, in 1952 and 1956. In 1953, Julius and Ethel Rosenberg were executed on charges of passing atomic secrets to the Soviet Union, in spite of protests and appeals from all over the world. J. Robert Oppenheimer, popularly known as the father of the atom bomb (he had been the head of the US Atomic Bomb project), was denied security clearance. He had opposed the Hydrogen Bomb project and was accused of having concealed his past connections with communists. The leader of this crusade against communism within the United States was Senator Joseph McCarthy. From 1950 to 1954, he is described as having "terrorized American public life" by branding many innocent people as traitors and levelling accusations even against the State Department and the military of harbouring "traitors". He himself was disgraced in 1954 and there was a gradual decline in the hysteria even though most victims of the hysteria were not rehabilitated.

Foreign Interventions

The 'containment' of communism remained the objective of US foreign policy for most of the period after the Second World War. The US policy in Latin America continued more or less as before and the US either sent her troops or actively aided rebels to overthrow regimes in many Latin American countries which she suspected of being leftists and, therefore, anti-American. John F. Kennedy, who was elected US President in 1960, inaugurated a period of new dynamism in US domestic policy. However, it was during his presidency that the US began to get directly involved in the war in Vietnam, the fiasco of the Bay of Pigs took place and the confrontation on Soviet missiles in Cuba occurred.

A major peace initiative was taken in 1963 when the US President Kennedy and the Soviet Union Premier Khrushchev signed a treaty banning nuclear tests in the atmosphere, in the outer space and underwater. President Kennedy was assassinated on 22 November 1963. The man who was believed to be his lone assassin was killed soon after while in police custody and millions of people saw this act of killing on their television screens as it took place. Later, doubts were raised about the view upheld by a judicial commission that there was only one person behind the killing of President Kennedy.

The war in Vietnam ended in the ignominious defeat of the US. The war had begun to escalate during the period when Lyndon Johnson was the US President (1963–69). It was further escalated during the presidency of Richard Nixon (1969–74). Cambodia was bombed and the government of Cambodia was overthrown, and a pro-US government under a military general was installed there. The US had also extended the war to Laos, the third country of Indo–China.

President Nixon started the process of normalising relations with China and China was admitted to the United Nations in 1971. In 1972, Nixon went to China. The SALT talks referred to earlier were started with the Soviet Union. In 1973, the US agreed to end the war in Vietnam and to withdraw her troops. However, the war continued for another two years and ended when the North Vietnamese troops and the troops of the National Liberation Front of South Vietnam entered Saigon, the capital of the pro-US regime in South Vietnam, in April 1975, soon after the last US planes and helicopters had left the city.

The war in Vietnam came to an end after Nixon had resigned as president after a major scandal popularly known as the Watergate scandal. He had been re-elected president in 1972 but was soon after accused of serious charges of corruption, and of authorising planting of spying devices and stealing of files from the office of the Democratic Party. Although he claimed that he was not a crook, he was faced with the prospect of impeachment and resigned.

The US support to many unpopular regimes sometimes created problems for the US and led to acts which were illegal under US law. The US had long supported and sustained the regimes of Ferdinand Marcos in the Philippines and Jean-Claude Duvalier, commonly referred to as Papa Doc, in Haiti. But these regimes became so unpopular that the US had to support the overthrow of these dictators. In the case of Iran, the US first took an adventurous step which ended in a fiasco and later US officials had dealings with Iran which according to her own laws were illegal. In 1979, the Shah of Iran who was one of the most important supporters of the US in Asia fled the country following a revolution in Iran. The government of Iran asked the US to hand over the Shah, who had come to the US for treatment. The Iranian government wanted to put the Shah on trial. On the refusal of the US, the Iranians held many Americans as hostages. In April 1980, Jimmy Carter who had become president in 1977, sent US commandos to rescue the hostages. The commando action ended in disaster. The hostages were finally released in early 1981 when the US returned the Iranian assets in US banks which had been frozen by the US government earlier. In the 1980s, during the presidency of Ronald Reagan (1981–88), a major scandal broke out. High US officials had entered into illegal deals to support the rebels against the government of Nicaragua. These officials were believed to have entered into the illegal deals with the approval of the president.

In 1989, when George Bush was the president (1989–92), US troops were sent to Panama. General Noreiga who ruled Panama was overthrown and brought to the US to stand trial on charges of drug trafficking. In 1991, supported by the troops of some other countries, the US went to war against Iraq following the occupation of Kuwait by the latter. The war which was authorised by the United Nations led to the ending of the Iraqi occupation of Kuwait. Though the US-led troops were victorious, Iraq was not occupied. However, the war had serious consequences for the people of Iraq. Many restrictions were imposed on Iraq, including restrictions on the sale of oil, which was the only export commodity available there. In 2003, Iraq was again invaded, this time on the pretext of developing weapons of mass destruction, by the US and its allies, and has since been under US occupation.

Poverty

An issue which succeeding administrations in the US have had to contend with is the persistence of poverty. In the most prosperous country of the world, about 15 per cent of the population (over 30 million people) were officially classified as poor in the 1980s. The incidence of poverty in different 'racial' groups reflected the continuing 'racial' inequality in US society. In the 1980s, about 33 per cent of African Americans, about 20 per cent Hispanics (or Spanish-speaking inhabitants and immigrants from Mexico, Puerto Rico, etc.) and 12 per cent Whites in the US were poor. Homelessness in urban areas has been another major issue.

Civil Rights Movement

The issue which rocked the US for over a quarter century after the end of the war and continues to be a major issue is of racial equality. We have discussed the oppression of the African American people and their movement for equality in the period before the Second World War. A powerful civil rights movement arose in the 1950s which, during the following two decades, achieved significant success. The major objectives of this movement were the ending of segregation and discrimination against the African American people, the exercise of the right to vote by them and the ending of their poverty. Even the US armed forces had been following the policy of segregation. This was ended during the presidency of Truman.

In the southern states of the US, schools, colleges and universities, buses and trains, cafes, hotels, theatres and other public places, were all segregated. Black people were not allowed to even register as voters. In 1896, the Supreme Court had legalised segregation and had put forward the doctrine of "separate but equal". In 1954, the US Supreme Court rejected that doctrine and said: "We conclude that in the field of public education the doctrine of 'separate but equal' has no place.

Separate educational facilities are inherently unequal". This led to efforts by African American children to gain admission to schools which were all-White. These efforts were sought to be put down by force by governors of some states. In 1957, 17 Black children were selected for admission to a school in the town of Little Rock in Arkansas. The governor of the state posted guards outside the school to prevent them from entering the school. The federal government was then forced to send 1000 paratroopers to Little Rock to prevent the governor and the state guards from violating the law. These paratroopers stayed there for the entire duration of the school year. A similar development took place in 1962 when an African American student was admitted to the University of Mississippi.

The most powerful leader of the civil rights movement was Martin Luther King. Deeply influenced by Mahatma Gandhi, he launched a movement of non-violent protest against the segregation of African Americans. The protest began in Montgomery in the state of Alabama where the African American people started a boycott of buses. The bus companies had to yield and ended segregation in buses. The movement extended to other areas and took new forms. In restaurants, for example, 'sit-ins' were started. People would go to the segregated restaurants and ask to be served and on being refused, would continue to sit there. Students played a very significant role in this movement. Groups of them, both African Americans and Whites, went on what came to be called "freedom rides" to non-violently protest against racial segregation and discrimination. A powerful movement was also launched for the registration of African Americans as voters. The participants in these movements suffered tremendous hardships and even physical injuries at the hands of police and white hoodlums. There were many killings. The famous song "We shall overcome" was the theme song of these freedom riders.

In 1963, a huge mass rally was organised near the Lincoln Memorial in Washington DC. It was at this rally that Martin Luther King made his stirring "I have a dream" speech. In the following years, many legislations on civil rights were passed which helped in establishing civil rights as legal rights. However, the legal rights by themselves were not very effective and the civil rights movement increasingly became a radical movement. Many civil rights leaders also became actively involved in the anti-war movement. A militant

Black movement called Black Power also began to gain ground. In 1968, Martin Luther King was assassinated. The assassination sparked off race riots in many cities of the US. Martin Luther King was posthumously awarded the Jawaharlal Nehru Award for International Understanding.

Similar movements have also arisen among the American Indians who number about 2 million and the Hispanics whose population is about 22 million.

Anti-War Movement

New radical groups began to emerge in the US in the 1960s, mainly among the youth and the intellectuals. A major factor behind their rise was the Vietnam War which had created a powerful anti-war movement. There were anti-war demonstrations in universities. Thousands of students refused to be drafted into the army. Many fled to Canada and other countries. There were many incidents of violence in university campuses and in many places the police resorted to the use of brute force in suppressing these demonstrations. In one university, the Kent State University, four students were killed by the police. The new radical groups, later, increasingly concerned themselves with various global issues such as peace, disarmament and environmental protection.

Recent Developments

Suicide Attacks on the US

Many serious developments has taken place during the recent years with the US and in the conduct of US foreign policy. An event which has been a major, if not the most important, influence during this period was the terrorist attacks on the US in 2001. On 11 September 2001, four commercial jet planes were hijacked. Two of these were crashed by the hijackers into the Twin Towers of the World Trade Centre in New York. The act of crashing with all its horror was seen as it took place on television screens the world over. The crashes and resulting fireled to the collapse of the towers and destroyed two other buildings in the area. Another place crashed into the building of the military headquarters of the US, the Pentagon, and the fourth plane in a rural area of Pennsylvania. This was the worst ever terrorist attack with civilians as its target. About 3000 people were killed and over 6000 injured in these attacks. The killed and the injured, most of them civilians, included, besides Americans citizens of various other countries. The hijackers, none of whom survived, belonged to an Islamic terrorist organisation called al-Qaeda, whose chief leader was Osama bin Laden of Saudi Arabia. The terrorist attacks have come to be referred as 9/11.

War in Afghanistan

Soon after 9/11, the US declared war on terrorism. George W. Bush Jr, who had become the US President in 2000, held Osama bin Laden as the "prime suspect" in the terrorist attacks. He was known to have been in Afghanistan at the time where, with the full support of the Taliban government there, terrorist training camps run by the al-Qaeda have been set up. The al-Qaeda has been formed in 1979 to fight against the Soviet forces in Afghanistan. After the withdrawal of Soviet troops in 1989, Afghanistan had seen fighting between various groups to dominate Afghanistan. Many of these groups had earlier been armed to the teeth by the US with sophisticated weapons to wage what was then seen as a "holy war" against the Soviet intervention. Taliban, literal meaning 'students' had been trained in what were suppose to be religious schools belonging to a particular theology in Pakistan. In 1996, the Taliban established their rule over most parts of Afghanistan. The fanatical Taliban government, which was recognised by only three governments in the world—Pakistan, Saudi Arabia and United Arab Emirates—ushered in a period of oppression and gross violation of human rights in the name of implementing their version of the Sharia law.

On 7 October 2001, the US troops invaded Afghanistan. They were joined by British troops and troops from some other NATO countries. The invasion was given the code name "Operation Enduring Freedom". The objective of the invasion included the capture of Osama bin Laden and the destruction of the al-Qaeda and the Taliban. The military operations mainly consisted of air strikes against al-Qaeda training camps and Taliban positions. They were supported on the ground by the forces of the most important anti-Taliban group in Afghanistan called the Northern Alliance. On

13 November 2001, Kabul was captured, the Taliban having fled the previous night. Subsequently, many parts of Afghanistan, mainly cities, were freed from Taliban rule. Later, a government headed by Hamid Karzai was set up. The government is recognised by most countries and has taken steps to undo the damage done to Afghanistan by six years of Taliban rule and to launch projects for the construction of the country. However, it has not been able to establish its effective control over large parts of the country.

In the meantime, the war in Afghanistan continues. The Taliban and al-Qaeda still remains strong in many parts of the country and form their enclaves in the border areas in Pakistan. The US forces have conducted military operations against them in the enclaves which are under their control in Afghanistan. Pakistan, which has been an ally of the US in the war against terror, has condemned these attacks in Pakistani territory. Thousands of Afghan civilians have been killed in the war, may of them during military operations by US-led forces directed against al-Qaeda and the Taliban.

The war in Afghanistan, except in the beginning when it was launched, has been extremely unpopular throughout the world, including in countries which have sent their troops to fight in the US-led war. It has led to the devastation of the country and starvation deaths. There has been numerous cases of human rights violation and torture of prisoners in the special jails set up in Afghanistan to question suspected al-Qaeda and Taliban fighters. Many prisoners were taken to a detention camp in Guantanamo in Cuba—the area has been under US occupation for over a century—and continued to be held there. Since 2003, when US invaded Iraq, the focus of the US foreign policy and military operations has shifted to Iraq. The war in Afghanistan has gone in for seven years and there are little possibilities of its coming to any end.

War in Iraq

A reference has been made about the war which the US and some of her allies, notably Britain, had waged against Iraq in 1991. In August 1990, Iraq invaded Kuwait and the Security Council of the United Nations immediately authorised the use of force against the Iraqi occupation of Kuwait. The United Nations had imposed comprehensive economic sanctions against Iraq in 1990 and these sanctions continued even after the Iraqi troops evacuated Kuwait. The sanctions were a disaster for the people of Iraq. For many years, she could not sell her oil or import even the most essential commodities. Even after the UN relaxed the sanctions under what was called Oil-for-Food Programme, the US and Britain made it extremely difficult for Iraq to import food items, medicines and medical equipments, and other materials which were essential for Iraq's agriculture, water supply, education and maintenance of hygienic condition. According to a UNICEF report, 500,000 Iraqi children under the age of five died between the years 1991 and 1998. The estimate of the people, including adults, who died during this period is over a million. The government of Iraq had no control over a large part of the country's airspace, while the US and British troops bombed the entire country. In the meantime, the US leaders began to increasingly talk about the objective of "regime change" in Iraq, that is, to overthrow Saddam Hussein, the President of Iraq.

The US, supported by a few other countries again invaded Iraq in March 2003 on the pretext of destroying Weapons of Mass Destruction (WMD) which Iraq was suspected to be harbouring. The war which is still raging has been the most devasting war since the end of the US war in Vietnam. The world-wide mass protests against the war, including those in the US, are comparable to the protests against the US war in Vietnam. According to one estimate, from early January 2003 to about mid-April 2003, about 36 million people took part in protest demonstrations against the war the world over.

After the 1991 war, the UN Security Council had passed a resolution which required that all Iraqi programmes for the development of chemical, biological, nuclear and long-range missiles be stopped and all such weapons destroyed. UN weapon inspectors had been sent to Iraq soon after the end of the war in 1991. The inspection was suspended in 1998 but was resumed in 2002. However, the weapon inspectors found no evidence of WMD. In spite of the reports of UN inspectors about the absence of any WMD, the US government in March 2003 announced that it, along with its allies, would proceed to free Iraq of the WMD, and asked the UN inspectors to leave Baghdad immediately. The invasion of Iraq began on 20 March 2003. The US, Britain and other countries who constitute what is called "coalition of the willing" did not find any WMD, though the entire country was soon under their occupation.

The war did not last long. It was given the codename "Operation Iraqi Freedom". The doctrine on which the war operation was based is called "Shock and Awe". It meant the use of such devastating airstrikes and an enormous number of precision guided weapons so that, in the words of one of the authors of the doctrine, "you have this simultaneous effect, rather like the nuclear weapons in Hiroshima, not taking days or weeks but in minutes". Within a few days of the invasion, on 9 April, Baghdad was occupied. By 15 April, the invasion was stated to be effectively over. Soon after the invasion started, George W. Bush, in his address to the nation, stated that the military operations had begun "to disarm Iraq, to free its people and to defend the world from grave danger". He told the nation: "We will accept no outcome but victory" and "we will defend our freedom. We will bring freedom to others. And we will prevail'.

One of the objectives of the invasion, besides the elimination of WMD, had been "regime change". Saddam Hussein, who had gone into hiding, was captured on 13 December 2003 and hanged after conviction by a court in the country which was under foreign occupation. Many of his associates and leaders of the Baath Party were captured and some of them were executed. The objective of "regime change" was made under the claim of establishing "democracy", with the US president claiming the spread of democracy in the world as the doctrine of his country's foreign policy. Another doctrine was the right of "pre-emptive strike", the right to invade another country on the ground that the other country pose a threat to the security of the US. Iraq under Saddam Hussein had been totally hostile to Al-Qaeda, the organisation which had been held responsible for the 9/11 attack. The US government, however, fabricated another ground for invading Iraq after that country had been invaded—to fight against Islamic terrorism led by Al-Qaeda. The US president also claimed divine inspiration behind his war. The *Washinston Post*, a leading American daily, reported Bush saving, "God inspired me to hit al-Qaeda, and so I hit it. And I had the inspiration to hit Saddam, and so I hit him".

The war in Iraq has still not ended. It has devastated the country. According to *The Lancet*, the reputed medical journal, up till July 2006, over 600,000 Iraqis had been killed as a result of the invasion. Since then another similar number of Iraqis have been killed. Apart from the loss of life various other forms of devastation remains unmeasured. Soon after the fall of Baghdad, there was a large-scale plunder of art objects and antiquities from the Baghdad museum. Iraq is one of the most ancient of world civilisations and was a great treasure house of art and antiquities. US forces showed little interest in securing Iraq's great heritage from pillage and destruction. They were busy in safeguarding and taking control of the oil fields and pipelines because, it is universally accepted that, the country was invaded and occupied mainly with a view to taking control of Iraq's rich oil resources. It may be noted that soon after the country was occupied, the UN sanctions against Iraq, which had led to untold misery for the people of Iraq, were lifted and the effective control of Iraq's oil passed on to the US. The occupation of Iraq has continued. There is no end to the insurgency against foreign occupation in sight. The foreign occupation and the revival under foreign auspices of political processes have led to violence and near civil wars between different communities and different regions of the country, subverting the existence of Iraq as one country. The reports of grotesque torture inflicted by the US troops on Iraqi prisoners have shocked the conscience of the people all over the world. The damage done to the US has also been enormous. It is estimated that about 4,200 US soldiers have been killed and thousands injured. There are reports of serious psychological ailments which soldiers who have returned from Iraq are suffering from. The number of American casualties compared with those suffered by the Iraqis is small. However, the damage that the war has caused to the US economy is very serious. According to Joseph Stiglitz, the eminent American economist who won the Nobel Prize many years ago, the war in Iraq has cost the US three trillion dollars.

USSR

Failures in Economy

The role which the Soviet Union played in the Second World War won her the admiration of anti-fascists all over the world. To the people of the Soviet Union, the war which they fought was the "Great Patriotic War" which they made every possible sacrifice to win. The Soviet Union suffered most as a result of the war. The economy was completely devastated. As soon as the war was over the Soviet Union launched a massive effort at reconstruction. In 1946, the Fourth Five Year Plan was launched and before the end of the 1940s, the industrial production had been restored to the pre-war level. Through greater mechanisation of agriculture and by having larger collective farms, agricultural production had also been restored to the pre-war level by the beginning of the 1950s. The development of the Soviet economy continued through a series of Five Year Plans in the subsequent period and it became the second most powerful economy, in terms of GNP, in the world.

In spite of its growth, however, the Soviet economy was continuously dogged by certain serious problems. The emphasis on heavy industries had helped build a strong infrastructure but the consumer goods industries fell far short of the requirements. The result of this disproportion was that in spite of its economic might, the rise in the standard of living of the people was far slower than in the developed countries of the West. Even in terms of the rate of economic development, the Soviet leaders began to admit in the mid-1980s that the economy had been stagnating for many years. The failure in agriculture had been particularly conspicuous. In terms of advances in technology, except in areas connected with defence and space research, the Soviet Union lagged behind advanced capitalist countries. This was in spite of the fact that in terms of numbers, the Soviet Union was ahead of any other country in technical and scientific manpower.

The Soviet Union's failures in economy are attributed to what was later described as the "command system". The kind of economic planning which was followed in the Soviet Union led to its over-centralisation and killed all initiative at the level of individual industrial enterprises. Certain sectors of industry produced goods in quantities for which there was no demand. Prices of products were fixed artificially and caused further strains. A serious debate began in the Soviet Union from the mid-1980s about devising new strategies for overcoming the ills of the economy and making it more responsive to the needs of the people. However, the changes which were introduced failed to end the stagnation. In 1991 the Soviet Union disintegrated. The failure in the economic field can be considered a major factor in the collapse of the Soviet Union.

Military Strength

One sector in which the Soviet Union was more or less equal, in its effectiveness, to the US was her military capability. The advances in technology relating to military requirements were much greater than in other areas, and were comparable to the highest in the world. The same was also true of developments in science and technology relating to space programmes. In fact, at one time Soviet space research was considered to be ahead of US space research as was evidenced by the first satellite launched in space and the first manned flight in space as well as the space station with cosmonauts on board over long periods. The massive expenditure on the military and the technology of armaments gave the Soviet Union parity in military strength with the US. It can be said to have maintained the 'balance of power' in the world. At one time, the priority given by the Soviet Union to military strength was justified on the ground that it prevented the US from imposing her will on the world. However, it became a major factor in weakening the Soviet economy diverting vast resources away from productive and useful channels.

Political Developments

Some of the features of the political development of the Soviet Union since the Bolshevik Revolution have been described earlier. By the late 1930s, Stalin had established his dictatorial rule in the Soviet Union. The ruthlessness of his dictatorship did not diminish after the war. Stalin ruled as the supreme leader of the Soviet Communist Party but the Communist Party and its various bodies such as the

Polit Bureau, had been reduced to no more than a rubber stamp of whatever Stalin decided. According to the party's constitution, a congress of the party was required to be held every four years. However, the first party congress after 1939 was held in 1952 after a gap of 13 years. Through the 1930s and 1940s, almost every leader of the Bolshevik Revolution had either died or had been liquidated. A system of repression had been institutionalised. Every dissent was considered an act of treason. Thousands of people had been sent to labour camps and thousands of others languished in prisons. The Soviet security police was an important instrument of the policy of repression. The repression caused grave damage to intellectual life and to art, culture and science. The science of biology was all but destroyed in the Soviet Union due to the suppression of what Stalin considered 'bourgeois' tendencies in the biological sciences. In January 1953, nine doctors were charged with the murder of a Soviet leader in 1948. It was alleged that they had also plotted to damage the health of several high military officers who were under their medical care. The arrest of these doctors was believed to be the starting point of yet another wave of repression. However, on 9 March 1953, Stalin died

End of Terror

A number of significant changes took place shortly after the death of Stalin. Nikita Khrushchev became the First Secretary of the Soviet Communist Party. The policy of large-scale repression was ended. The doctors were released and it was stated that they had been arrested illegally. Thousands of people who had been charged with all kinds of offences against the state and had been sent to labour camps and prisons were released and rehabilitated. In February 1956, the Twentieth Congress of the Soviet Communist Party was held. This Congress has become famous for many major departures that it made in political and economic policies at home and in foreign policy as well as for Khrushchev's report on Stalin's crimes against the party and the people. Although this report was made at a secret session of the Congress and was not released, its main contents became known throughout the world soon after. Though these developments did not lead to the establishment of a democratic political system and the restoration of full intellectual freedom and civil liberties, the period of terror and of large-scale repression was definitely over. Two literary works which symbolised this change were a novel by Ilya Ehrenburg entitled, *The Thaw* and a novel by Alexander Solzhenitsyn entitled *One Day in the Life of Ivan Denisovitch*, which dealt with life in a labour camp. Solzhenitsyn who was later awarded the Nobel Peace Price for literature lived abroad for many years and returned to his homeland in 1994. He died in 2008. However, restrictions continued to be imposed on civil liberties, publications, travel abroad and many repressive measures continued to be resorted to for almost thirty years after the Twentieth Congress.

In 1964, Khrushchev was ousted and Leonid Brezhnev became the First Secretary of the Communist Party. From the early 1970s, he became the supreme leader of the Soviet Union. A number of economic reforms were initiated during the 1960s and 1970s but they failed to bring about any notable improvement in the economy. The period of Brezhnev's rule which lasted till 1982 is now generally considered a period of stagnation.

The system of repression began to be fully demolished and a truly democratic system established in its place only in 1985 when Mikhail Gorbachev was elected the leader of the party and, later, President of the Soviet Union. The changes initiated by Gorbachev were often referred to as marking the second Soviet revolution. These changes are best described by two Russian terms—*glasnost* (openness) and *perestroika* (restructuring). The policy of glasnost meant free and frank discussion of every political, economic and social issue, and removal of restrictions on civil liberties. The hold of the Communist Party was loosened and in 1990 non-Communist parties were allowed to be formed. Perestroika was an effort to end the stagnation in Soviet economy. However, little was achieved in this regard and, in fact, the economic situation worsened further. The loosening of the hold of the Communist Party did not immediately lead to the establishment of a stable democratic political system. In the meantime, there was a demand for greater autonomy, and in some cases independence, by the republics which constituted the Soviet Union. Very soon, the Soviet Union broke up.

Foreign Policy

The foreign policy of the Soviet Union had been deeply influenced by the fact that right from her birth she was surrounded by countries which were quite openly hostile to her and to the social and economic system that she was trying to build. She had been the only major power in the 1920s and 1930s which extended full support to the peoples of the colonies in their struggle for freedom. During the 1930s she had also been consistent in her opposition to fascism and fascist aggressions until she entered into a non-aggression pact with Germany. The main allies she had in that period were the communist parties in various countries who considered the defence of the Soviet Union their duty.

The Soviet Union had played the leading role in the defeat of fascism. The tremendous good will that she had won for her role in the war, however, suffered due to the policies that she followed in the countries of Eastern Europe where, with her backing, the rule of the communist parties was imposed. In some of these countries, the communists enjoyed much popular support at the time of liberation and as partners in the coalition governments which were formed in these countries after their liberation. However, they began to be alienated from the people when, through undemocratic means, they established their exclusive control over the governments. Afterwards, under Stalinist influence and pressure, similar types of repressive systems were built in these countries as Stalin had built in the Soviet Union.

In 1948, Yugoslavia was expelled from the world communist movement for her refusal to accept Soviet control. Following this, some of the most prominent leaders of the communist parties in the countries of Eastern Europe were expelled on the charge of being agents of Tito, the leader of the Yugoslav communists. Many of them were jailed and many executed. The policy of interference in the governments and communist parties of Eastern Europe continued throughout the period up to Stalin's death.

In the immediate post-war period, communist parties in some countries tried to engineer revolutions. Some of these attempts were believed to have been instigated by Stalin. In fact, except in countries which had been liberated by Soviet troops (Eastern Europe and North

Korea), the success of the communists in capturing power (China, Vietnam, Cuba) was not the result of Stalin's or the Soviet Union's instigation or interventions. It may be remembered that during this period, all the imperialist countries had the backing of the military might of the US and that the US made frequent use of the military to put down nationalist and revolutionary regimes and install despotic governments in many countries. The Soviet policies, however, did little to diminish the Cold War or to end the situation of Great Power confrontation.

A major change took place in Soviet foreign policy after Stalin. The most significant shift was in the new emphasis on "peaceful coexistence" between countries following different social, economic and political systems. The policy of peaceful coexistence which was the most significant feature of the policy of non-alignment adopted by newly independent countries like India was, as far as Soviet foreign policy is concerned, the contribution of Khrushchev. The communists had always believed that though they were opposed to war as an instrument of national policy, war was inevitable as long as imperialism existed. The policy of peaceful coexistence meant the giving up of the theory of the inevitability of war. The Soviet leaders, along with the leaders of the Non-Aligned Movement, stressed that war in the present day would destroy all humanity and must, therefore, be replaced by a policy of peaceful coexistence and a policy of peaceful competition between different social, economic and political systems.

The Soviet Union made many important proposals for disarmament throughout the period from the late 1950s, but little progress was achieved in the direction of disarmament or in outlawing war. It may be necessary to mention here that the Soviet Union also almost consistently supported the various initiatives taken by the Non-Aligned Movement regarding disarmament and some non-aligned countries expressed the view that the Soviet Union and other socialist countries were the "natural allies" of the Non-Aligned Movement. The Soviet foreign policy also became an important factor in strengthening the national independence of many newly independent countries and many freedom movements through the material and political support which was given to them by the Soviet Union. The economic relations of the Soviet Union with newly independent countries were also seen as a major contribution to their efforts at building their national economies.

The advocacy of the policy of peaceful coexistence became a major cause of the split in the communist movement which began in the late 1950s. The Chinese Communist Party under the leadership of Mao Zedong continued to believe in the theory of the inevitability of war. Mao Zedong stated that even in a nuclear war, though many millions would die, socialism would be victorious. Some Chinese communist leaders and their supporters in the communist parties of different countries were of the view that the policy of peaceful coexistence would weaken the struggle for socialist revolution.

In spite of the policy of peaceful coexistence, the Soviet Union did not cease her efforts at building an arsenal of destructive weapons to match those of the US. She did, however, take many unilateral decisions. For example, she declared that she would never use the nuclear weapons first and she appealed to the US to make a similar commitment. She ceased underground tests of nuclear weapons and declared that she would not resume those tests as long as the other side did not hold these tests.

In spite of the stress on peaceful coexistence, the Soviet policy towards Eastern Europe did not undergo any basic change. It can be said that she continued to regard Eastern Europe as her sphere of influence. On two occasions she resorted to massive military intervention—in Hungary in 1956 and in Czechoslovakia in 1968—to overthrow the communist leadership in those countries which wanted to change the policies of their respective countries in the direction other than those suggested by the Soviet leadership. In fact Brezhnev, who had replaced Khrushchev, had declared that it was the duty of a socialist country to interfere in another socialist country if in that country the continuance of socialism was threatened.

There were basic changes in Soviet foreign policy after Gorbachev came to power. A reference has been made earlier to Soviet military intervention in Afghanistan. This had led to the Soviet Union's involvement in a protracted civil war. It had also embittered Soviet-US relations and hampered the process of detente. In 1988, the Soviet Union began to withdraw her troops from Afghanistan and by 1989 all Soviet troops were withdrawn. However, the withdrawal of Soviet troops did not lead to the establishment of peace in Afghanistan and the civil war in Afghaistan continued unabated. In 1996, the Taliban captured power and in 2001, US-led forces invaded Afghanistan. The Soviet Union also signed two important agreements on arms control with the US. Another important development during this period was the end of Soviet control over the countries of Eastern Europe. This led to the end of the rule of the communist parties in all these countries. The Warsaw Pact, the military bloc headed by the Soviet Union, was also formally dissolved in 1991.

Gorbachev's policies, both internal and external, were acclaimed throughout the world. His foreign policy initiatives can be said to have been crucial in bringing the Cold War to an end. He was awarded the Nobel Peace Prize in 1990.

Break-up of the Soviet Union

Gorbachev's economic policies was a failure and the republics of the union started demanding greater autonomy in internal and also external policies. By the end of 1990, it was clear that the Soviet Union could not continue as a single state. The three Baltic states—Estonia, Latvia and Lithuania—had decided to become independent and the other republics had decided to assert the supremacy of their laws over the laws of the union. To prevent the break-up of the Soviet Union, Gorbachev negotiated a new treaty with ten republics. The new treaty would have granted greater autonomy to the republics but maintained the union. However, before the new treaty could be signed, some leaders of the Soviet Communist Party tried to stage a coup against Gorbachev on 19 August 1991 by removing him from the presidentship of the Soviet Union and putting him under house arrest. There was widespread opposition to the coup, and even the army was opposed to it. It was fanally thwarted on 21 August 1991. Though Gorbachev resumed office as the president, the attempt at a coup accelerated the process of disintegration. Boris Yeltsin, who had been elected President of the Russian Republic, emerged as the most powerful leader during this period. He had played the leading role in foiling the coup. Gorbachev resigned from the Communist Party and all activities of the Communist Party were ordered to be suspended. Gorbachev's effort to preserve the Soviet Union on the basis of a new treaty came to naught. By November 1991, 13 of the 15 republics had declared their independence. Early in December 1991, Boris Yeltsin, the Russian President along with the presidents of two other republics announced that the Soviet Union had ceased to exist. They invited other republics to join a new federation called the Commonwealth of Independent States. On 25 December 1991, Gorbachev resigned as president and the Soviet Union formally ceased to exist. Its place was taken by 15 independent states which had constituted the USSR. Twelve of them, including four Asian republics, became members of the Commonwealth of Independent States.

Ten Days that Shook the World was the title of an American journalist John Reed's firsthand account of the Russian Revolution of 1917. The kind of socialism, or what is now generally called the "really existing socialism", which was built over the vast territory of the Soviet Union, formerly the Russian empire, was for long viewed as an alternative to the capitalist system of society. The collapse of the "really existing socialism" and the break-up of the Soviet Union was anticipated by few and happened rather suddenly and almost without any resistance. The impact of these developments, it was believed, may turn out to be as world shaking as the Russian Revolution of 1917. These developments certainly marked the end of an era in world history.

Russia after the Break-up

The collapse of the Soviet Union has been followed by a period of turmoil in many former Soviet republics. In some of them, the former heads of government who were leaders of the Communist Party established authoritarian regimes of their own. Some others are still striving to establish stable democratic political systems. In Russia the period till end of 1999, when Yeltsin was the president, was one of serious economic crisis, rise of mafia-type economic oligarchs who plundered the country to become billionaires, extreme hardships for the common people and near collapse of law and order. Under the presidentship of Vladimir Putin, there was economic recovery and the position of Russia as a major economic and military power began to be restored. Some of the worst features of the breakdown that followed the collapse of the Soviet Union were eliminated and a sense of security and stability was restored to the country. Russia once again started playing an important role in world affairs. One of the major issues that have some to the fore in recent years has been the Western policy of expanding NATO to include the former allies of the Soviet Union as members and installing US missiles in the Czech Republic and Poland. There have also been strains in relations between Russia and some of the former Soviet republics, such as Ukraine and Georgia. According to the Russian constitution, the president cannot continue more than two terms in office. After the elections held in 2008, Medvedev became the President of Russia. Putin became the prime minister.

EUROPE

For a more fuller understanding of the developments in Europe during the post-war period it will be better to deal with each country separately.

Portugal, Spain and Greece

The first major feature of post-war Europe till the 1980s was the division of Europe with the countries of Eastern Europe coming under the rule of the communist parties allied with the Soviet Union, while the Western part of Europe following a variety of democratic political systems with a capitalist economy and were under the influence of the US. The main exceptions to the latter were the three backward countries of Europe—Portugal, Spain and, for many years, Greece.

In Portugal, the dictatorial rule of Salazar which had been established as far back as 1932 had continued till 1968 when ill health forced him to retire. In 1974, the dictatorial government was overthrown by a group of junior army officers with the support of Portuguese socialists, communists and other democrats and a new democratic constitution was promulgated.

In Spain, the fascist dictatorship established by Franco after his victory in the civil war continued till his death in 1975. His death was followed by the beginning of liberalisation and the release of political prisoners. In 1977, the first free election was held after over forty years. The Socialist Party in Spain emerged as a major political force in the country.

In Greece, the end of the civil war did not lead to the establishment of a stable democratic political system. In 1967, a group of army officers seized power and established a tyrannical regime. For many years the restoration of democracy in Greece became a major issue exercising the people of Europe. A number of famous Greek political and cultural figures had fled the country and many others languished in prisons in Greece. While a movement of resistance grew inside the country, it was supported by a powerful protest movement outside the country. In 1974, the rule of the colonels, as the Greek military dictatorship was called, ended and Greece once again became a democracy.

Western Europe

In most of the countries of Europe, particularly France and Italy, socialists and communists had been major political forces, but their influence, particularly of the communists, has declined in recent years. In West Germany and many other countries of Europe, social democratic parties have been a major political force and very often they have formed governments, either independently or with coalition partners. In Britain, the Labour Party has come to power at different times.

The Second World War had a radicalising influence on the political thinking of the people of Europe. Soon after the war, left-wing governments had come to power in many countries of Europe. In France and Italy, till 1947, communists were also part of the government. These governments had introduced many important legislations which helped end many gross inequalities that characterised most European societies before the war. Some important sectors of industry in these countries were nationalised. The existence of powerful labour unions prevented any major reversals in welfare programmes even when conservative or centrist parties came to power.

A reference has been made earlier to the European Recovery Programme. This plan helped the economies of Western Europe to recover to their pre-war level. This was followed by a tremendous growth in the economy of these countries with France and West Germany emerging as industrial giants. The economic development of West Germany was particularly spectacular and it outstripped all other countries of Europe.

Peace Movements

For many years after the war, Europe became the main centre of Cold War conflicts. Most of the West European countries were members of the NATO military alliance and had NATO troops and military bases, equipped with nuclear weapons and missiles supplied by the US, in their territories. These further added to tensions in Europe. The removal of NATO bases became a major demand of the peace movements which grew powerful in many countries of Europe from the late 1950s. Britain and France began to develop their own nuclear weapons or "independent nuclear deterrents", as they called them. Britain still continued to believe that she was a great world power and, therefore, it was necessary for her to have her own nuclear weapons besides those of the US in her territory. One of the most powerful peace movements in Europe emerged in Britain. Led by the Campaign for Nuclear Disarmament (CND), it demanded the closing of the US bases in Britain and unilateral nuclear disarmament by her.

End of Europe's Hegemony

The most significant feature of the post-war world was the end of European hegemony around the world. Within about two decades after the end of the war, most of the European empires in Asia and Africa had collapsed. The European imperialist countries were not willing to give up their empires and in some cases they got involved in protracted wars with the nationalist movements. For example, the French continued to fight a war to retain Indo-China from 1947 to 1954 and Algeria from 1954 to 1962. In this regard we can mention that Portugal—the most backward country of Europe—held on to her empire the longest. The nationalist armed resistance against the Portuguese rule in Angola and Mozambique lasted as long as the dictatorship in Portugal lasted. After the revolution, the new Portuguese government entered into negotiations with the freedom movements of Mozambique and Angola. Mozambique became free in 1975 and Angola in 1976.

European Unity

A significant development which would help the rise of Western Europe as a great world power was the emergence of a movement for the unification of Western Europe. To begin with, the major country to take a lead in this direction was France. She believed that she was the natural leader of a united Western Europe. The first major step in this direction was taken in 1957 with the setting up of the European Economic Community (EEC). The countries comprising the EEC— France, West Germany, Belgium, Holland, Luxemburg and Italy— set up what is known as the "Common Market". This was to be a prelude to the formation of a federation of West European countries. Initially Britain kept herself out of the EEC but in 1961 when she wanted to join, France did not let her join. She was finally admitted to the EEC in 1973 along with two other countries—Denmark and Ireland. The nine members of the EEC later set up the European Parliament. Later, Greece, Spain and Portugal were also admitted to the EEC.

During the next few years, the emergence of a united Western Europe as a political entity has become a real possibility. Already, plans are afoot to introduce a common currency in the EEC countries and to do away with the requirement of a passport for Europeans to travel from one EEC country to another. In the meantime, Germany has emerged as the strongest economic power in the EEC. With her unification, the influence of Germany is likely to grow even further. In spite of the loss of their empires, the countries of Western Europe together have emerged as a new power in the world. Their economic dependence on the US has diminished and they are likely to play an increasingly independent role in world affairs.

On 1 November 1993, the EEC was transformed and became the European Union. From a grouping of mainly Western European countries, it became, by 2007, a union of 27 European nations. Its objectives included enhancing political, economic and social cooperation as well as guaranteeing freedom of movement of people, goods and services and capital between different European countries. In 2004, seven countries of Eastern Europe—Estonia, Latvia,

Lithuania, Poland, Czech Republic, Slovakia (the former Czechoslovakia by then had broken up into two independent countries), Poland and Hungary—which had been earlier ruled by communist parties and had been allied to the Soviet Union joined the European Union. Soon after, they were joined by former communist countries, Bulgaria and Romania, and Slovenia (which had broken away form Yugoslavia). It is interesting to note that all these countries had transformed themselves into free market economies. Also, all these new member countries of the European Union have become member countries of NATO. In two of them—Poland and Czech Republic—missiles have been deployed which the leaders of the Russian Federation think are directed against their country. This development is becoming a source of new tension in Europe. Some other countries such as Turkey and the former republics of Yugoslavia, have been seeking the membership of the European Union. Turkey has already been a member country of NATO.

Some significant steps have been taken in the direction of integrating Europe into a single entity. Fifteen member countries of the European Union now have a common currency—the euro. In most member countries, there is free movement of people without any passport. A common institutional framework have also been developing. There is, for example, a European parliament which is composed of members elected from various countries comprising the European Union but their grouping in the parliament cut across the national boundaries. There is a European Court of Justice which can, on certain matters, hear complaints form individual citizens of member countries of the European Union. On some issues concerning international relations, the European Union has developed a common position. But on various other issues, each country has adopted its own position. Britain, for example, has been a close ally of the US in the Iraq War while some other countries, such as France, have been totally opposed to the US invasion of Iraq, and Spain which had sent its troops to Iraq when the war broke out withdrew them when the country elected a Socialist government.

Eastern Europe

In the European countries which were liberated by Soviet troops, Communist parties and their supporters had established their exclusive control. These countries were allied to the Soviet Union as members of the Warsaw Pact. They were often described as 'satellites' of the Soviet Union. The latter frequently imposed its will, sometimes with the use of armed forces, on the communist parties and governments of these countries.

These countries did not receive the benefits of the European Recovery Programme and had to rely mostly on their own resources. The Soviet Union was in no position to provide the kind of massive aid which the US had given to Western Europe. The kind of socialism that was sought to be built in these countries was based on the Soviet model. The economies of these countries were closely linked with the Soviet economy and suffered from many ills of the latter. Most of these countries had been backward agricultural economies. Although the level of their economic development was not comparable to that of the advanced West European countries, the industrialisation of these countries was a significant development. The evils associated with the concentration of economic power in private hands were avoided and the hold of the old ruling classes and big landlords eliminated in these countries. .

A reference has already been made to the end of the rule of the communist parties in Eastern Europe. The events in the Soviet Union after 1985 had a direct impact on the political developments in these countries. In almost all these countries, communist rule came to an end between 1989 and 1991.

Romania and Albania

Two of these countries—Romania and Albania—had freed themselves of Soviet control in the 1960s following the split between the Soviet Union and China. Albania had also withdrawn from the Warsaw Pact. However, there was no change in the exclusive control of the communist parties in these countries. In fact, the communist rule in these countries can be said to have been more authoritarian than in most other countries of Eastern Europe. In December 1989 there was a popular upsurge in Romania against the government which was headed by Nikolai Ceausescu. Many army units also came out against the government. Ceausescu and his wife were captured, tried and executed. A coalition government came to power after the elections. In Albania, the communist rule came to an end in 1992.

Poland, Hungary and Czechoslovakia

In Poland, the movement against the Communist Party was led by an organisation called Solidarity. In 1989, an agreement was reached between Solidarity and the communist government. After the free elections, a non-communist became the Prime Minister of Poland. In Hunguary there was a revolt in 1956 which was crushed by Soviet troops. In 1990, free elections were held and a non-communist government was formed there. In Czechoslovakia, after the armed intervention by Warsaw Pact countries in 1968, the Communist Party had removed Alexander Dubcek who had started introducing political and economic reforms. In December 1989, following mass demonstrations and strikes, the dominant role of the Communist Party came to an end. An eminent Czech writer, Vaclav Havel, became the President of Czechoslovakia. The country had emerged as an independent state in 1918. Since 1968, she had been a Federal Republic comprising Czech Republic and Slovak Republic. Following the end of the communist rule, the two republics decided to form two separate independent states. The Czech Republic and the Slovak Republic came into being in 1993.

East Germany

The end of the division of Germany has been discussed in the previous chapter. This was the result of a series of developments which began in 1989. There was change in the leadership of the Socialist Unity Party, in the ruling party of the German Democratic Republic (GDR), and in the government in 1989. In November 1989 the new leaders of East Germany (GDR) announced the opening of the Berlin Wall. Soon after, political parties and organisations which were not controlled by the ruling party of East Germany began to function freely. Early in 1990, the East German government made it known that it was in favour of unification of Germany. Talks were held between the governments of East Germany and West Germany and on 3 October 1990, after which Germany became a unified state. A new coalition government came to power in unified Germany after country-wide elections in December 1990.

Immediate Problems

The end of the communist regimes in Europe, and the speed with which it came about, is one of the most important developments since 1989. What has been remarkable in this development is that it took place, except in the case of Romania, more or less in a peaceful manner. However, the change-over has not been without problems. In some countries, the collapse of the highly centralised economies has not been followed by significant economic development based on free enterprise. In some countries, there has been some aggravation of immediate economic problems. In the former East Germany, the change-over had led to the collapse of many industrial enterprises which led to increased unemployment. The communist parties in most of these countries were reorganised as democratic socialist parties. In some countries, they have become a powerful force, winning majority support in the elections.

The move towards European unity and the formation of the European Union have been mentioned earlier. It may be remembered that the concept of United Europe is no longer confined to the countries of Western Europe.

Break-up of Yugoslavia

A major development in recent years has been the break-up of Yugoslavia and the tragic violence that has accompanied it. It may be recalled that Yugoslavia emerged as an independent state at the end of the First World War. During the Second World War, the people of Yugoslavia had waged a heroic war of resistance against the Nazi occupation. She became a federation of six republics after the Second World War. Though ruled by the communist party, she had rejected Soviet control. Josip Broz Tito, who had led the Yugoslav resistance against Nazi occupation and subsequently headed the government of Yugoslavia was, along with Jawaharlal Nehru, Nasser and Sukarno, the pioneer of the Non-Aligned Movement. At the end of the 1980s, as in other communist-ruled states in Europe, there was a demand for ending the control of the communist party. By early 1990, non-communist governments had come to power in most of the republics of Yugoslavia.

In the meantime, many republics had started demanding independence. By early 1992, Croatia, Slovenia, Macedonia and

Bosnia-Herzegovina had declared their independence, and Serbia and Montenegro together formed the new state of Yugoslavia.

The declaration of independence by Bosnia-Herzegovina was been followed by terrible violence in which thousands of people have been killed. This republic is inhabited by Serbians, Croats and Muslims. The Bosnian Serbs, supported by Serbia, controlled a large part of Bosnian territory. The various ethnic groups were hostile to the idea of a multicultural independent state of Bosnia-Herzegovina. A bloody war has been going on since 1992 between Bosnian Serbs and Bosnian Muslims in spite of the presence of the UN Peace Force. The war was characterised by what came to be called as a war for "ethnic cleansing". It is an obnoxious term which has been used to justify the extermination of one ethnic group by another.

The ethnic conflict that led to the break-up of Yugoslavia were encouraged by the US and some countries of Europe with tragic consequences for the population. The US-led NATO troops conducted horrible reads on Serbia. Many hundreds and thousands

STATES OF FORMER YUGOSLAVIA

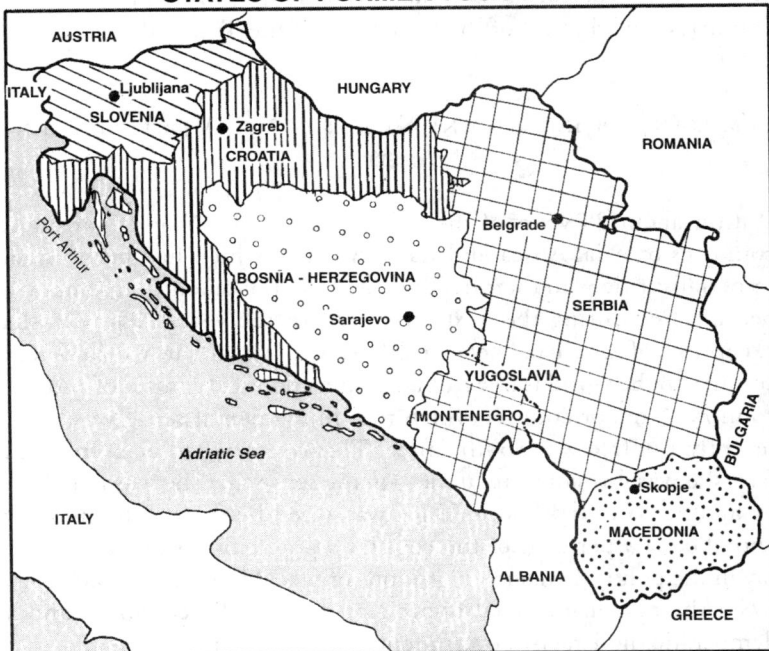

of people were displaced from their homeland and thousands were killed and their homes burned down. By 2000 Serbia and Montenegro remained as the successor states of Yugoslavia. In 2006, Montenegro also became independent. Kosovo was an autonomous province of Serbia. The ethnic Albanians had set their army and thousands of Serbs had to leave their homes. There was a NATO-led peace keeping force which was suppose to help preserve the autonomy of Kosovo as a province of Serbia. However, early in 2008, the ethnic Albanian-led government declared Kosovo's independence which was soon recognised by the US and some countries of Europe. This has added to the tensions between the countries that supported Kosovo's independence and various others, notably Russia and China, who were opposed to it. Earlier in 2001, the pro-Western government of Serbia had handed over Milosevic, the former President of Yugoslavia, to the UN War Crime Tribunal, to stand trial for the crimes alleged to have been committed by him during the war in Bosnia. The trial had gone on for five years, when in 2006 he was found dead in his cell as a prisoner. Recently, in July 2008 Karadzik, a leader of the Kosovo Serbs, has been extradited to the Hague to stand trial. Some countries are sceptical of the legitimacy of the Tribunal.

EMERGENCE OF INDEPENDENT NATIONS IN ASIA, AFRICA AND LATIN AMERICA

Within about 25 years of the end of the Second World War, most countries of Asia, Africa and Latin America which had been under imperialist rule won their freedom. Most of the others that remained became free during the next few years. In the year 1995, with the exception of small pockets in different parts of the world, every country in the world is free from the direct political control of another country. A major country which in a fundamental sense was, until recently, not free was South Africa. This country had been free—in fact, she was formally a republic—in the sense that she was not ruled by another country. South Africa was ruled by the White minority and about 80 per cent of the country's population was denied any say in the political system on grounds of race. However, by early May 1994, the system of racial oppression had finally collapsed and a democratic, non-racist government came into being.

Another country where a somewhat different system of oppressive rule had been imposed was Palestine. In this country, a 'Jewish' state, Israel, was set up by people, most of whom had come there from other parts of the world, mainly from Europe. After establishing their rule, they had displaced the inhabitants of the country and those Palestinians who continued to live in the territories occupied by Israel were subjected to colonial type rule. During the mid-1990s, some steps were agreed to which were expected to lead to the creation of a Palestinian state. However, the hopes aroused in the 1990s have come to a nought.

With the ending of the system of White rule in South Africa and the creation, when it happens, of an independent state of Palestine almost the entire world will become free.

During the twentieth century both the continents of Asia and Africa witnessed the rise of nationalism and the growth of nationalist movements. These nationalist movements played an important role during the Second World War and the defeat of Axis Powers. The Second World War had been viewed everywhere as a war to defend freedom and democracy. It had strengthened the forces of the freedom movements in countries which were under colonial rule of the allied power fighting fascist aggressions. Even in colonial countries which were occupied by the Axis Powers, there occurred movements for freedom and independence. In Asia, for example, the British rule over India had continued, but in many other countries, the British, the French and the Dutch had been ousted by the Japanese. (In the case of French colonies, formally the ruling power continued to be Vichy France.) In all these countries, nationalist movements had grown powerful during the war and there was a wave of anti-imperialist upsurge in all these countries. When the war ended the old imperialist powers tried to re-establish their rule over their colonies, but were met with strong resistance, and in some cases armed resistence. Some of the conflicts between the imperialist countries and the nationalist movements became ttransformed into Cold War conflicts, with the US coming in support of the imperialist powers. In many parts of Africa where nationalism had begun to emerge during the inter-war period, powerful nationalist movements took shape after the war.

Weakening of Imperialism

Many other factors helped in speeding up the collapse of imperialism after the war. The Second World War had, besides destroying fascism, weakened the imperialist countries of Europe. Many of these countries were themselves victims of fascist aggressions. For example, three imperialist countries of Europe—France, Belgium and Holland (the Netherlands)—themselves had been under German occupation during the war. Their military power as well as economies had been shattered during the war. Britain, which had the biggest empire, had also emerged from the war with a shattered economy. None of these countries was a great power any more. In their place the greatest powers in the world now were USA and the Soviet Union. The setting up of socialist governments in Eastern Europe under the rule of the communist parties also was a factor which weakened the power of the imperialist countries. They were no longer in a position to sustain a protracted colonial war. The countries which carried long colonial wars faced serious internal problems. For example, France's colonial war in Indo-China and Algeria created serious political crises in France which at one time threatened her political system. The colonial wars waged by Portugal in Africa were a major factor in the downfall of the Portuguese dictatorship.

In the changed political climate, imperialism was no longer considered a mark of a 'superior' civilisation. On the contrary, it was now associated in the minds of the people everywhere, including the colonial countries, with brute force, injustice and exploitation, and was considered inhuman and immoral. The dominant ideas in the world after 1945 were ideas of self-determination, national sovereignty, equality and cooperation between states. Thus, the efforts to maintain colonial rule were no longer popular with the people even of the imperialist countries. The colonial wars waged by France were opposed by vast sections of the French people. Some of the biggest anti-government demonstrations in Britain were seen in 1956 when Britain, along with France and Israel, invaded Egypt.

The imperialists now put forward other reasons for holding on to their colonies. They started saying that their control on the colonies is important in order to prepare the people in the colonies for peaceful transition to independence, prevent fratricidal and tribal wars, safeguard the interests of the minorities, resist terrorism and communism, educate the people of the colonies for a democratic system of governance, etc.

Most scholars also hold the view that the cost of maintaining their control over the colonies had become too high for the colonial countries to afford. It was also no longer necessary to establish direct political control over a country in order to exploit its economy.

Solidarity of the Anti-Imperialist Movements

An important factor which strengthened movements for freedom was the growth of solidarity among the freedom movements of different countries. Each country's freedom movement supported the freedom struggles in other countries. In India, for example, mass demonstrations were held in 1946 in support of the independence of Indonesia and Indo-China, and against the Indian troops who were being sent by British colonial rulers of India to restore the Dutch and the French rule in Indonesia and Indo-China respectively.

This solidarity played a crucial role as countries gained independence. As a country became independent, she actively aided the independence movements in other countries. The forums of the Commonwealth and, much more importantly, of the United Nations, were used by the newly independent countries to support the cause of the countries still under foreign rule.

Anti-colonialism and anti-imperialism were among the most important objectives of the Non-Aligned Movement. It pursued these objectives by extending support to the movements of national independence in the colonies. It is not surprising that the South West Africa People's Organisation (SWAPO) which led Namibia's struggle for independence was a member of the Non-Aligned Movement since long before Namibia became independent in 1990. The Palestine Liberation Organisation (PLO) became a member of the Non-Aligned Movement in 1976.

The independent states of Africa have played a crucial role in strengthening the struggles for freedom in Africa. In 1963, they set up the Organisation of African Unity (OAU) with "the eradication of all forms of colonialism from the continent of Africa" as one of its purposes. The freedom movements also received the support of the Soviet Union and other socialist countries.

ASIAN COUNTRIES WIN INDEPENDENCE

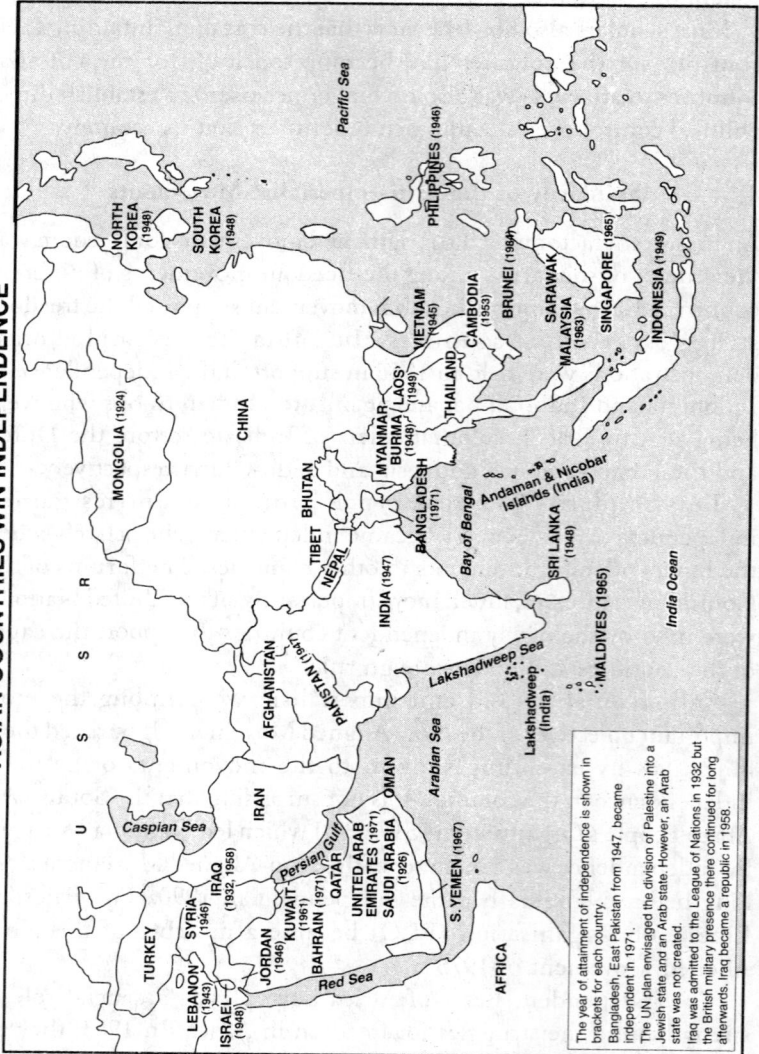

U   S   S   R

MONGOLIA (1924)

NORTH KOREA (1948)

SOUTH KOREA (1948)

CHINA

Pacific Sea

PHILIPPINES (1946)

BRUNEI (1984)

SARAWAK

SINGAPORE (1965)

MALAYSIA (1963)

INDONESIA (1949)

VIETNAM (1945)

CAMBODIA (1953)

MYANMAR BURMA (1948)

LAOS (1949)

THAILAND

Caspian Sea

IRAN

AFGHANISTAN

TIBET   BHUTAN

NEPAL

PAKISTAN (1947)

INDIA (1947)

BANGLADESH (1971)

Bay of Bengal

Andaman & Nicobar Islands (India)

SRI LANKA (1948)

India Ocean

MALDIVES (1965)

Lakshadweep Sea

Lakshadweep (India)

Arabian Sea

OMAN

S. YEMEN (1967)

SAUDI ARABIA (1926)

UNITED ARAB EMIRATES (1971)

QATAR

BAHRAIN (1971)

KUWAIT (1961)

JORDAN (1946)

IRAQ (1932, 1958)

SYRIA (1946)

TURKEY

LEBANON (1943)

ISRAEL (1948)

Red Sea

AFRICA

Persian Gulf

The year of attainment of independence is shown in brackets for each country.
Bangladesh, East Pakistan from 1947, became independent in 1971.
The UN plan envisaged the division of Palestine into a Jewish state and an Arab state. However, an Arab state was not created.
Iraq was admitted to the League of Nations in 1932 but the British military presence there continued for long afterwards. Iraq became a republic in 1958.

Role of the Untied Nations

The United Nations also has been a major force in promoting the process which has brought about the ending of colonialism. The United Nations Charter and the Universal Declaration of Human Rights symbolise the universal aspirations of the international community. The question of colonies was taken up by the United Nations from the very beginning of its foundation. As the number of former colonies joining the United Nations, the question of ending colonialism received great importance in the United Nations and it played an increasingly active role in facilitating the achievement of independence by the colonies. Its role was crucial in bringing about the independence of Nambia.

India's Role

One of the first countries to achieve independence after the Second World War was India. Though the British rulers had succeeded in partitioning the country, India's independence was of great historic importance. India's freedom movement had been a source of inspiration to freedom movements in all colonial countries of Asia and Africa. Even before independence, the leaders of India's freedom movement had brought together the leaders of many Asian countries on a common platform at the Asian Relations Conference which they organised. This conference symbolised the emergence of Asia as a new factor in the world. Independent India became a source of strength to all peoples fighting for their independence.

SOUTH-EAST ASIAN COUNTRIES ACHIEVE INDEPENDENCE

Early in 1948, Burma (now Myanmar) on 4 January and Ceylon (now Sri Lanka) on 4 February, became independent. Malaya, which had been reoccupied by the British troops in 1945 after the defeat of Japan, became independent in 1957. In 1963 she, along with Sabah (formerly north Borneo), Sarawak and Singapore formed the Malaysian Federation. However, in 1965, Singapore declared herself a separate independent state.

In Indonesia, soon after the surrender of Japan, the Republic of Indonesia had been proclaimed by the nationalists. However, the

Dutch, supported by British troops, came back to re-establish their rule and a war followed. The war ended in 1949 and on 27 December that year, Indonesia became independent.

The war in Vietnam, which ended in the defeat of France and the US, has been referred to earlier. It ended on 30 April 1975 when Saigon, the capital of the US-sponsored regime in South Vietnam, was liberated. In 1976 Vietnam was united. Saigon was renamed Ho Chi Minh city, after the great leader of the Vietnamese people who had launched the freedom movement in Vietnam and had led it till his death in 1969.

Laos, one of the three countries comprising Indo-China, had proclaimed her independence in 1945. However, first French and later US intervention in Laos continued. The US intervention in Laos was ended in 1973.

In Cambodia, the third country of Indo-China, also, the French returned after the defeat of Japan. The French finally left in 1953 and Cambodia became independent. In 1970, the US installed a puppet government there and the US war in Vietnam was extended to Cambodia. The pro-US government was overthrown in 1975. However, a barbarous government came to power in Cambodia. This government was formed by Khmer Rouge, a communist group of Cambodia. It was headed by Pol Pot. It followed a policy of genocide against its own people. It is estimated that between one to three million Cambodians were killed by this government. This barbarous government was overthrown with the help of Vietnamese troops in 1979.

The conflict in Cambodia continued for many years. There were three main political groups—the Khmer Rouge, the group led by Prince Sihanouk whose government had been overthrown in 1970 with US support, and the group which formed the government after Pol Pot's government was overthrown with the help of Vietnamese troops. The Khmer Rouge had continued the war against the Vietnamese-supported government from the territories it controlled inside the country, and from across the border. In 1989, the Vietnamese troops were withdrawn from Cambodia. In 1991, the three opposing groups were brought together and an agreement was signed under the auspices of the United Nations. In 1993, elections were held in Cambodia and a coalition government was formed. The Khmer

Rouge, however, refused to join the government and continued its policy of war. Its war activities did not last very long. Most of its leaders were captured and tried for the crimes they have committed against their worn people.

NATIONALIST STRUGGLES IN THE ARAB COUNTRIES

During the twentieth century there was a rise of Arab nationalism in a few Arab countries. Lebanon, a mandate of France, had been formally made a separate state by the French. During the war, the French authorities in Lebanon were allied with Vichy France but had been ousted and the country was occupied by Free French forces. In November 1943, the independence of Lebanon was recognised, though the French troops continued to stay there till 1946. Since the 1950s, Lebanon has seen many turmoil and political instability. Besides the violent clashes and civil wars between different Lebanese groups, the country has been devastated by frequent air raids by Israel.

In Syria, there was an uprising against the French who were supported by the British. On 17 April 1946, Syria became independent and the French troops were withdrawn. In Egypt, the monarchy was overthrown when a group of military officers led by General Neguib and Colonel Gamal Abdel Nasser seized power in 1952. The new government asked for the withdrawal of British troops which were stationed in the Suez Canal zone in Egypt. In July 1956, the British troops left but in October 1956, British and French troops invaded Egypt, along with the Israeli troops. They were soon forced to withdraw. Nasser became the leading figure of Arab nationalism. He was also one of the founders of the Non-Aligned Movement. From 1958 to 1961, Syria and Egypt were joined together as one state called the United Arab Republic. There was also a revolution in Iraq which overthrew the pro-British government and the monarchy.

Kuwait had come under British control at the end of the nineteenth century. Her vast oil resources were controlled by British and US oil companies. On 19 June 1967, Kuwait became a fully sovereign state. North Yemen had become an independent state after the destruction of the Ottoman empire but in South Yemen, the British had consolidated their rule. The city of Aden had been made a part of British India, but had become a separate colony in 1937. It was made a part of the new state of South Arabia which the British had created. In 1963, an armed revolt began in South Yemen. In November 1967, South Yemen became an independent state and the British troops left the country. The two Yemens were unified in 1990.

In Tunisia and Morocco, French rule came to an end in 1956. Libya had come under Italian rule and, during the war many important battles were fought there between the German and the Allied troops. The country was later occupied by British and French troops. She became an independent monarchy on 24 December 1951. !n 1969, the monarchy was overthrown and Libya became a republic.

After the end of the Second World War, the Arab League, comprising the Arab states, was formed. For many years, the Arab League played a very important role in bringing the Arab states together, in promoting Arab nationalism and strengthening the self independent role of Arab states in world politics.

One of the main concerns of all Arabs has been the question of Palestine where with the support of the US and some other Western contries, the state of Israel was created and sustained and the formation of an independent Palestinian state prevented. The Arab nationalists looked upon Israel as an outpost of imperialism in their territories. In 1964, the Palestine Liberation Organisation (PLO) which, under the leadership of Yasser Arafat, has been carrying on the struggle for the creation of an independent state of Palestine, was set up. Subsequently, the PLO proclaimed the setting up of a government of Palestine which was recognised by many countries.

The creation of an independent state of Palestine comprising West Bank and Gaza Strip depends on the vacation by Israel of the territories occupied by Israel. In the 1990s, after what are known as the Oslo Agreements between Israel and Palestine Liberation Organisation (PLO), possibilities for the creation of an independent state of Palestine and the establishment of peace in the region were opened up. The Palestine Liberation Organisation which led the struggle for the creation of an independent state of Palestine formed the Palestinian Authority in 1994 to administer West Bank, excluding areas that remained under Israeli occupation, and Gaza Strip, with its capital at Ramallah. Security functions in the rural areas under Palestinian Authority also remained under Israeli control. Thus, the power which the authority was permitted to enjoy was mainly what may be described as municipal powers. It may be mentioned in this context that even these agreements were not to the liking of the right-wing forces in Israel. In 1994, Israeli Prime Minister Yitzhak Rabin was given the Nobel Peace Prize, along with Yasser Arafat and Shimon Peres, then foreign minister of Israel, for his role in starting the peace process of which the Oslo Agreements were viewed as a major strp. In 1995, Rabin was assassinated by an Israeli.

The Palestinian Authority was visualised as an interim body for five years during which period negotiations for settling the status of Palestine as an independent state were to take place. Yasser Arafat, the most important leader of the Palestinian people, headed the Palestinian Authority from 1994 till his death in 2004. He was succeeded by Mahmoud Abbas. However, no progress was achieved for the creation of an independent state of Palestine. Israel has refused to vacate large parts of West Bank with Israeli settlements; Israeli settlements in the West Bank, in fact, have been expanding while restrictions are imposed on the movement of Palestinians. It withdrew from Gaza Strip in 2005. However, being in control of water the air space and all passages, Gaza Strip also remains a virtually occupied territory. There have been frequent bombings of areas that are under the formal control of the Palestinian Authority, inflicting heavy casualties and damage to the Palestinian infrastructure. The Israeli position on the status of Jerusalem is another stumbling block to any peaceful settlement. An independent Palestine state had been declared in 1988. It is recognised by over hundred countries. However, this remains as no more than symbolic. A new factor has been the rise of a new organisation, the Hamas, which has been gaining in popularity. It has emerged as the leading force among Palestinians. It presently controls the Gaza Strip. The hopes aroused by the Oslo Agreements fifteen years ago have been belied. The cause of Palestinian independence is the most important issue for the Arabs. It is supported by most countries. Its solution is central to the ending of tensions in West Asia. The continuing injustice done to Palestinian is seen as a factor which is used by Islamic terrorists to legitimise their activities. For the US, to pursue its policies in the region, Israel is its staunchest ally. Israel is believed to be in possession of nuclear weapons and has adopted threatening postures, along with the US, towards Iran. This has further added to the tension in the region.

ALGERIA'S STRUGGLE FOR FREEDOM

One of the longest struggles for freedom was launched in Algeria. The French occupation of Algeria had begun in 1830. After the Second World War, France was engaged in a protracted colonial war to retain her rule over Algeria. Unlike other French colonies, a large number of French *colons* (settlers) had settled in Algeria. In 1960, they numbered about a million. They controlled most of the economy and the administration of Algeria and were determined to hold on to their domination even when the people and government of France favoured a settlement. The situation was comparable to some other colonies, such as South Africa and Southern Rhodesia, where White settlers were for long totally opposed to any settlement which would end their domination. In 1954, the nationalist movement in Algeria gave a call for a popular uprising. Soon after, a full-scale war of national liberation began. The National Liberation Front (FLN) of Algeria set up its own liberation army which had its regular armed troops as well as guerrilla units. The French army in Algeria now numbered over 800,000 soldiers who resorted to large-scale atrocities and tortures. The FLN set up its Provisional Government which was recognised by many countries.

In 1958, a revolt by the French settlers and the French army in Algeria led to the overthrow of the Fourth Republic, as the French government since 1946 was called. General de Gaulle came to power in France and a new constitution creating the Fifth Republic came in force. The French settlers and the army in Algeria had hoped that the new government would support the war to maintain French rule in Algeria. However, when they discovered that de Gaulle favoured a settlement with the Algerians, they organised unsuccessful revolts. In March 1962, de Gaulle's government opened negotiations with the FLN which led to a ceasefire in Algeria. An agreement was also reached on Algeria's independence and the complete withdrawal of French forces from Algeria. A referendum was held in France on the question of Algerian independence in April 1962 and the French people voted overwhelmingly in favour of Algeria's independence. In a similar referendum held on 1 July 1962, 99 per cent of the people in Algeria voted in favour of complete independence. On 3 July 1962,

Algeria's independence was recognised by France. About 1,500,000 Algerians had been killed by the French troops in the war of national liberation.

FREEDOM MOVEMENTS IN SOUTHERN AFRICA

Ghana and Guinea

Just after the end of the Second World War, nationalist organisations were formed in almost all countries of southern Africa (sub-Saharan Africa). The imperialist countries had realised that they would not be able to hold on to Africa for long. The first country to gain independence in southern Africa was Ghana (formerly Gold Coast). The struggle for freedom in Ghana was led by Kwame Nkrumah. He was an outstanding leader of African nationalism and played an important role in uniting the African people for freedom as well as for asserting their national sovereignty and independent role in world affairs. In 1949, he fromed the Convention People's Party. In 1956, this party won more than 70 per cent seats in the elections and on 6 March 1957 Ghana became independent. In 1958, Guinea became the first French colony in southern Africa to become independent.

The Africa Year

In 1960, 17 countries of Africa became independent. This has given that year the title of the 'Africa Year'. Out of them, 13 had been French colonies. These 17 countries were Mauritania, Mali, Niger, Chad, Senegal, Ivory Coast, Upper Volta (now Burkina Faso), Nigeria, Togo, Benin, Cameroon, Gabon, Congo (formerly French), Democratic Republic of Congo (formerly Belgian Congo, it was renamed Zaire until 1997), Central African Republic, Somalia and Madagascar. The wave of anti-imperialism that engulfed Africa in 1960 influenced even the British Prime Minister Harold Macmillan. During a tour of British colonies in Africa in March 1960, he spoke about the wind of change which was blowing throughout the continent and said, "whether we like it or not this growth of national consciousness is a political fact and our national policies must take account of it".

The Struggle in Kenya

British imperialism had long been trying to prevent this 'wind of change' from blowing. In Kenya the nationalist movement had been launched in the 1920s and one of its leaders who emerged into prominence was Jomo Kenyatta. In 1943, was formed the Kenya Africa Union which later became the Kenya African National Union which, besides Jomo Kenyatta, was led by Odinga Oginga. In 1952, the Mau Mau rebellion broke out in Kenya. This rebellion was mainly a peasant rebellion of the Kikuyu tribe whose lands had been taken away by the British colonial authorities. Some Western writers have described Mau Mau rebels as terrorists who committed inhuman atrocities. The British suppressed the rebellion with the use of brute force, killing about 15,000 Kenyans. In 1953, Kenyatta was arrested and sentenced to seven years' imprisonment on the charge of leading the Mau Mau rebellion. The British were compelled to end their repression which had won them world-wide condemnation. In 1961, Kenyatta was freed. On 12 December 1964, Kenya became a republic with Jomo Kenyatta as its first President.

End of Colonial Rule in Africa

Most of the remaining British colonies in Africa became independent in the 1960s. These included Tanzania (formerly Tanganyika and Zanzibar) and Sierra Leone in 1961, Uganda in 1962, Zambia (formerly Northern Rhodesia) and Malawi (formerly Nyasaland) in 1964, Gambia in 1965, and Botswana, Swaziland and Lesotho in 1968. Ruanda (present Rwanda) and Burundi which had been under Belgian rule since the end of the First World War became independent in 1962. By the end of the 1960s, most countries of Africa had become free. The countries where the struggle for independence continued beyond the 1960s was the Portuguese colonies of Angola, Mozambique, Guinea Bissau and Cape Verde Islands. All these countries became free in the 1970s. Namibia (South West Africa) which had been ruled as a colony by South Africa since the end of the First World War became independent on 21 March 1990.

The World Since 1945

AFRICAN COUNTRIES ACHIEVE INDEPENDENCE

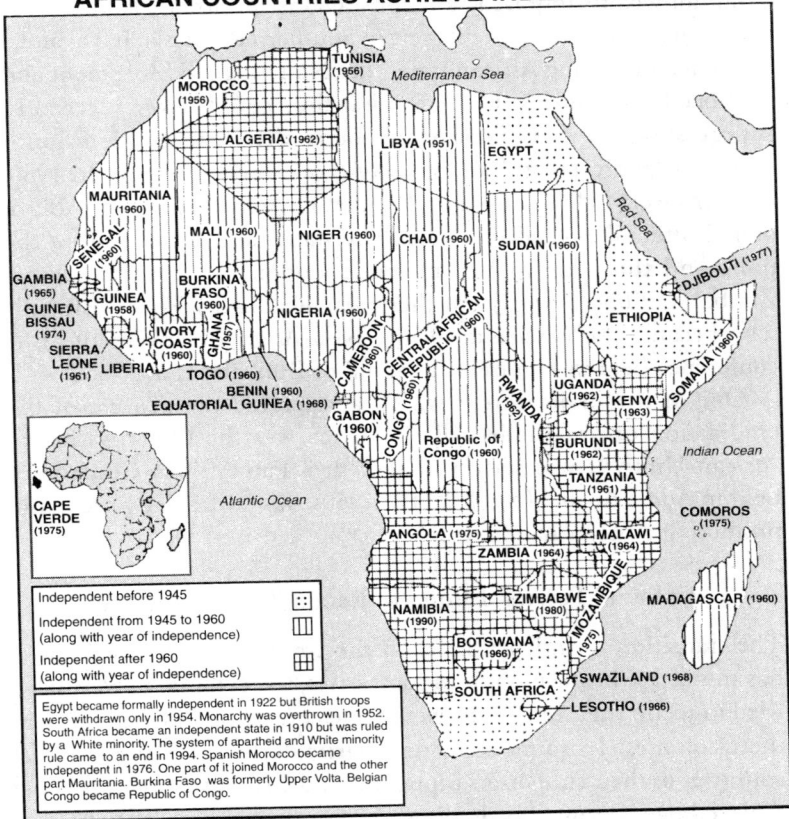

Independent before 1945

Independent from 1945 to 1960
(along with year of independence)

Independent after 1960
(along with year of independence)

Egypt became formally independent in 1922 but British troops were withdrawn only in 1954. Monarchy was overthrown in 1952. South Africa became an independent state in 1910 but was ruled by a White minority. The system of apartheid and White minority rule came to an end in 1994. Spanish Morocco became independent in 1976. One part of it joined Morocco and the other part Mauritania. Burkina Faso was formerly Upper Volta. Belgian Congo became Republic of Congo.

Zimbabwe

Another country which had to undergo a long period of struggle before she became independent was Zimbabwe (formerly Southern Rhodesia). She had been a British colony but the White settlers there, under the leadership of Ian Smith, captured power in 1965. They were alarmed at the prospect of the country being granted independence which would have meant Black majority rule. A White minority government was established there on the pattern of South Africa and with South African support and it declared what it called the Unilateral Declaration of Independence (UDI). Most countries of the world at the instance of the United Nations and the

Commonwealth imposed sanctions against Southern Rhodesia. A powerful guerrilla movement grew in Southern Rhodesia. It was aided by the neighbouring African states, the Non-Aligned Movement and the socialist countries. Realising that they could never succeed in suppressing the war of national independence, in spite of South Africa's support, the White minority government gave up. In 1980, elections were held in Southern Rhodesia in which everyone—Black and White alike—had one vote. The nationalist parties swept the polls and the country became independent with a new name, Zimbabwe. The government there was headed by Robert Mugabe who became the Chairman of the Non-Aligned Movement at its conference held in Harare, the capital of Zimbabwe, in 1986.

One of the major forces which accelerated the process of the eradication of imperialist rule in Africa was the Organisation of African Unity. It was set up in 1963 at a Pan-African Conference held in Addis Ababa. Its role in the 1960s was particularly crucial in promoting African nationalism.

Colonial Powers' Efforts to Retain Their Influence

The transition to independence in the countries mentioned above has in no case been smooth. In most cases, the colonial powers have tried to retain their influence even while conceding independence to their colonies. In some countries, particularly when the colonial countries or their supporters thought that the colonial rule was being replaced by governments dominated by radical leaders, they tried to intervene more directly.

Guyana

In 1953, under a new constitution, elections were held in British Guiana (now Guyana) in which the Progressive People's Party (PPP) won 18 of the 25 seats. The party, led by Dr Cheddi Jagan and Forbes Burnham, had been the main anti-imperialist party in Guyana and drew its support from all sections of the population, mainly people of Indian origin and Black people. Cheddi Jagan became the prime minister and he started implementing, a radical social and economic programme. However, after about four months the government was dismissed and the constitution suspended. British troops landed there and the leaders of the PPP—Jagan and Burnham—were arrested. All this was done in the name of 'repelling' communism. After that, the British fomented ethnic conflicts in Guyana and the PPP was split. In the 1957 elections, Dr Jagan's party again won and intensified the demand for independence. In the 1961 elections his party again won a majority, but the government was denied financial help and ethnic disturbances and violence were fomented. In the 1964 elections, Bumham's party—he had broken away from the PPP—polled less votes than the PPP but by allying with another party, he became the Prime Minister of Guyana. In 1966, Guyana became independent with Bumham as prime minister (and later as president). In the 1992 elections, Dr Chhedi Jagan was elected president.

Democratic Republic of Congo

In the Democratic Republic of Congo (formerly Zaire and much earlier called the Belgian Congo), the freedom movement was led by Patrice Lumumba who had set up the National Congolese Movement (MNC). On 30 June 1960, Congo became independent with Lumumba as the prime minister. However, soon after, the governor of the province of Katanga, supported by Western companies which controlled the vast mineral (copper) resources of the province, announced the secession of the province from Congo. A number of mercenaries were employed to support the secession. On the request of the government of Congo, United Nations troops were sent to Congo to end the secession and the foreign interventions. However, they failed to protect Lumumba, who was murdered. Later, however, they succeeded in ending the secession of Katanga. In 1965, Colonel Mobutu who headed the army of Congo captured power and became the president of the country, which was renamed Zaire. Lumumba was regarded as one of the greatest leaders of the nationalist resurgence in Africa and his murder, it is believed, had been planned by the US intelligence agency, CIA. Mobutu's authoritarian rule continued till 1997, when he was overthrown. In 1996, a genocidal war broke out between the Hutus and Tutsis in Rwanda, with Mobutu supporting the Hutus. Kabilas, who had the support of various opposition groups and of the Tutsis, overthrew Mobutu in 1997 and became the president. He had also secured the help of foreign companies by giving them rights over the country's natural resources. He was assassinated in 2001 and was succeeded by his son.

Similar efforts were made in Angola where a government led by Agostinho Neto was formed after independence. However, this government was sought to be overthrown by the US and South Africa aiding and arming rival groups of Angolans. The South African troops also entered Angolan territory and fought against the Angolan troops. Angola requested Cuba's help in resisting foreign invaders and attempts at destroying Angola's independence were thwarted. After many years, agreements were reached on the ending of foreign intervention in Angola and the withdrawal of Cuban troops from there.

South Africa: The Emergence as a Democratic Nation

The most vicious system of racial oppression was set up in South Africa. The system of racial segregation, called apartheid, was enforced in the country by the government of the White minority led by Daniel Malan, who came to power in 1948, and by the successive governments. The non-Whites, over 80 per cent of the population, were denied the right to vote, strikes were banned, Africans were deported from some specified areas, education was segregated, mixed marriages were declared illegal (and immoral) and all dissent was banned under what was called the Suppression of Communism Act. Some of the greatest works of world literature, and not just political writings, were banned under the Suppression of Communism Act. Strict restrictions were imposed on the movement of Africans and they were required to carry a pass permitting them to do so. South Africa left the Commonwealth when the policy of apartheid came under attack at the conference of the Prime Ministers of Commonwealth countries.

The system of apartheid created widespread revulsion everywhere and most contries banned all relations with South Africa. The United Nations called for the imposition of military and economic sanctions against South Africa and under pressure from world opinion and from their own people, the Western countries also began to apply these sanctions.

However, despite the condemnation of her policies, South Africa, for a long time, was not deterred from pursuing her inhuman policy with a brutality comparable only to that of the Nazis. In 1960, an anti-apartheid rally at Sharpeville was dispersed by resorting to brute force. Later, many other acts of brutal repression took place. By the early 1960s, most leaders of the anti-apartheid movement were arrested and sentenced to long terms of imprisonment. The others worked to overthrow the oppressive regime either from underground or from other countries.

The struggle against apartheid and the White minority rule was led for many decades by the African National Congress (ANC) which had been formed in 1912. In 1955, a Congress of the People was held which adopted "The Freedom Charter". This Charter laid down the basic objectives of the South African people's struggle. The Charter declared:

> We, the people of South Africa, declare for all our country and the world to know:
> that South Africa belongs to all who live in it, black and white, and that no government can justly claim authority unless it is based on the will of all the people:
> that our people have been robbed of their birthright to land, liberty and peace by a form of government founded on injustice and inequality;
> that our country will never be prosperous or free until all our people live in brotherhood, enjoying equal rights and opportunities;
> that only a democratic state, based on the will of all the people, can secure to all their birth right without distinction of colour, race, sex or belief;
> And therefore, we, the people of South Africa, black and white togehter —equals, countrymen and brothers—adopt this Freedom Charter. And we pledge ourselves to strive together, sparing neither strength nor courage, until the democratic changes here set out have been won.

The African National Congress had so far followed a policy of peaceful non-violent struggle. In the face of the brute force with which all peaceful protest was suppressed, it decided to launch an armed struggle. It trained its guerrillas and soldiers inside South Africa and in the independent states of Africa. Some of the prominent leaders of the ANC had been able to escape arrest. A powerful underground movement was built up and many daring acts of sabotage were committed. In its struggle the ANC received full support from the African states, the Non-Aligned Movement and the socialist countries in its struggle.

With her almost total isolation in the world and the growing strength of the struggle inside the country, the White rulers of South Africa were forced to open negotiations to end the policy of apartheid. Nelson Mandela, who was the vice-president of the ANC, was released from jail in 1990 after about 26 years. He had become the indomitable symbol of the struggle of the South African people. When he visited India in October 1990, he was given the honour of Head of State. He was also awarded the Jawaharlal Nehru Award for International Understanding. Nelson Mandela's release was followed by the lifting of ban on ANC and repeal of many apartheid laws. Subsequently, agreement was reached to put an end to the system of racial oppression and for holding democratic elections on the basis of one person one vote.

No event in recent history has been acclaimed the world over as much as the elections and the formation of a new government in South Africa. In April 1994, the first ever democratic elections were held in that country. The ANC swept the polls and in May 1994, Nelson Mandela became the president of the first non-racist democratic government of South Africa. This is known as the Government of National Unity (GNU) and almost every major political party of South Africa is represented in it. The emergence of a democratic South Africa can be truly considered a glorious event in recent world history. With this, the liberation of Africa was complete.

JAPAN

Japan was occupied by the US forces after her defeat in the war. A number of reforms were initiated in the political system of Japan and in the economy and society which laid the foundations of the post-war development of Japan. The power of the big landlords was broken. Workers' unions were given freedom to function. The educational system was reformed and its misuse for inculcating militaristic and chauvinistic values was prevented. In May 1947, a new constitution prepared mainly by the occupation authorities (the US), came into force. It introduced a democratic parliamentary form of government and universal adult franchise in Japan. Though the institution of monarchy was retained, the emperor was divested of all his powers and was viewed as just "the symbol of the state". The new Japanese constitution renounced war as a national policy. It also prohibited Japan from having a standing army or navy. In 1952, the US occupation of Japan was ended, though by a security pact she retained the right to station her troops in Japan.

The country has been almost throughout ruled by the conservative Liberal Democratic Party which, in spite of many cases of corruption involving the prime ministers of the country, has been generally returned to power. The second most popular party is the socialist party which advocates nationalisation of industry and wants the security pact with the US scrapped which has aligned Japan with the US. The Japanese Communist Party also has a substantial following. These two parties along with others are opposed to any revival of militarism in Japan. The security pact with the US provoked countrywide protests in Japan when it was renewed in 1960.

A number of small right-wing groups have emerged in recent years in Japan which advocated the revival of the greatness of Japan as a military power, and inculcation of the traditional values some of which are closely related to militarism.

Japan has, during the post-war decades, emerged as a great world economic power, challenging US supremacy in many areas of the economy. Her economic growth is often referred to as a 'miracle'. Lacking most of the natural resources herself, she has made tremendous advances in technology which has become her main asset. In many fields of manufacture requiring high technology, she has surpassed every other country in the world. As one of the economic 'giants' in the world today, she is closely allied with the most advanced capitalist economies of the West. In her foreign policy, she has generally followed the US. She started normalising her relations with China, formerly her main victim since her rise as a modern nation, in the early 1970s, and subsequently with the Soviet Union (and after her break-up, with Russia).

SOME IMPORTANT DEVELOPMENTS IN ASIA

A reference has been made to some developments within and between Asian countries in the context of the Cold War. It is necessary to mention a few other developments and events which are important in the history of the region.

Main Trends in Political Development

The political development of Asian countries since their emergence as independent nations has followed many different trajectories. While it may be said that the general direction of political developments in Asia has been towards the establishment of democratic systems, this has neither been smooth nor has it been without reversals. Not many countries in the region throughout the period since their independence have had a stable democratic political system. The Indian political system is among the few which has remained democratic throughout its history as an independent nation. In some countries, such as Pakistan, there has been military rule for long periods. Democracy was restored with the holding of elections there recently, after about ten years of rule by General Pervez Musharaf as president. Burma (renamed Myanmar in 1989) started as a political democracy in 1948 but came under one-party rule in the early 1960s, with the armed forces playing a dominant role. In May 1990, elections were held in Myanmar and the party led by Daw Aung Saun Suu Kyi, who had been put behind bars, swept the polls. However, no change was effected in the government even after the elections. Suu Kyi was awarded the Nobel Peace Prize in 1991 for being an 'important symbol in the struggle against repressions. She continued to be under house arrest for six years and was released in July 1995, only to be rearrested again. Almost all through the following years, she has been under house arrest and a few times in jail. In 2008, her house arrest was extended by another year. All efforts by the United Nations in recent years to secure her release have failed.

In some countries in the region, there has been frequent political turmoil, often accompanied by violence. The overthrow of monarchies in some countries has been referred to earlier. This has, however, not always led to the establishment of democratic regimes.

There has been growing secularisation of political and social life also been trends which are the reverse of secularism. In some countries, religion has been used as a basis of political activities and even of nationhood. An early example of such countries is Pakistan which was created on the basis of the Muslim League's claim that Muslims in India constituted a separate nation and, therefore, should have a separate state. In some parts of the region, religio-political movements, with the active participation of religious leaders, have arisen. These movements exercise, or seek to exercise, influence and even dominance on the state. They lay stress on the inviolability of their religious principles and advocate the view that these principles should form the fundamental basis of state policy in all spheres. Their conception of religion is often highly dogmatic and obscurantist. Some of them do not hesitate to use terrorist methods against those who do not agree with them and for gaining their ends. These movements are often referred to as movements of religious fundamentalism.

There are also powerful socialist and communist movements in some countries of Asia. In three Asian countries—China, North Korea, and Vietnam—communist parties have been the ruling parties in their respective countries. In Mongolia, which adopted a parliamentary system of government, the former communist party is a major political force.

Developments in China

The victory of the Communist Party of China in the civil war and the proclamation of the People's Republic of China on 1 October 1949 have already been referred to. The communist victory in the most populous country in the world was considered a world-shaking event. During the first few years of its rule, the Communist Party carried out radical land reforms and launched programmes for industrialisation. She received economic, technical and military aid from the Soviet Union with whom she had entered into an Alliance. China also developed close relations with India. The two countries entered into an agreement in 1954 according to which Chinese suzerainty over Tibet was recognised by India and China reaffirmed the status of Tibet as an autonomous region. The five principles of peaceful coexistence, known as "Panchsheel", were also a part of this agreement.

From the late 1950s, Chinese policies began to change. A reference has been made to the emphasis laid on peaceful coexistence by the Soviet leadership after the death of Stalin. The Chinese Communist Party, under the leadership of Mao Zedong, opposed this and the relations between the two countries began to deteriorate. By the early 1960s, the split between them was complete. The Sino-Soviet split led to splits in many communist parties the world over. The Chinese started incursions into Indian territory in the late 1950s. The Chinese policy in Tibet also changed and in 1959 the Dalai Lama and thousands of his followers had to flee to India where they have lived ever since as refugees. In 1962, there was a border war between India and China when the latter invaded Ladakh in the north-west and Arunachal Pradesh in the north-east. In her internal policies, this period is known for what was called the Great Leap Forward. It aimed at accelerating the growth of economy. This was also the period when the growth of the personality cult of Mao Zedong began. His thought was extolled for its invincibility.

The period from 1966 to 1969 was called the Cultural Revolution. There was political turmoil in China during this period. In the name of continuing the revolution, thousands of people were disgraced and removed from their jobs by mobs of students and Red Guards. Centres for higher education were closed down and severe restrictions imposed on literary and cultural activities. China's economic life was seriously disrupted. In the early 1970s China was admitted to the United Nations. Her relations with the United States also improved. By then, China had become a nuclear power.

Mao Zedong's death in 1976 was followed by a fierce power struggle in China. By 1980, Deng Xiaoping had become the most important leader in China.

From the late 1970s, vast changes began to take place in China in every sphere. The damage done to the economy, political system, education and cultural life during the Cultural Revolution and its aftermath was undone. Her relations with the Soviet Union were normalised and there was a significant improvement in her relations with India. There were significant advances in her economic life and there was an amazing acceleration in the growth of the Chinese economy, particularly from the 1990s. For many years, the annual growth rate has been about 11 per cent. During the recent years, the economy of Chinese has been the fastest growing economy in the world and has become the fourth largest economy in the world. The economic policies and the 'economic reforms' that China has pursued during this period mark a sharp departure from the kind of policies that were followed earlier in the name of building socialism. There was not only the beginning and increasing spread of private (capitalist) enterprises but also massive foreign investments. Officially the new system is described as 'market socialism'. Along with economic growth, inequalities in society have also grown giving rise to new tensions. The disparities in the living standards of the rural and urban populations have been particularly marked.

A major significant event has been the transfer of Hong Kong to China by Britain which came into effect in 1997. It may be recalled that Hong Kong which was a part of China had become a British colony in 1842 after the First Opium War. In course of time, it had become a leading financial capital of the world. It became a part of China as a Special Administrative Region retaining a great deal of internal autonomy as well as its character as an advanced capitalist economy. Hong Kong becoming a part of China while retaining its autonomy and capitalist system, is described as 'one country, two systems'.

It may be noted that while vast changes of a basic nature have taken place in the economic policies of the country, China's political system continues to be under the exclusive control of the Communist Party of China. While the kind of regimentation which characterised China's political and cultural life for many years has come to an end, there has been little progress in the direction of political democracy. In the late 1980s, there was widespread upsurge for democratic rights in Beijing and some other major cities of China. It began with protest demonstrations by students in April 1989 in Beijing with Tiananmen Square in the city becoming as the rallying centre of what was described as the Democracy Movement. There were massive demonstrations in Beijing in May 1989 by students, who were joined by others, with hundreds of students going on hunger strike. To clear the Tiananmen Square of the demonstrators, the troops of the PLA (China's army known as the People's Liberation Army) were brought in on 3 June who resorted to indiscriminate firing. On 4 June, the Square was cleared of demonstrators and the movement was crushed.

According to foreign media and observers, several thousand people were killed in the Tiananmen Square and elsewhere in the city. There has been little change in the country's political system since the events of 1989. By the early years of the twenty-first century, however, China had emerged as one of the most powerful countries of the world.

Conflicts and Wars

There have been many other conflicts and wars between Asian countries after 1945. In most of these the two major superpowers of the world were not directly involved. There have been three wars between India and Pakistan. The first war took place in 1947 soon after the two countries became independent. After Jammu and Kashmir had acceded to India, the invasion of Kashmir launched from and with the support of Pakistan was halted by Indian troops. In 1965, there was another war when Pakistan sent her infiltrators into Kashmir. The third war took place in 1971 over the question of Bangladesh which will be referred to separately. In the 1980s, relations between the two countries were strained because of the aid which Pakistan gave to terrorists in Punjab.

Since the late 1980s, a major issue of conflict between the two countries has been the Pakistani support to the secessionist elements in Jammu and Kashmir, particularly Pakistan's training and arming of terrorist groups operating in Kashmir. Though there have been talks between the leaders of the two countries with both countries committing themselves to resolving the Kashmir issue through negotiations, the infiltration of armed groups trained in camps located in Pakistan, particularly in territories of Kashmir which are under Pakistan occupation [POK], into Jammu and Kashmir across the Line of Control has not ceased. In 1998, war broke out between the two countries in the Kargil region of Kashmir. There had been large scale infiltration by Pakistani soldiers in this mountainous region in May 1998. Indian armed forces, including the air force, succeeded in defeating the Pakistani forces and inflicting heavy casualties on them. The war ended in July 1998, with most countries blaming Pakistan for violating the Line of Control [LOC]. The war remained confined to the Kargil area and did not lead to a general war between the two countries. In 1999, Pervez Musharaf, chief of Pakistan's army, overthrew the civilian government and became the President of Pakistan. In 2001, there was a summit meeting between him and Indian Prime Minister at Agra but it ended without any formal agreement between the two countries. Pervez Musharaf had to resign as president in 2008 after the elections in Pakistan. The elections had been preceded by the assassination of Benazeer Bhutto who had been Pakistan's prime minister twice and had led the movement for the restoration of democracy in the country along with other political parties and groups.

In the meantime, many citizen groups in both countries have been active in promoting people to people contacts to create an atmosphere of peace and harmony between the peoples of the two countries. Some steps towards normalisation of relations between the two countries have been taken by the governments of the two countries. For example, train services between Delhi and Lahore (the train is appropriately known as Samjhauta Express) and bus services between the two cities have been resumed. Road transport between Srinagar and Muzaffarabad (the latter in POK) has been started. The end of army rule and the restoration of democracy have opened up possibilities of further steps in promoting relations of peace and harmony between the two countries. Both the countries since 1998 are countries with nuclear weapons and this has made the establishment of peaceful and cordial relations between them more imperative than ever before.

In 1980, war broke out between Iran and Iraq. There had been some disputes over boundary between the two countries as well as political differences. The war continued for eight years taking a toll of hundreds of thousands of lives in both the countries and causing serious damage to their economies.

In 1991, there was a war between Iraq and a number of other countries including USA. In August 1990, Iraq had occupied Kuwait. On her refusal to end her occupation, the United Nations authorised the use of force against her. On 17 January 1991, war broke out in which there was large-scale use of missiles by both sides. This was the first major war in which the US troops were directly involved after the end of the Cold War. It came to an end on 28 February 1991 after the forces of the US and her allies in the war had entered the territory of Iraq and Kuwait and Iraq had ordered the withdrawal of her troops from Kuwait. It had a shattering effect on the economy of Iraq besides taking a huge toll of human lives.

Bangladesh as an Independent Nation

Pakistan, which was created with the partition of India in 1947, was divided two parts—East Pakistan and West Pakistan. The two parts were separated by about 1600 km of Indian territory. The only bond which united the two parts was religion—the majority of the population in both parts was Muslim.

Soon it was clear that religion could not be the basis of nationhood. Almost immediately after the creation of Pakistan, there had been a movement for autonomy by the people of East Pakistanis. The Awami League led by Sheikh Mujibur Rahman spearheaded the movement. While the people of East Pakistan comprised more than half the population of Pakistan, the government and the armed forces were dominated by West Pakistanis. East Pakistan was also economically exploited by West Pakistan and her language, Bengali, and culture were sought to be suppressed. In the elections held in December 1970, the Awami League swept the polls in East Pakistan, winning 168 out of 169 seats. It was expected that Pakistan would now frame a new federal constitution which would guarantee greater autonomy to East Pakistan. It was also expected that with the Awami League as the majority party in Pakistan, Mujibur Rahman would form the government at the centre. However, the meeting of the newly elected assembly was not allowed to be held leading to widespread demonstrations in East Pakistan. To suppress the protest demonstrations, the army was sent to East Pakistan and Mujibur Rahman was arrested in West Pakistan. Soon after, the independent state of Bangladesh was proclaimed with its own guerrilla army to fight against the Pakistan army. Thousands of people were killed and millions of Bangladeshis entered India as refugees. The influx of millions of refugees into India created a difficult situation for India and she intervened in support of the people of Bangladesh on 3 December 1971. Pakistani troops unconditionally surrendered on 16 December. In January 1972, Mujibur Rahman was released and on his return he became the first prime minister of the independent state of Bangladesh.

The emergence of Bangladesh as an independent nation was an event of great historical significance, particularly for the Indian subcontinent. It was a serious blow to the theory of nationhood on the basis of religion.

The period after independence has been marked by long periods of political instability and military rule in Bangladesh. On 15 August 1975, Sheikh Mujibur Rahman, popularly known as Bangabandhu, who had led the struggle for independence and was the President of Bangladesh, was assassinated along with most members of his family. This was followed by army rule with General Ziaur Rahman as president. Zia was assassinated in 1981 and was followed by General Ershad. He resigned and in 1991 elections were held which brought Khaleda Zia, Ziaur Rahman's widow to power as prime minister. In 1996, Sheikh Hasina the surviving daughter of Mujib and leader of the Awami League, won the election and became prime minister. In 2001, the Awami League was defeated and Khaleda Zia again came to power. There have been wide spread political disturbances in the country. The forces of religious fundamentalism have been growing in strength. Elections that were due to be held in 2006 were not held. In January 2007, a caretaker government, with the active backing of the army, took over power and a promise of holding elections. A large number of political workers and leaders, including Sheikh Hasina and Khaleda Zia, were arrested and put behind bars. It is almost two years since the caretaker government took over power but there is still no firm announcement of elections.

Regional Groupings

In spite of tensions and conflicts, a number of regional groupings have emerged in Asia to promote common political, economic, social and cultural interests and cooperation among its members. The Arab League, which has 21 Arab states, including Palestine, as its members, was set up in 1945. ASEAN (Association of Southeast Asian Nations), comprising six countries of Southeast Asia— Malaysia, Thailand, Singapore, the Philippines, Brunei and Indonesia—was set up in 1967. Most of these countries are among the fastest growing economies in the world and ASEAN has played an important role in the economic development of each of its members. Vietnam became the seventh member of ASEAN in July 1995. Another major regional grouping which was set up in 1985 is SAARC (South Asian Association for Regional Cooperation). It comprises seven countries— India, Pakistan, Nepal, Bhutan, Bangladesh, Sri Lanka and Maldives. Because of strains in the relations between some of these countries, SAARC's actual achievements have so far been limited.

Commonwealth of Nations

Commonwealth of Nations was formed before the Second World War but acquired a different character after the end of the Second World War. It had started as an association of self-governing British colonies and was referred to as the British Commonwealth and Empire. After India became independent, followed by the independence of other British colonies, its character changed. It was no longer 'British' and 'Empire' but an association of independent nations which had once been British colonies. Its members, now numbering fifty independent countries, follow their own' independent policies in their domestic and foreign affairs. Its multiracial character as well as the variety of political, social and economic systems that its members represent have made the Commonwealth an extremely useful body for discussing important issues and for promoting cooperation in various fields.

BRITISH AND DUTCH COLONIES IN SOUTH AMERICA

Britain had continued to retain a few colonial possessions in South America and the West Indies. Beginning in the 1960s, these countries became independent—Jamaica, and Trinidad and Tobago in 1962, Guyana and Barbados in 1966 and Grenada in 1976. Another colony, Suriname, situated to the east of Guyana, which had been under the rule of the Netherlands since the early years of the nineteenth century, became independent in 1975.

Developments in Latin America

Most Latin American countries continued to suffer from most of the same ills as before the war. The emergence of regimes which promised

LATIN AMERICA

UNITED STATES

North Atlantic Ocean

Mexico

Gulf of Mexico

Bahamas ■

Puerto Rico(U.S)

Cuba

Virgin Is.(U.S. and Br.)
Antigua and Barbuda ■
Guadeloupe(Fr.)
Martinique(Fr.)
Santa Lucia ■
Barbados ■

Belize ■ Jamaica Haiti Dominican
Republic

Guatemala
El Salvador

Honduras
Nicaragua Caribbean Sea ■ Grenada

Trinidad and Tobago ■

Costa Rica

Panama
Panama Canal Colombia

Venezuela

Suriname

Guyana

French Guiana

North Pacific Ocean

Ecuador

Peru

Brazil

Bolivia

Paraguay

Formerly British Colony ■
Formerly Dutch Colony ▲

Country	Year of In Dependence
Belize	1981
Guyana (Formerly British Guiana)	1966
Suriname (Formerly Dutch Guiana)	1975
Trinidad and Tobago	1962
Barbados	1966
Santa Lucia	1979
Antigua and Barbuds	1981
Bahamas	1972
Grenada	1974
Jamaica	1962

Chile

Argentina

South Atlantic Ocean

South Pacific Ocean

Uruguay

The year of independence shown above
are only of those countries which became
independent after the Second World War

ANTARCTICA

to introduce radical economic and social changes were always
considered a threat to the United States and led her to intervene in
the political affairs of the Latin American countries. These countries
faced much the same problems as the developing countries of Asia
and Africa and often suffered from political instability which had
become a common feature of many developing countries' political
life. The US had vast economic interests in almost every country in

Latin America; in the case of some countries, the US companies almost totally dominated their economy. To maintain their domination, these companies, with the support of the US government, encouraged undemocratic regimes with a powerful influence exercised by the army. The US policy, besides the threat it always perceived from the radical regimes in Latin America, also began to see these regimes as being communist-inspired or under communist control and, therefore, a danger to her security. In many cases, the US interference in Latin America directly or through the CIA's covert operations, was sought to be justified by an alleged communist threat. Very few countries in the region have had a continuous history of elected governments since the end of the Second World War.

US Interventions against Radical Regimes

Since the late 1940s, in the political life of most Latin American countries radical and left-wing trends have become powerful. They have been able to form governments and introduce reforms, and stay in power for varying lengths of time, only to be, in most cases, overthrown through coups, almost invariably with the support of the US. The two major exceptions have been Mexico and Cuba. The case of the latter has already been mentioned in the context of the Cold War.

Guatemala

Guatemala, for over a hundred years, had been ruled by military dictators. The first free elections were held in 1944 and a reformist government came to power. From 1950, this government was led by Jacobo Arbenz Guzman. It introduced many social and economic reforms in the country and expropriated the United Fruit Company, a US company which dominated the economy of Guatemala. This alarmed the US government. Dulles believed that the government of Arbenz was potentially communist. A US-supported military coup overthrew this government in 1954. The resentment against the US was so deep that when Richard Nixon, the then US Vice-President, visited Latin American countries in 1958, he was "greeted in city after city by angry, hostile, occasionally dangerous mobs".

Cuba

The most important event in Latin America in the 1950s which inspired radical and left-wing movements throughout the region was the revolution in Cuba. On 1 January 1959, after Batista, a military dictator who had been a close ally of the US, fled the country, Fidel Castro who had led the revolutionary movement formed the government. The revolution in Cuba had not been led by Cuban communists and Castro himself was not a communist. However, when the government started implementing radical land reforms and taking over foreign companies, the US government turned hostile to it. It was only in 1965 that the organisations with which Castro and other Cuban revolutionaries were associated and the Cuban communists came together to form the Communist Party of Cuba. The US had been the main importer of Cuba's sugar, which was Cuba's main item of export. This was stopped. Gradually, the Cuban government established close links with the Soviet Union. Many attempts were made by the CIA—a member of the US Congress had some years ago listed 15 attempts—to assassinate Castro. The Bay of Pigs fiasco and the missile crisis during the presidency of Kennedy have been mentioned earlier. Against the heavy odds the Cuban revolution has survived for over forty years now.

One of the most inspiring leaders which the Cuban revolution produced was Che Guevara. He was born in Argentina but had joined Castro in 1956. He played a leading role in the revolutionary movement in Cuba which led to the fall of Batista's dictatorship. He became a minister in the new Cuban government, but left Cuba in 1965 to help organise a revolution in Bolivia. He was captured and killed by Bolivian troops in 1967. He became a major source of inspiration to the radical youth in Latin America and elsewhere in the world.

Chile

An event which shocked the world in the 1970s was the overthrow of the government headed by Salvador Allende in Chile. One of the founders of the Chilean Socialist Party, he was elected President of Chile in 1970. Like other radical regimes in Latin America which had come to power in the past, Allende also started introducing radical land reforms and nationalising industries. On 11 September 1973, a military junta headed by General Pinochet, again with the support of the CIA, overthrew the government of Allende. Allende himself was killed in his Presidential Palace while fighting. A brutal military regime was established in Chile which remained in power till recently. Civilian rule was restored in Chile in 1990 when a democratically elected government came to power. There were demands to prosecute him for violation of human rights, including kidnapping, murder, torture and corruption. He escaped prosecution because of the immunity he enjoyed as a senator. He went to Britain for medical treatment and was arrested there. He was supposed to be extradited to Spain to stand trial for human rights violation. He was however released by the British authorities on grounds of health. Back in Chile he was arrested, but the court declared him mentally unfit to stand trial. In 2006, he was again arrested, but before his trial could begin, he died.

The events mentioned above indicate a major trend of developments in Latin America. The US has intervened in many more countries than have been mentioned above—in Honduras, Panama, Nicaragua, El Salvador, Grenada, etc. There have been too many military coups, mainly directed against elected governments which tried to introduce social and economic reforms.

Recently, the US sent troops to Haiti to restore Aristide, who had been elected president in 1990, but had been overthrown the next year. However, in 2004, he had to leave, when the US President announced that US marines would be sent there to, what he called, "restore peace". One of the significant developments has been the change in the attitude of the Catholic clergy in Latin America. Traditionally hostile to all radical ideologies and movements, the church and the clergy have become more responsive to the need for social and economic reform. Many priests have actively involved themselves in radical social and political movements.

Recent Changes in Latin America

The US perceived as their legitimate rights to intervene, both overtly and covertly, in the internal affairs of the Latin American countries. There Latin American countries were perceived by the US to have established radical regimes which meant regimes that sought to implement policies that were in the interest of the common people and diminished or eliminated the interests of the US companies in the economies of their respective countries. Cuba defeated the US-sponsored invasion and in spite of serious economic problems that it faced due to the economic blockade foisted by the US, continued on the path it has chosen for itself. In most other countries the US succeeded in maintaining its hegemony. In recent years, however, the US has suffered considerable loss of influence in the region. The loss of US influence over Latin America has been increasing and the process appears to be irreversible. A large number of countries—Brazil, Venezuela, Ecuador, Paraguay, Bolivia, Uruguay, Nicaragua, Guatemal, Chile, and others—now have elected government which may be broadly described as 'leftist'. They have come to power through free and fair elections, replacing in most cases authoritarian and dictatorial regimes and are implementing in varying degrees programmes of radical social and economic development. One of the most charismatic leader to emerge in Latin America is Huga Chavez in Venezuela. He was elected president in 1998 and again in 1999 when a new constitution came in force. He was re-elected in 2000 but was deposed in a US-sponsored military coup in 2002. He was again elected in 2004 and 2006. He is an ardent supporter of Cuba (a close friend of Castro) and a staunch opponent of US domination. Venezuela, unlike Cuba, has the resources of possessing enormous oil resources which is an important factor that may enable Chavez to pursue his policies of social and economic change in Venezuela and to promoting in collaboration with other leaders of Latin American countries, close relations of cooperation of Latin America.

THE NON-ALIGNED MOVEMENT

Many references have already been made to the rise and growth of the Non-Aligned Movement and the role played by it in international affairs. It arose at a time when many countries, particularly of Asia and Africa, had first emerged as independent states. They were deeply interested in preserving their own independence and playing an independent role in shaping the world and in speeding up the process of destruction of colonialism. The world had already been engulfed in the Cold War, with military alliances and race for weapons of mass destruction, which posed a threat to their independence as well as the survival of humanity. The world economic order in which they found themselves was based on gross inequalities and exploitation and the requirements of their development made fundamental changes in the world economic order a necessity. It was in these conditions that the Non-Aligned Movement emerged and shaped itself.

The Asian Relations Conference

While the Non-Aligned Movement was formally set up in 1961 when the first conference of non-aligned countries was held in Belgrade, Yugoslavia, its antecedents can be traced back to the early post-war years. The leaders of the Indian freedom movement convened the Asian Relations Conference in March 1947 in Delhi. At this Conference, Jawaharlal Nehru, who was to become the first prime minister of independent India in a few months' time, declared:

> Far too long have we of Asia been petitioners in Western courts and chancelleries. That story must now belong to the past. We propose to stand on our own legs and to cooperate with all others who are prepared to cooperate with us. We do not intend to be the playthings of others.... The countries of Asia can no longer be used as pawns by others: they are bound to have their own policies in world-affairs.

He warned of the new dangers that threatened the world and said,

> The West has ... driven us into wars and conflicts without number and even now, the day after a terrible war, there is talk of further wars in the atomic age that is upon us. In this atomic age Asia will have to function effectively in the maintenance of peace.

Bandung Conference

By the end of the 1940s, the Western countries' military alliance, NATO, had been set up, and in the early 1950s, military alliances had begun to be formed in Asia. The Cold War was being extended throughout the world leading to tensions and conflicts. In this context India, along with China, enunciated the Panchsheel or the five principles of peaceful coexistence. These principles were incorporated in the preamble to an agreement which India and China signed in 1954. They became integral to the Non-Aligned Movement.

Many outstanding leaders had emerged in Asia in the early 1950s who wanted to build the unity of Asian and African countries to bring about the end of colonialism and imperialism and to keep themselves aloof from Cold War confrontations. In 1955 Ahmed Sukarno of Indonesia hosted a conference of Asian and African countries at Bandung from 17 to 24 April. The conference was attended by 29 Asian and African countries. Among the outstanding leaders who participated in this conference were Jawaharlal Nehru, China's Prime Minister, Chou En Lai and Gamal Abdel Nasser, then prime minister, and later president, of Egypt. Although the conference was attended by many countries including Pakistan, Iran, Iraq, the Philippines, Turkey, Thailand, who were members of the US-sponsored military alliances, the communique unanimously adopted at this conference clearly stated ideas which expressed some of the fundamental principles of non-alignment. The Bandung Conference was a major milestone in the history of the Non-Aligned Movement.

It was also the biggest conference of the countries of Asia and Africa representing half of the population of the world.

Belgrade Conference

From the mid-1950s, leaders of some non-aligned countries had started holding meetings. Gradually, the idea grew that a conference of all non-aligned countries should be held. The 1960 session of the UN General Assembly was a historic one. Seventeen newly independent countries of Africa were admitted to the United Nations that year. The growing members of new nations, recently become free, brought about significant changes in the United Nations which became a truly international organisation at which, in course of time, almost every country in the world was represented. At this time, when the process of ending colonialism had been accelerated, the United Nations started playing a crucial role in furthering that process. On 14 December 1960, the United Nations adopted the historic

"Declaration on Granting Independence to Colonial Countries and Peoples". This historic session of the United Nations was attended by leaders of five leading non-aligned nations—Jawaharlal Nehru of India, Sukarno of Indonesia, Nasser of Egypt, Tito of Yugoslavia and Nkrumah of Ghana. They took the historic decision of convening a conference of all non-aligned countries in the following year.

DECLARATION ON THE ESTABLISHMENT OF A NEW INTERNATIONAL ECONOMIC ORDER

The new international economic order should be founded on full respect for the following principles:

(a) Sovereign equality of States, self-determination of all peoples, inadmissibility of the acquisition of territories by force, territorial integrity and non-interference in the internal affairs of other States.

(b) The broadest cooperation of all the States members of the international community, based on equity, whereby the prevailing disparities in the world may be banished and prosperity secured for all.

(c) Full and effective participation on the basis of equality of all countries in the solving of world economic problems in the common interest of all countries, bearing in mind the necessity to ensure the accelerated development of all the developing countries, while devoting particular attention to the adoption of special measures in favour of the least developed, land-locked and island developing countries most seriously affected by economic crises and natural calamities without losing sight of the interests of other developing countries.

(d) The right of every country to adopt the economic and social system that it deems the most appropriate for its own development and not to be subjected to discrimination of any kind as a result.

(e) Full permanent sovereignty of every State over its natural resources and all economic activities. In order to safeguard these resources, each State is entitled to exercise effective control over them and their exploitation with means suitable to its own situation, including the right to nationalization or transfer of ownership to its nationals, this right being an expression of the full permanent sovereignty of the State. No State may be subjected to economic, political or any other type of coercion to prevent the free and full exercise of this inalienable right.

(f) The right of all States, territories and peoples under foreign occupation, alien and colonial domination or apartheid to restitution and full compensation for the exploitation and depletion of, and damages to, the natural resources and all other resources of those States, territories and peoples....

[Adopted by the General Assembly of the United Nations on 1 May 1974]

The first conference of heads of state or governments of non-aligned countries was held at Belgrade, Yugoslavia, from 1 to 6 September 1961. It was attended by 25 countries as full members. These member countries were Afghanistan, Algeria, Burma (now Myanmar), Cambodia, Sri Lanka, Republic of Congo, Cuba, Cyprus, Ethiopia, Ghana, Guinea, India, Indonesia, Iraq, the Lebanon, Mali, Morocco, Nepal, Saudi Arabia, Somalia, Sudan, Tunisia, United Arab Republic (then comprising Egypt and Syria), Yemen and Yugoslavia. Algeria had not yet become independent but the provisional government set up by the FLN was admitted as a full member, as later SWAPO and PLO were admitted as full members. The conference adopted a declaration which stated that "the principles of peaceful coexistence are the only alternative to the Cold War and "to a possible general catastrophe" and that lasting peace would be achieved only in "a world where the domination of colonialism, imperialism and neocolonialism in all their manifestations is radically eliminated". The conference also addressed letters to Nikita Khrushchev, the Prime Minister of the Soviet Union, and John F. Kennedy, the President of the United States, and urged them to resume negotiations aimed at reducing the risk of war and at ensuring peace.

Basic Objectives

The basic objectives of the Non-Aligned Movement were laid down at the first conference itself. Some of these objectives were later elaborated and made more specific. The most important objectives included ending of imperialism and colonialism, promotion of international peace and security and disarmament, creation of a New International Economic Order, ending of racism and racial discrimination, and ending of information imperialism.

During the past forty-seven years, the membership of the Non-Aligned Movement has increased to 118. South Africa had become the 109th member in 1994. Almost all of them are members of the United Nations and thus constitute about sixty per cent of the total membership of the United Nations. All countries of Africa are members of the Non-Aligned Movement. The Charter of the Organisation of African Unity has as one of its principles 'Affirmation of a policy of non-alignment with regard to all blocs'. Fourteen summit conferences of the Non-Aligned Movement have been held: Belgrade (1961), Cairo (1964), Lusaka (1970), Algiers (1973), Colombo (1976), Havana (1979), Delhi (1983), Harare (1986), Belgrade (1989) and Jakarta (1992). Cartagena de Indias – Columbia (1995), Durban (1998) Kuala Lumpur (2003) and Havana (2006). At the Fourth Summit conference held at Algiers, it was decided to establish a Coordinating Bureau which was later charged with the task of coordinating their joint activities aimed at the implementation of the programmes adopted at the summit conferences, at ministerial conferences, at meetings of groups of non-aligned countries in the United Nations and at other meetings of the non-aligned countries.

There were doubts about the relevance and future of the Non-Aligned Movement after the end of the Cold War. These doubts were set at rest at the Tenth Summit held at Jakarta in 1992. This was the first summit which was held in the new world situation. The Tenth Summit, as the Jakarta Message adopted by the heads of state or governments of the Non-Aligned Movement stated, was held at "a time of profound change and rapid transition, a time of great promise as well as grave challenge, a time of opportunity amidst pervasive uncertainty". It stressed that the improvements in the international political climate had vindicated the validity and relevance of non-alignment. Pointing out that the world was "still far from being a peaceful, just and secure place", it stated:

> Simmering disputes, violent conflicts, aggression and foreign occupation, interference in the internal affairs of States, policies of hegemony and domination, ethnic strife, religious intolerance, new forms of racism and narrowly conceived nationalism are major and dangerous obstacles to harmonious coexistence among States and peoples and have even led to the disintegration of States and societies.

The message reiterated the commitment of the Non-Aligned Movement "to the shaping of a new international order, free from war, poverty, intolerance and injustice, a world based on the principles of peaceful coexistence and genuine interdependence, a world which takes into account the diversity of social systems and cultures".

The period after the Jakarta summit was one of far reaching changes in the world situation which gave rise to questions regarding the relevance of the movement. There was an acceleration in the process of globalisation and the spread of free market economies that accompanied it. The problem of terrorism was also becoming an important issue in many regions. There was also the manifestation of the consequences of the world which was believed to have become 'unipolar', such as 'unilateralism' and the proclamation of the right by the sole superpower and its allies to interfere in the affairs of other countries and the effect 'regime change'. The Kuala Lumpur Summit (2003) laid emphasis on the revitalisation of the Non-Aligned Movement. The Havana Summit (2006) in its declaration reaffirmed it "commitments to the ideals, principles and purposes upon which the movement was founded". "On a political level", it said, "there is a need to promote the good of creating a multipolar world order, based on respect for the application of the principles of International Law and the UN Charter and the reinforcement of multilateralism." It further stated, "Now more than ever it is essential that our nations remain united and steadfast and are increasingly active in order to successfully confront unilateralism and interventionism." The Declaration asserted the principles by which the nations associated with the movement will be guided. Some of these principles were,

1. "No State of group of States has the right to intervene either directly of indirectly, whatever the motives, in the internal affairs of any other State."

2. "Rejection of attempts at regime change."

3. "Rejection and opposition to terrorism in all its forms and manifestations, committed by whomever, wherever and for whatever purposes, as it constitutes one of the most serious threats to international peace and security. In this context, terrorism should not be equated with the legitimate struggle

of people under colonial or alien domination and foreign occupation for self-determination and national liberation."

The membership of the Non-Aligned Movement comprises almost all the developing countries of the world and notwithstanding differences on some specific issues, there are many issues, including the fulfilment of the right to development, that bind them together and make for the continuing relevance of the movement.

Index

A

Abbas, Mahmoud, 229
Abdel Karim, 100
Abdullah, King of Palestine, 95
Adowa, battle of (1896), 19
Afghanistan, 61, 82, 187; between
the two wars, 94; Soviet
intervention, 197, 208–9; and
US war, 197–98
Africa: Africa Year, 231; African
National Congress (ANC),
103, 237–38; anti-colonial
resistance, 46–47; emergence of
independence, 220–25, 232; in
First World War, 44–47;
between the two wars, 98–104;
in Second World War, 135, 172,
173; since 1945, 162, 257. *See
also* Asia. Latin America
Alaska, 31
Albania, 22, 24; in World War II,
143; since 1945, 165, 186, 216–
17, 220
Algeria, 19, 141; since 1945, 213, 222,
257; struggle for freedom, 230–31
Allende, Salvador, 251
Allied Powers, 51–52, 53, 54, 55
61, 62, 65–70, 112–13, 124,
127, 141, 148, 150, 164, 165;
victories in Europe, 142–43;
war aims, 153–59

al-Qaeda, 197–98, 200
Alsace-Lorraine, 23, 52, 67;
annexed by Germany, 132
Amanullah Khan, 94
American Federation of Labour
(AFL), 37
American Indian tribes, 31, 47
Anglo Iranian Oil Company, 95, 177
Anglo-German-Russian-French-
Japanese-American force, 19
Anglo-Japanese Treaty or Alliance,
43
Anglo-Russian agreement, 1907, 94
Angola, 19; Portugal rule, 213–14
Anti-Comintern Pact, 84, 127
Anti-Fascist People's Freedom
League, 153
Arab: Arab League, 228; Arab
Palestinian Congress, 97; Israel
war, 182, 183; nationalist
struggles, 180–83, 227–29
Arabia, 45
Arafat, Yasser, 228–29
Armenia, 78
Asia: in First World War, 44–47;
between the two wars, 87–91;
in the context of Cold War,
239;—West Asia, 94–95; since
1945, 162, 239–48; emergence
of independence, 220–25;
political developments, 240–41;